Contents

A GUIDE TO PRISONS AND PENAL POLICY

Prisons Unlocked

Rachel Vipond

First published in Great Britain in 2023 by

Policy Press, an imprint of
Bristol University Press
University of Bristol
1–9 Old Park Hill
Bristol
BS2 8BB
UK
+44 (0)117 374 6645
bup-info@bristol.ac.uk

Details of international sales and distribution partners are available at
policy.bristoluniversitypress.co.uk

© Bristol University Press 2023

British Library Cataloguing in Publication Data
A catalogue record for this book is available from the British Library

ISBN 978-1-4473-6541-9 hardcover
ISBN 978-1-4473-6542-6 paperback
ISBN 978-1-4473-6543-3 ePub
ISBN 978-1-4473-6544-0 ePdf

Cover design: Nicky Borowiec
Front cover image: Adobe Stock/Normform
Bristol University Press and Policy Press use environmentally responsible
print partners.
Printed and bound in Great Britain by CPI Group (UK) Ltd, Croydon, CR0 4YY

For Drew

Contents

List of figures and tables

Figures

Tables

Abbreviations

AP	approved premises
BAME	Black and minority ethnic
BLM	Black Lives Matter
CJS	criminal justice system
CNA	certified normal accommodation
CRE	Commission for Racial Equality
FTE	full-time equivalent
HMCIP	His Majesty's Chief Inspector of Prisons
HMIP	His Majesty's Inspectorate of Prisons
HMP	His Majesty's Prison
HMPPS	His Majesty's Prison and Probation Service
IEP	incentives and earned privileges
IPP	imprisonment for public protection
MBU	mother and baby unit
MoJ	Ministry of Justice
NOMS	National Offender Management Service
PEF	Prison Education Framework
PR	progression regime
PSI	prison service instruction
ROTL	release on temporary licence
SCH	secure children's home
STC	secure training centre
UOC	useable operational capacity
YOI	young offender institution

About the author

Rachel Vipond is Lecturer in Criminal Justice and Social Policy at the University of York. Rachel has been a lecturer in criminology since 2012. Prior to this she was a student of criminology and has studied the discipline at undergraduate, postgraduate and doctoral levels at Lancaster University. She is an experienced researcher and has both taught and researched inside several prisons across England. She is currently delivering a module in partnership with HMP Buckley Hall whereby students from the University of York and the prison come together to study social policy on the prison site.

Acknowledgements

This book is the culmination of several years of researching, teaching and experiencing prison from the perspective of an outsider. I am grateful and thankful for all those at HMP Buckley Hall who have given me their time over the years, especially Debbie Poles and Andy Mielczarski. I would like to thank the many individuals who have shared their experiences with me during their time in prison. Ikky, Trey, Dave, you taught me a lot about hope and change – thank you.

I would like to thank the publishers for their support with this project as well as my colleagues and friends from the University of York for their encouragement and guidance. Sharon and Lisa, I appreciate all the support you have given me during my time at York.

I would like to thank my family for their unwavering support, DrHennyPondCastle, you are all amazing, thank you for your constant positivity and love. My darling husband, Drew, you are my constant strength. Thank you for believing in me and helping me to achieve this goal.

This book would not have been possible without the influence and love of my mother, Susan. Mum, you have always said I could do it; well, here it is, for you. Thank you.

1

Orienting the prison

This book is about prisons and the broader penal policy in which they sit. Many of us are drawn to the study of criminology and subsequently penology because we are interested in how we should respond to individuals who break the law. The book is centrally concerned with the prison system in England and Wales (Scotland and Northern Ireland have separate systems). The word 'prison' conjures up questions about the aims of punishment, and they naturally diverge opinion as the central issue of what we should do with people who break the law remains one of the most challenging and divisive issues in our society. The UK spent approximately £5.63 billion on its prison system in 2020/21, one of the highest amounts in the last ten years (HM Treasury, 2021). It has a workforce of over 50,000 individuals and a total prisoner population that has stayed at the 80,000 mark for several years. How this system operates, what the prison experience is like for prisoners and the prospects for reducing reoffending are addressed in this guide. The aim of this chapter is to provide further context for the book as well as to discuss key terminology and how the book is organised.

The word 'penal' stems from the broader term 'penology', which refers to the study of punishment. The use of the word punishment here is key, as according to Oxford Dictionaries (2022), 'punishment' is defined as the 'infliction of a penalty or sanction in retribution for an offence'. This is one example of a definition but the decision on which definition to use will have an impact on how broad or narrow your understanding of penology is. The Oxford Dictionaries (2022) definition of punishment refers to punishment as being about inflicting retribution; this is a narrow definition. The infliction of punishment can do much more than this and punishment within the English and Welsh criminal justice system (CJS) is multi-faceted in its aims. The penal system, therefore, is the collection of agencies whose role it is to carry out the sentence of the court. His Majesty's Prison and Probation Service (HMPPS) under which the prison system in England and Wales sits has the primary role in regard to managing all sentences handed out by the criminal courts; these can range from imprisonment for short prison sentences of less than a month to long-term prison sentences of anything from four years to life to community payback and probation supervision. HMPPS has the responsibility in regard to adults but for young people who are sentenced at court, the responsibility for their sentence sits with the Youth Custody Service and youth offending teams. If the penal system was considered at its broadest definition, it could also include the significant number of organisations that work in and around it, including those companies that provide the electronic monitoring of individuals, and the charities that provide resettlement support and rehabilitation programmes, as well as the large number of volunteers who support the delivery of a vast amount of the work the system does. There should also be recognition made at this point of those whose role it is to inspect and report on the work of the penal system; the work of HM Inspectorate of Prisons (HMIP) is vital in terms of illuminating what goes on behind the locked gates of our prison system.

So why, then, is it important to examine prisons? The answer to this question is variable and will depend on the nature of someone's interest in the subject and the kind of work they are undertaking. For the vast proportion of students, the study of prisons and penal policy will sit alongside broader discussions of the CJS. As prison is the final stage in the process of criminal justice, it is important to recognise and understand the impact of what goes on beforehand and the effect it can have on an individual once inside. For those who may have been wrongly accused, mistreated in police custody, poorly represented at court and/ or harshly sentenced, their experience of the penal system will be shaped by their sense of justice or injustice in these instances. It will also have a bearing on how successful the CJS can be at deterring individuals from further offending and rehabilitating them.

In the now-famous words of Nelson Mandela (UNODC, 2022), '[N]o one truly knows a nation until one has been inside its jails. A nation should not be judged by how it treats its highest citizens, but its lowest ones.' By their very nature prisons are closed institutions and unless you work there or have been sentenced to serve there, they are inaccessible to the public. It is this very inaccessibility that drives some of our curiosity about them; rarely, other than perhaps a police station, are there places within modern society that we cannot enter to see for ourselves what they are like. In this instance, we are dependent on the work of HMIP, researchers and academics along with those who work there and are serving their sentences to share insights as to what life behind bars is truly like.

There are few more contentious issues within our CJS than the question of what we should do with people who break the law. Perhaps the only question in similar contention is: do prisons work? Given that the vast proportion of people will not break the law let alone end up in prison, the answers to these questions are unique ones. The lack of having experienced prison potentially precludes one from having an informed opinion of it and whether it works or not. Prison is a highly contentious and challenging topic area and can be understood differently depending on a person's political, ideological or philosophical viewpoint on the broader issue of the aims of punishment.

Scope of the book

This book focuses on the English and Welsh prison system. Despite this, much of what the book centres on is relevant to prison systems around the world, particularly in the West. An international look is taken at prison systems to provide a useful comparison (see Chapter 9) to the English and Welsh experience; the question of who does prison best as a nation remains open for debate. It is also important to explain that the book, unless otherwise specified, focuses on the prison experience for adult male prisoners over the age of 22. The reason for this is that it is these individuals who dominate the prison system in terms of prisoner numbers. The book does, however, recognise that different groups experience prison differently due to social characteristics, with Chapter 4 focusing on women, ethnically minoritised prisoners and older prisoners as population groups who arguably have more challenging experiences in the prison system. Most of the book's focus is on the publicly run prison estate.

The book is not intended to act as a replacement for lectures, other textbooks, journal articles or official statistics but is designed to complement and work alongside such other material. It aims to help you understand the organisation and function of the prison system and to provide insights from both a prisoner's and a prison officer's perspective as to what it is like inside. The term 'prisoner' is used throughout; this is based on the author's experience of researching and teaching in prison. When asked, it is the term that most individuals in prison, in the author's experience, prefer to be called. Other terms such as 'offender' are seen as somewhat offensive and counterintuitive to the rehabilitative aims that prison purports to have. The term is also factually accurate; someone in prison by that very fact is a prisoner. That is why this term is used throughout the book.

Themes that help us to understand prisons and penal policy

There is, no matter what text you read about prisons, a key set of running themes that recur throughout the literature. Some themes shape and mould the policy approaches to imprisonment; they, therefore, have an influence directly on the behaviour and practice of those working in these institutions and subsequently the experience of prisoners. The book is written from the standpoint that the prison system in England and Wales does not work in regard to its stated aims, that it is unjustly punitive and dangerous and does little to provide individuals with the support and experience they need to rehabilitate. This is not a reflection on the significantly hard work that the vast number of individuals working within the prison system do daily but rather a reflection on the overwhelmingly flawed policies and practices that are apparent within the system. The book argues that a lack of a clear policy vision and the politicised nature of criminal justice has hampered any potential reform and progress that could have been made with prisons for decades now. To try to understand prisons and broader penal policy, three key themes should be thought about as they often have a clear impact on the topic being analysed:

1. Power: this is a useful term when exploring prisons and broader penal policy because understanding who has the power to punish and who does not helps us to understand how the experience of prison is shaped. Critically, an understanding of the fact that the power to punish individuals and subsequently the use of imprisonment is disproportionately deployed against

those who are from the lowest socioeconomic backgrounds (poor people, in other words). Power is an essential dynamic in regard to imprisonment and an imbalance of power is often at the very heart of some of the issues that prisons face.

2. Legitimacy: intrinsically linked to the concept of power, questions over whether prisons are legitimate and therefore morally acceptable are difficult but worthwhile to ask. Prisons exert power over prisoners but whether they have the moral right to do so remains questionable. Given the squalor, high levels of violence, self-harm, self-inflicted deaths and reoffending rates that prisons currently have, it is hard to argue that they are legitimate institutions whereby prisoners should comply with the rules. Prisons are arguably deficient in legitimacy because they suffer from a lack of clear aims and objectives in the overall goals of imprisonment.

3. Rehabilitation: despite it not being written in any policy or Act of legislation, rehabilitation is often considered one of the main goals of imprisonment. As a philosophical justification of punishment, rehabilitation seeks to restore the person to the state they were in before they committed the crime. It is often used within penal policy interchangeably with other words such as 'resettlement', 'reintegration' and 'reform'. The influence of the rehabilitative ideal has been present within the penal system for a considerable time; the idea that these institutions can change a person dates back to Victorian times. It remains a goal of the system despite the word itself not being used, the stated aim of imprisonment being 'to encourage and assist prisoners to lead a good and useful life' (The Prison Rules, ch.3, 1999).

How to use this book

The chapters that follow aim to provide a succinct and critical discussion of different elements that are key to understanding the prison system in England and Wales.

- Chapter 2 sets out the historical journey of the 'prison', providing the reader with an insight into the nature of punishment before imprisonment and insights into what prison was like before the 20th century.
- Chapter 3 describes the modern context of prisons; it draws on a range of data to provide a sense of the current state of the prison system. The chapter discusses how many prisons are in operation, types of prisons including prison privatisation, who is in prison and in prison for what. It explains the processes involved in sending people to custody and the different types of sentences individuals may be given.
- Chapter 4 explores how different groups experience prison differently based on their age, gender and ethnicity. While it is not an exhaustive exploration of all the different groups that are recognised under diversity legislation, the chapter outlines how these groups experience prison differently, and discusses,

critically, the extent to which the prison system caters for and meets the needs of different prisoner populations.

- Chapter 5 provides insights into what day-to-day life in prison is like for the vast majority of men who are there. It focuses on what the average prison regime is and how prisoners fill their time while incarcerated. It also discusses the key concerns of healthcare in prison, focusing on both physical and mental health.
- Chapter 6 introduces how the experience of being in prison can be seen when looking at broader philosophies of punishment. It explores the four main theories behind the use of prison as a punishment: incapacitation, deterrence, just deserts and rehabilitation. The chapter moves on to consider the 'pains of imprisonment' and the impact of being in prison through exploring levels of violence, self-harm and self-inflicted deaths in custody.
- Chapter 7 moves on to look at imprisonment through the eyes of those who work in prison, for the first time in the book. A discussion of the different individuals who work in prison is had, including the work of prison governors, before a specific focus is taken to explore the role of a prison officer.
- Chapter 8 considers the process of leaving prison through an examination of the concept of desistance – the theory of stopping offending. It explains the processes of being released and includes an analysis of the work of the Parole Board. What happens when individuals fail to comply with the terms of their release is also discussed before moving on to a broader discussion on how we can assess whether or not prison works.
- Chapter 9 takes a global look at imprisonment and the general trends and rates of incarceration on a worldwide scale. The reader is taken on a tour of six different countries with their approaches to imprisonment being described to allow for comparisons and contrasts with the English and Welsh approach. Finally, the chapter explores which nation does prison best and what lessons can be learnt from taking a global look at imprisonment.
- Chapter 10 concludes the text by asking what the future is for prisons in England and Wales. It revisits the issue of the purpose of prison and suggests potential routes to solving the penal crisis.

Aims of the book

This book is designed as a useful reference guide to prisons and penal policy; by focusing on the prison system the broader issues in penology can be illuminated and explored. For those who are new to the prison system and the study of penology, it aims to serve as an introduction and can be used to bridge the gap between more detailed academic sources and practice-focused texts.

The fundamental aim of the book is to stimulate your thinking and to help you get the most from your studies. Each chapter concludes with suggested questions for discussion. Further suggested reading is also presented, some with additional annotations to explain their inclusion and why they are worth a read. There are also useful websites to visit and other sources of information that you could engage with to further your knowledge and understanding.

Prisons and penal policy sit in an ever-changing political world, where policy and subsequently practice can be changed in an instant on the basis of reactive policy making (see Chapter 6). It is worth, therefore, familiarising yourself with the HMPPS website alongside the various sources of government statistics so that the most up-to-date information is always used when completing assignments.

Before you go any further ...

Consider what your current views of the prison system are. Do you think we are too harsh in the way that we punish people? Do you think that prisons should be tough, unpleasant places to do time? What do you think the goals of imprisonment should be and does our current system help or hinder them? Make some notes in answer to these questions. We will return to them at the end of the book, to see if your views have changed.

2

The birth of the prison

Key learning outcomes

By the end of this chapter, you should be able to:

- Explain the key developments in history in relation to prisons

- Describe the work of two key penal reformers

- Understand how the development of the prison is entrenched in broader developments of penal policy

Introduction

This chapter focuses on the birth of the prison starting with an exploration of what punishment was in the 18th century before prisons were established. There is a brief discussion of transportation, the punishments that were used to inflict pain and the public spectacle of punishment – the death penalty. The chapter moves on to discuss what Foucault (1977) called the punishment of the soul and the centralisation of imprisonment as the main method of punishment. It presents the work of the Victorians, who are credited with the invention of the modern prison, using a series of examples to illustrate the shifts in approaches to punishment. There is also a discussion of early prison reformers, namely John Howard and Elizabeth Fry, as a way of introducing the notion that the current problems faced by prisons are not new but have been ingrained in their very fabric from their creation.

Punishment in an era before prison

Prisons, as we have come to know them, were an invention of the 19th century. Much of what we now associate with prisons – such as the separation of male prisoners from female prisoners, and young people from adults; the provision of work and education; and above all, a term of imprisonment being used as a sentencing decision and therefore as a punishment – were developments that were only gradually established over time in an often uneven, messy and chaotic process of transformation. The Victorians mostly undertook these changes, and so prison as the institution that we now know and recognise came into being around the same time as postage stamps, trains, cameras and the flushing toilet. This is not to imply that prisons did not exist before the 19th century; until then,

7

the roles that these places performed and how they were organised internally were markedly different.

The word prison comes from the Latin word *carpare*, meaning to seize. Prisons have long existed in England and Wales in one form or another and are used for different purposes. They were first formally recognised when William I ordered the building of the Tower of London as the first royal prison in 1066. Before the 18th century, prison was one of the ways people could be punished but it was by no means the most popular choice. There was a wide range of sentences available, much more choice than there is in modern times. The punishments ranged from the death penalty – the most severe corporal punishment – which was usually carried out by particularly gruesome and public means, to essentially being given a verbal warning or a strong telling-off. In between, lay a range of other corporal punishments, which involved whipping, branding and other forms of mutilation. Other punishments could be categorised as acts of public shaming such as the use of the pillory; yet others were essentially acts of slavery such as being sent to the workhouse or subject to transportation (Spierenburg, 2005).

The Assize of Clarendon, an Act issued by King Henry II in 1166, instructed his government representatives, the county sheriffs, to build a jail (or gaol) in their counties. The Act paved the way for the CJS to become structured, more like we know it today, with the creation of the process of trial by jury alongside other significant developments including the creation of local jails. The use of the word 'jail', often associated now with the US penal system, is significant here, as they had a specific function, different from what was to become a 'prison'. Jails were used to hold those awaiting trial along with those who had been convicted but were awaiting punishment; the punishment was not to be imprisonment but some other form, so the jails were used as places to hold people. The conditions individuals were kept in were primitive; everyone in the jail slept on the bare earth and they were given bread and water every other day. Those awaiting sentencing were charged fees for everything, items that today we would consider to be a human right, such as food, blankets and even to have manacles removed. Given that individuals were often from the poorest parts of society they often could not pay, meaning that their experience of jail was brutal.

Following the creation of jails, houses of correction became the next type of establishment to be created in 1556 to control poor people and those who were unable to work such as beggars and vagrants. After the passing of the Elizabethan Poor Law in 1601, James I mandated for each English county to have a house of correction, more commonly referred to as a bridewell (after the first was established at Bridewell Palace in London). These facilities were to be used as a punishment for those who largely were in debt; they were sentenced to serve a short period in these institutions, undertaking hard labour while there. Significantly, both types of establishment were governed by local magistrates and authorities, showing the start of devolution from the state (Johnston, 2016). At the turn of the 18th century, England was still a small and insular place with most people living in the countryside and working in agriculture. Individuals who owned the land were often also the local magistrates and therefore the enforcers of the law. In 1723, a system that became known as the 'Bloody Code' was established whereby over 200 separate offences were legislated for, mostly property offences, for which the punishment was the death penalty. The punishment of death was to be carried out by public hanging, continuing the theme of earlier methods of corporal punishment being a public spectacle. The public nature of hanging was thought to act as a deterrent, warning people that this is what would happen if they transgressed the law. There was little public debate at this time on punishment and no legal safeguards against wrongful conviction. Capital punishment legislation boomed haphazardly during this period to deal with individual crimes as they arose. For example, destroying Westminster Bridge was the same kind of offence as destroying Fulham Bridge, but each offence had a separate capital statute (Act), making the law ever more complicated to understand and subsequently defend oneself against (National Justice Museum, 2019). Some of the offences on the list were as follows:

- murder
- arson
- forgery
- cutting down trees
- stealing horses or sheep
- destroying turnpike roads
- stealing from a rabbit warren
- pickpocketing goods worth a shilling (roughly £30 today)
- being out at night with a blackened face
- being an unmarried mother concealing a stillborn child
- stealing from a shipwreck
- wrecking a fishpond (National Justice Museum, 2019)

Yet, despite its name and the implied brutality, approximately only 10 per cent of those sentenced to death under the Bloody Code were executed. Hay (1975) describes the Bloody Code as an ideological system of social control, which combined:

- majesty: the power and authority of the law
- justice: everybody could be prosecuted under the rule of law
- mercy: local elites gained pardons through petitions to the monarch

One of the other main methods of punishment during this time was transportation. The Transportation Act 1718 introduced transportation for individuals who broke the law – a first experiment in the privatisation of criminal justice. From 1718 to 1775, commercial shippers made large profits transporting people to the USA; over 30,000 people were transported during this time. Meanwhile, decommissioned ships, named prison hulks (often referred to as 'floating hells'), were anchored at London, Portsmouth and Plymouth where prisoners were put to hard labour during the day and then loaded, in chains, onto the ship at night. These ships acted as warehouses for people who had broken the law while the government sought alternatives to transportation to the USA, which had ended following the American War of Independence. The pause in transportation was only temporary; it was resumed 12 years later following the establishment of a penal colony in Australia and continued into the 19th century.

Developments from the 18th century onwards

As the 18th century developed, industrialisation and a boom in the population started to change how people were living their lives. There was growing opposition to the death penalty for all but the most serious crimes and a movement towards the increased use of imprisonment as punishment (Spierenburg, 1998). Cohen (1985: 13) contends that new patterns of social control were developed during this period, which paved the way for the prison to become the centralised method of punishment. He suggests that these patterns of social control consisted of:

* increasing classification of deviants by experts;
* increased incarceration of deviants into 'asylums' – penitentiaries, prisons, mental hospitals and reformatories;
* increased involvement of a centralised state; and
* the mind replacing the body as the object of penal repression. (Cohen, 1985: 13)

There was movement in broader understandings of the causes of crime; immorality was starting to be seen as the main cause of offending. As this view started to gain traction within government circles so too did the idea that those who broke the law could potentially be reformed, paving the way for prisons to be seen as more than just a place of detention. For this emerging penal philosophy and viewpoint to take shape, prisons required reform because for much of the 18th century no matter what the type of institution, be it a bridewell, workhouse or local jail, they could be characterised as places of squalor, disorder and mistreatment. It was the highlighting of these poor conditions by early penal reformers, such as John Howard and Elizabeth Fry, which started the process of change. The reformers advocated for classification, isolation and sanitation as initial improvements to the emerging prison system.

To enact the reforms that Howard suggested, William Blackstone, the appointed Justice of the Court of King's Bench at the time, introduced the Penitentiary Act 1779. Blackstone (cited in Ignatieff, 1978: 94) described the legislation:

> In framing the plan of these penitentiary houses, the principle objects were sobriety, cleanliness and medical assistance by a regular series

of labour, by solitary confinement during the intervals of work, and some religious instruction to preserve and amend the health of the unhappy offenders and to ensure them to the habits of industry, to guard them from pernicious company, to accustom them to serious reflection and to teach them both the principle and practices of every Christian and moral duty.

John Howard: the first penal reformer

John Howard was appointed as High Sheriff of Bedfordshire and with this came the responsibility for the local county jail. On visiting the jail, he was appalled by the conditions he found. This prompted him to visit other prisons in the UK and Europe, at a time when travel was uncomfortable and dangerous, to explore different penal establishments and the conditions people were held in. He travelled nearly 49,000 miles on horseback and spent some £30,000 of his own money in his determination to improve prison conditions. Howard made seven large-scale journeys between 1775 and 1790, the first two of which are described in his book *The State of the Prisons in England and Wales*. The publication in 1777 of his comprehensive investigations of prison conditions in the UK and Europe aroused considerable public interest and soon led to calls for institutional change. John Howard campaigned for improvements to prisoner health and hygiene as well as independent systems of inspection. He championed the rights and wellbeing of prisoners for years, so much so that the Howard League for Penal Reform charity was set up to honour his legacy and continues his work to this day (Howard League for Penal Reform, 2021).

Elizabeth Fry: highlighting the plight of women

Elizabeth Fry was a social reformer, philanthropist and Quaker; she was the first penal reformer to devote her attention solely to the plight of imprisoned women. During a visit to Newgate Prison, she was struck by the terrible conditions that the female prisoners were living in. To raise awareness as to the situation that women faced she visited other prisons and tried to encourage other middle-class women to do so. She overcame considerable male opposition to her stance and set about organising education classes for women. In 1818 Fry gave evidence to a House of Commons committee on the conditions prevalent in British prisons, becoming the first woman to present evidence in Parliament. She was instrumental in the Gaols Act of 1823, which mandated the sex segregation of prisons and female warders for female inmates to protect them from sexual exploitation. Elizabeth kept diaries of her visits to prisons and her work, detailing extensively the conditions she found. Fry was one of the earliest documented people to advocate for rehabilitation rather than punishment, which was acknowledged by some of the operators of jails within London. Fry had a significant influence on the development of prisons, particularly in London and particularly for women. There are many commemorations to her across the UK, the most famous being that from 2001 to 2016 Fry was depicted on the reverse of £5 notes issued by the Bank of England. She was shown reading to prisoners at Newgate Prison. The design also incorporated a key, representing the key to the prison that was awarded to Fry in recognition of her work.

The Penitentiary Act 1779 paved the way for a new institution, the penitentiary, to be created. Formerly named the Penitentiary, Millbank Prison was the first national prison in England to be built and opened. It was a gloomy, foreboding place built on the south bank of the River Thames where the Tate Gallery now stands; it was the first government-run prison to be built. The prison building was based on the work of Jeremy Bentham who had in 1791 produced his ideas for prison management, the Panopticon. The design was a round prison with cells on the circumference facing a core at the centre where guards would sit and view all cells, thereby creating the appearance of constant surveillance. Bentham had been unable to secure funding for the prison; the government took over the contract, completing it in 1821 and abandoning Bentham's panopticon design in the process. The prison was doomed from its initial opening; this big 'monument of ugliness became a maniac-making machine' (Webb and Webb, 1922: 48). It was the largest prison in England, designed to hold 1,000 prisoners, yet it was beseeched with problems. It was overcrowded and criticised consistently for its huge cost, poor location, staff shortages, corruption, poor conditions and disease. The prison operated a strict regime whereby the first half of one's sentence was spent in seclusion and the latter half was spent undertaking hard labour. However, in later years of its operation the regime became stricter, focusing largely on solitude and isolation. The demise of Millbank Prison paved the way for the establishment of a new institution driven by a new direction and understanding of crime led by the Victorians.

Victorian prisons

The Victorians were worried about the rising crime rate: offences went up from about 5,000 per year in 1800 to about 20,000 per year in 1840. They were firm believers in punishment for criminals but faced a dilemma in that they could not decide on what the punishment should be. The prisons that were in existence during the early stages of the Victorian era were largely used, as previously stated, for confinement purposes only. The common punishments of the time continued to include transportation – sending the offender to the USA, Australia or Tasmania – or execution. Hundreds of offences carried the death penalty.

Yet, by the 1830s, people were having doubts about both punishments. The government at the time was being challenged to come up with an alternative solution because the public was starting to be unconvinced by the death penalty and transportation was costing too much. The answer they came up with was prison. Between 1842 and 1877, 90 prisons were built or added to. It was a massive building programme costing millions of pounds, but represented a change in direction and focus in terms of how people were to be punished. No longer were prisons to be used just to hold people but the process of being imprisoned became the main way in which individuals were to be punished for breaking the law. Despite the perceived failure of HMP Millbank, the Victorians persisted with the creation of more institutions, a vast proportion of which are still in operation today as some of our most well-known and well-used prisons; HMP Pentonville is such an example.

HMP Pentonville (informally known as 'The Ville') was opened in 1842, in the London Borough of Islington. It was built to hold 520 prisoners in single cells and is one of England's oldest and most famous institutions. It is a prime example of Victorian design and architecture; its structure has largely been unchanged in the 180 years it has been operational. Pentonville was not just an experiment in architectural design for the Victorians but also in the creation of a regime. The Victorians had clear ideas of what they wanted prisons to be like: foreboding, unpleasant places where nobody would want to be. They should act as a deterrent to deter people from committing crimes. A regime and an environment were created that reinforced such a perspective. The design of Pentonville was such that it isolated prisoners and the separate system regime was enforced to further that isolation. The principle of the regime, which had previously been used in the USA (see Henriques, 1972), was to encourage individuals to face up to their actions and reform their behaviour, with Christian chaplains being used to encourage prisoners to live a more crime-free lifestyle. It was thought that, by isolating individuals and leaving them in their cells for long periods, they would reflect on their crimes and be reformed. Isolation was further enforced when individuals were made to wear hoods whenever they were required to move around the institution; they could not communicate with each other, thus making the prison experience one of total segregation. This was why prisons were also known as penitentiaries: they were places where individuals who broke the law were sent, to give penance and repent. Religious services were the only places where the silence of the separate system could be interrupted, although prisoners who attended services were made to sit in separate stalls, which meant they still could not talk to one another or make eye contact. Due to the isolation of the regime, it is widely documented that a number of individuals held at Pentonville and other similar institutions at the time were driven insane. By 1865, the Prisons Act came into law, amalgamating various institutions that were operating as prisons into a clear system of local and national prisons. As the popularity of transportation declined and ultimately ceased, long-term imprisonment (penal servitude) with hard labour became the preferred punishment. Under the guidance of Sir Edmund Du Cane, assistant director of prisons from 1863 and chairman of the prison commissioners (1877–95), further developments to the regime of these institutions were enacted. Prisons became clear places of punishment, as Du Cane encouraged a regime that was focused on breaking prisoners' wills by continuing to keep them in total silence and making them do long, pointless hard labour. He promised the public that prisoners would get 'hard labour, hard fare and hard board':

- Hard labour: back-breaking, often pointless work that demanded physical strength to complete
- Hard fare: a deliberately monotonous diet, with the same food on the same day each week
- Hard board: wooden board beds replaced the hammocks that prisoners had slept on previously

There were two main forms of hard labour used, one of which was the treadwheel, also known as the treadmill or 'everlasting staircase'. The device was a wide hollow cylinder, usually composed of wooden steps built around a cylindrical iron frame, and was designed in some cases to handle as many as 40 prisoners. As the device began to rotate, each prisoner was forced to continually step along the series of planks. The power generated by the treadwheel was commonly used to grind corn and pump water, although some served no purpose at all other than punishment. This was done in silence; due to the hard fare and hard board prisoners were often weak and there are documents which show a high number of individuals died during this work. The other form of hard labour that was mainly used was the crank. Cranks were housed in individual cells; early ones were made of wood and filled with sand with scoops or paddles fitted to a central spindle. A prisoner would have to turn the crank in his cell a set number of times to earn his food. Unlike the treadwheel, which in most circumstances served a purpose in the prison, the crank simply turned paddles in a box of sand. Again, the Victorians mandated that this was done in silence; this was strictly enforced. Prison officers could tighten the crank wheel to make the task more arduous and there are reports that officers would regularly alter the settings and reset the prisoner's target as a method of inflicting mental torture. The nickname 'screws' for contemporary prison officers comes from the action of officers tightening the crank wheel: 'turning the screw', hence the name screws.

By the 1890s, changes to attitudes in broader society meant the severity of the prison regimes was increasingly being called into question. It was becoming clear that the harsh regimes could not be applied equally to all prisoners; some groups required protection due to key social characteristics such as age and gender. It was also becoming clear that the harsh and strict prison regimes under the control of Edmund Du Cane were not working, in the sense of reforming the individuals subjected to them. Du Cane was increasingly viewed as having too much power and control over the prison system with there being few ways to hold him to account for his decision making (Harding, 1988). In addition, while the numbers of people sent to prison were declining due to a range of reasons that included a move towards increased use of non-custodial sentences and an overall fall in the crime rate, the numbers of people reoffending were increasing; this caused considerable concern (Johnston, 2016). Criticisms from sources that included a series of articles in one of the mainstream papers at the time, the *Daily Chronicle*, alongside significant media coverage of the trial and sentence of Oscar Wilde, which resulted in him being imprisoned for two years with hard labour, left the government with no choice but to address the failing prison system. A departmental committee led by Herbert Gladstone was established to examine the prison system. The Gladstone Report concluded that the prison system had significant problems and that reform was needed to return it to its primary purpose of deterrence and reformation. For Gladstone (1895, cited in Radzinowicz and Hood, 1986: 577):

> prison discipline and treatment should be more effectually designed to maintain, stimulate or awaken the higher susceptibilities of prisoners, to develop their moral instincts to train them in orderly and industrial habits and whenever possible to turn them out of prison better men and women, both physically and morally, than when they came in.

After publication of the report, Du Cane resigned from his post as chairman of the prison commissioners. Changes were made to the prison regime to replace hard labour with 'productive labour'; prisoners no longer had to work in silence and the provision of education was made compulsory.

The 20th century: what works?

The turn of the 20th century and the findings of the Gladstone Report marked a broader shift in penal policy than was anticipated. The adoption of a more positivist approach to criminology whereby the causes of crime were starting to be understood as being driven by the environment and family circumstances in which people grew up and lived led to a shift in thinking. It was believed that criminal behaviour could be 'treated' and cured through psychological interventions and the provision of social welfare. Garland (1985) refers to the period of 1895 to 1914 as being when the formation of the modern 'penal-welfare' complex was established. The turn of the century marked significant developments to the wider CJS: the probation service was established (1907), borstals were created for young offenders, sentencing practices changed and direct alternatives to custody were made available for first-time offenders. There was also recognition within policy that those who were mentally ill or under the age of 16 needed special treatment in recognition of their perceived vulnerability. All these elements worked to reduce the prison population; by 1938 the population in prisons was just over 11,000, which meant that England and Wales had the smallest prison population in Europe (Wilson, 2014). Despite positive changes, including educational and work facilities being made available in all prisons, prison conditions remained punitive. As significant challenges faced the world during and after both the First and Second World Wars, prison conditions fell into insignificance in penal policy with the use of enforced separate confinement, penal servitude and hard labour, the very things that were of concern in the Gladstone report, not being abolished until 1948.

The Second World War had a devastating impact on a lot of the prison system infrastructure with buildings significantly damaged during air raids and bombings. For instance, HMP Pentonville was bombed in 1941 resulting in the deaths of 17 people – both staff and prisoners. Prison officers had been called up to serve in the war, bringing about a staffing crisis that became increasingly pertinent as the prison population started to rise. After the end of the war, a building programme was launched to build 17 new prisons and borstals. Some of the policies that had been proposed before the war were enacted, including the creation of open prisons and the recognition that prisoners could be divided into different security categories and subsequently different prisons. Throughout the 1950s and 1960s the focus was on offender rehabilitation, with various experts creating models of treatment where the goal was to concentrate on individuals' different reasons and risk factors for offending. It was viewed that prisons could reform individuals within them; this positive approach, however, was not to last. As the problems that have always plagued prisons once again took hold, namely overcrowding, a lack of resources and security challenges, the rehabilitative aims and objectives of prisons fell out of favour. A series of reports suggested changes were required to the organisational structure of prisons and a renewed focus was needed for them. When Margaret Thatcher became prime minister in 1979 a new sentencing policy was created to try to stem the significant overcrowding that was occurring in the penal estate. Under the policy, bifurcation was to occur, whereby prison would be used for violent offenders only, with them receiving lengthy custodial sentences. Community sentences were to be used for less serious offenders and the 'short, sharp shock' treatment was to be used for young offenders. It was starting to be recognised that perhaps prisons could be nothing more than places of containment and that providing individuals were held humanely this was acceptable (Bottoms, 1990). However, penal bifurcation failed and overcrowding continued as prison numbers continued to rise. Following major riots that occurred at HMP Manchester (Strangeways) from 1 to 25 April 1990 and other disturbances at five different prisons, David Waddington, then-Home Secretary, commissioned Lord Justice Woolf to investigate what had happened. The riots at HMP Manchester, commonly referred to as the Strangeways riots, were the longest-running disturbances in penal history in England and Wales. The reasons for the riots and how they were concluded were to be the subject of the inquiry. The Woolf Report is regarded as one of the most important official reports on prisons since the Gladstone Report of 1895. On publication, the report set out a blueprint for prison policy for the next three decades, making 12 major recommendations and 204 proposals on how to overhaul the prison system. The recommendations called for:

- greater cooperation between different parts of the CJS;
- more visible leadership of the Prison Service by the director general;
- increased delegation of responsibility to governors of individual prisons;
- an enhanced role for prison officers;
- a 'compact' or 'contract' for each prisoner, setting out the prisoner's expectations and responsibilities;
- a national system of accredited standards;
- a cap on prison overcrowding;
- an end to 'slopping out' and better in-prison sanitation;
- better ways for prisoners to maintain contact with family;
- a division of prison establishments into small and more manageable units;
- a clearer process for remanding prisoners; and
- improved standards of justice. (Adapted from the Prison Reform Trust [PRT], 1991)

The government responded by publishing the White Paper *Custody, Care and Justice: The Way Ahead for the Prison Service in England and Wales* whereby all of Woolf's recommendations apart from the cap on overcrowding were accepted. Prison conditions somewhat improved in the immediate aftermath of Woolf's report but as media and public interest faded so too did the interest in reform. Given that no additional financial resource was given to prisons, some of the more ambitious elements of Woolf's report were never achieved. During the 1990s, as more embarrassing incidents occurred in prisons with several high-profile escapes gaining media attention, the focus turned to security. New resources were invested in the provision of CCTV, alongside new legislation and policies to allow for other security measures to take place such as increased strip-searching, enforced segregation, closed visits and the regular opening and searching of prisoners' mail and belongings. As the prison population swelled in the 1990s so did the need for further prisons. Privatisation came to the fore, with the focus on creating cost-efficient institutions. When New Labour came to power in 1997, they brought a new approach to prisons based on risk management and encouraged by a penal populist attitude that prisons should be places of incapacitation. Since then, penal policy has been tied up with political imperatives. Lacey (2008) argues that the embracing of neoliberal market economics by Conservative and Labour governments alike has tended to prioritise penal exclusion over penal welfare. This is the position we find the prison system in today.

Summary

This chapter has provided a historical overview of key developments in relation to prisons. While not an in-depth exploration (see the further reading list for suggestions of texts that do this), what the chapter has sought to show is how the development of prisons is entwined with shifts and approaches to broader penal policy. It has also shown that the problems faced by modern prisons are ones that have always been present; they are not something new.

Questions to consider

1. How and why have there been changes in the focus and format of punishment, that is, from corporal punishment to incarceration?
2. Why do you think the Victorians favoured transportation and that it was private companies who delivered it?
3. What lessons do you think policy makers could learn from looking back in history at the development of the prison?

TAKING IT FURTHER

The following texts explore the history of prisons and penal policy in further detail:

- Brown, A. (2003). *English Society and the Prison: Time, Culture and Politics in the Development of the Modern Prison, 1850–1920*. Woodbridge: Boydell.

- Foucault, M. (1977). *Discipline and Punish: The Birth of the Prison*. Harmondsworth: Penguin.

- Ignatieff, M. (1978). *A Just Measure of Pain: The Penitentiary in the Industrial Revolution 1750–1850*, London: Macmillan.

The Ballad of Reading Gaol, a poem written by Oscar Wilde, chronicles his experience of being imprisoned and doing hard labour. It is well worth a read.

If you are particularly interested in the history of imprisonment and would like to see what life was like in a Victorian prison then the Prison & Police Museum in Ripon, North Yorkshire, is well worth a visit (https://riponmuseums.co.uk/prison-police-museum). You can step inside a cell, see a treadwheel and even have a go at turning the crank.

3

Prison: the modern context

Key learning outcomes

By the end of this chapter, you should be able to:

- Explain the modern organisation of the prison estate in England and Wales

- Describe how prisoners are categorised

- Understand who is sentenced to prison and what for

Introduction

This chapter focuses on the modern context of prisons. It draws on a range of data to provide a sense of the current state of the prison system. The chapter discusses the size of the prison estate, types of prisons including prison privatisation, and who is in prison and for what offence. The chapter explains the processes involved in sending people to custody and the different types of sentences individuals may be serving.

The prison estate in England and Wales

His Majesty's Prison and Probation Service (HMPPS) is an executive agency, sponsored by the Ministry of Justice. Its stated aims are to carry out sentences given by the courts, in custody and the community, and rehabilitate people in their care through education and employment (HMPPS, 2021a). These stated aims have been delivered and commissioned together with the Probation Service since 2004 after HMPPS was restructured from the National Offender Management Service (NOMS). There are 117 prisons in England and Wales, most of which are publicly operated (104) but some are privately run (13). The public sector prison service is split into seven geographical regions, each of which is led by a deputy director. There is a separate director for each of the specialist functional areas of the prison estate: namely, high security, young people and women.

Prison functions and categorisation

The prison estate is made up of a range of different buildings that vary in size, age, the types of prisoners held and security category. No two prisons are identical. The type of institution an individual is sent to depends on their age, gender and potential escape risk. The adult prison estate consists of different types of institutions which have different purposes, so alongside having a security category they also have a designated function.

High security prisons (category A)

There are 13 high security prisons in operation in England and Wales, of which there are two types. 'Core locals' serve a population as described further on (see 'Local prisons') but can also hold category A prisoners. 'Dispersals' spread category A prisoners to ensure that the most dangerous prisoners are not held in a single establishment (Beard, 2021: 8). Moreover, HMP Frankland has a specialist role in having a separation centre which houses radicalised and dangerous extremists. This was established in 2017 as part of the government's strategy to deal with extremism in prisons (see Chapter 5 for more information). The high security estate held only 946 category A prisoners in 2017 despite having an operational capacity of 3,283 (Ministry of Justice, 2017). The policy of dispersing category A prisoners across different prisons rather than having them all in one establishment was established after the publication of the Radzinowicz Report of 1968 (McEwan, 1986). The regime in high security prisons is the most severe in terms of security across the prison estate with prisoners subjected to increased cell and personal searches, more restrictive movement, limits on visits and increased monitoring of communications within and outside prison. Those individuals who are considered the most disruptive, challenging and dangerous are placed in a close supervision centre, which is essentially a prison within a prison. They are held in single cells, with limited stimuli and human contact; these units have been subject to a range of criticisms including that the conditions and treatment of the individuals within them amount to torture (UNHR, 2021). Despite being more severe in terms of security, high security prisons are considered to have better living conditions, less overcrowding, improved staff:prisoner ratios and more time out of the cells.

Spotlight prison: HMP Full Sutton

Full Sutton is a category A and B publicly run prison based in the small village of Full Sutton, outside York. It is a relatively modern prison, purpose built in 1987, and can hold up to 626 prisoners; the average population is around 560. In its most recent inspection report, it was awarded a 'reasonably good' grade for respect and rehabilitation and release planning, while safety had improved to the highest grade: 'good'. However, purposeful activity had declined to 'not sufficiently good' (HMIP, 2020a). The population at the prison has high levels of mental health issues with some of the country's most complex and dangerous individuals being held there. It is often thought that the men held at this prison have access to lots of things, particularly televisions and PlayStations, but as the individuals who live there will be doing so for a long time – and in some cases, forever – it is perhaps understandable that, in comparison with other prisons, additional provisions to occupy the men's time are supplied, subject to appropriate behaviour.

Local prisons (category B)

Originally, local prisons were designed to hold individuals who were on remand or awaiting sentencing. However, given the difficulties over the past decade regarding the sheer numbers of people sentenced to custody and the estate struggling to cope, most local prisons now hold individuals sentenced to short-term prison sentences (less than four years) or individuals who cannot be placed in a training prison because there is no space. Local prisons are by nature closed institutions, most of which are category B but they can hold men who are classed as category C or D prisoners, again due to a lack of space in training and/or open prisons. There are currently 30 male local prisons (HMPPS, 2021b) in operation in England and Wales, some of which are privately run but the vast majority are publicly owned. There is a lot of diversity in the prison estate in terms of the age of the institutions. Some of the prisons in this category are more than 150 years old – for instance, HMP Birmingham (built in 1849) and HMP Hull (opened in 1870) – meaning that it is often questioned whether they are fit for purpose. Due to their high population turnover, local prisons are often the least stable in terms of the environment. Common issues include some of the highest levels of violence, overcrowding and drug use in the estate; in local prisons they are often features of everyday prison life. Jewkes (2008: 156) described the local prison estate as 'old and shabby, chronically over-crowded, poorly resourced and with higher suicide rates than any other prison [type]'.

Spotlight prison: HMP Leeds

HMP Leeds is a classic example of an inner-city Victorian prison. Built in 1847, it holds on average 1,051 adult men despite having a certified normal accommodation use of 687 (HMIP, 2020b), meaning that the vast proportion of those held there are in overcrowded conditions. In its most recent inspection report (HMIP, 2020b), it was found that the prison was rated as 'reasonably good' in terms of respect and rehabilitation and release planning but 'not sufficiently good' in terms of safety and purposeful activity. 'Levels of violence had also reduced and serious violence had gone down considerably, though over a third of prisoners said they felt unsafe and intimidated by staff. Prisoners suggested that the use of force by staff was sometimes excessive, and inspectors found evidence to support their view' (HMIP, 2020b). It is argued in the HMIP (2020b) report that a number of the problems that the prison has are driven or aggravated by the constant turnover in terms of population and the age of the institution.

Training prisons (can be either category B or C)

In a similar vein to high security prisons, training prisons have a specific function: to provide the men with full employment and training so that they can progress through the estate to release on licence. Training prisons hold men who have at least four years of their sentence left to serve and are thus considered to be medium- to long-term sentenced prisoners. Individuals serving their sentences at a training prison will not be released from there; in most circumstances, they will be moved either to a resettlement or an open establishment to complete their sentences. There are 30 training prisons in the prison estate, most of which are category C in terms of security level. Less overcrowded than local prisons, they have more stable populations due to lower turnover rates. Several training prisons have specialist facilities or they hold certain types of offenders; for instance, HMP Whatton houses sex offenders, HMP Gartree has the main 'lifer' unit in the system and HMP Grendon has a therapeutic unit. Training prisons tend to be more remote in terms of their location; this can result in prisoners being further away from their families.

Spotlight prison: HMP Buckley Hall

HMP Buckley Hall is a category C training prison in Rochdale, Lancashire. It is a relatively modern facility having been rebuilt in 1995; it holds on average 450 adult men. Buckley Hall was the fourth prison to be contracted-out in the UK in 1995 but it came back into public sector management in 2000, and in 2003 it became a closed female training prison. In 2005 it was reassigned to become a male category C prison. It has a population of men serving four years or more and a high number are serving indeterminate or life sentences. Buckley Hall is considered to be an excellent prison. It was rated as 'good' in three out of four areas with inspectors commenting that it is a 'very safe' prison (HMIP, 2019a). Staff–prisoner relationships are a strength of the prison; often this is due to the length of time prisoners spend there, allowing for relationships to form and trust to develop.

Resettlement (category C or D)

Resettlement prisons are another type of prison in the secure estate that have a specific purpose: to equip the men with the knowledge and skills they need for release. They are often category C or D prisons but they can also be training prisons, making it challenging to identify which among them have the 'resettlement' focus. These prisons hold category C prisoners serving sentences of between 12 months and four years and will in the last three months of their sentence help them work towards release. The specific aim is to increase an individual's level of personal responsibility towards the end of their sentence, thereby preparing them for independent living within the community on release. Three key areas are focused on: accommodation, employment and financial security. This type of prison was a specific policy creation of the Transforming Rehabilitation agenda, which saw 70 prisons designated as resettlement prisons (Taylor et al, 2017) and the introduction of the privatisation agenda into probation. This also brought about the extension of mandatory community supervision to all those who had spent more than one day in custody, meaning that all individuals in custody were required to have effective resettlement support in place before their release. The overall goal of this was to reduce reoffending and increase successful rehabilitation post-prison, yet it was viewed that rebranding penal institutions as 'resettlement' or 'reform' prisons does little to address the fundamental problems that have been a feature of the prison system for many years (Taylor et al, 2017).

Spotlight prison: HMP Wormwood Scrubs

HMP Wormwood Scrubs was built by prisoners from Millbank Gaol between 1875 and 1891 and is in west London. It is a reception and resettlement prison holding adult men and some young adults. It holds approximately 1,000 prisoners of whom an estimated third are foreign nationals, more than half are ethnically minoritised and two thirds are unsentenced (HMIP, 2021a). The prison has an infamous reputation for its poor conditions, which culminated in an inspection report describing its 'intractability and persistence of failure' (HMIP, 2017). However, more recent inspection reports (HMIP, 2019b; 2021a) show the prison has improved, noting there was a better atmosphere than there had been in the past (HMIP, 2021a). It was rated as 'good' in terms of safety but 'not sufficiently good' in the other three areas, showing there was still more room for improvement. Given its allocation as a resettlement prison it is of concern that it was still rated as 'not sufficiently good' in terms of rehabilitation and resettlement planning, especially given it was reported that there were no accredited programmes to reduce the risk of reoffending at the prison (HMIP, 2021a).

Open prisons (category D)

Open prisons have one of the most specific functions in the secure estate, which is to allow individuals who have been in custody for long periods to gradually have more interaction with the community. To do this, open prisons do not have many overt security features like other prisons; most, for instance, do not have a perimeter fence. To be transferred to an open prison individuals must be assessed as a minimum security risk and be unlikely to escape. There are 13 designated open prisons in operation in England and Wales. Prisoners often leave the prison on a temporary licence to undertake employment, voluntary work or visit family. The goal is to encourage prisoners to gradually resettle into the community, which is particularly important given that lengthy incarceration can cause individuals to become institutionalised. Evidence shows that for life-sentenced prisoners, gradual reintegration reduces the risk of potential reoffending by as much as three times (Pennington and Crewe, 2015). Recently, concerns have been raised about open prisons and the process of release on temporary licence (ROTL) due to a number of individuals committing further serious crimes following release (HMIP, 2014). The outcome of a review (HMIP, 2014) into ROTL was that the use of the scheme was tightened as well as the procedures for releasing people from open prisons. ROTL has subsequently become, despite the vast amount of evidence showing its effectiveness as a tool for reducing the risk of reoffending, a privilege rather than a right, with there being a greater emphasis on risk assessing the individual before any decision to release is made (Pennington and Crewe, 2015).

> ## Spotlight prison: HMP/YOI Thorn Cross
> HMP/YOI Thorn Cross was purpose built in 1985 as an open establishment for male, juvenile and young prisoners. It was re-rolled in 2008 to become a prison for 18- to 25-year-old men but, due to the decrease in prisoners under 25, this upper age limit was removed in 2013 and it is now classed as a category D open resettlement prison for young adult and adult male prisoners. It is a relatively small facility that can hold up to 330 men. The fundamental purpose of Thorn Cross is to prepare prisoners for return to the community and previous inspections found that it had performed this role consistently well (HMIP, 2021b). In its most recent inspection report, Thorn Cross was viewed as an impressive establishment with a culture and physical environment that supported rehabilitative endeavour and delivered positive outcomes for prisoners (HMIP, 2021b).

Female prison estate

The female prison estate is much smaller in terms of the number of institutions yet geographically much more dispersed around England. There are no female prisons in Wales. Due to the nature of the female prison population (see Chapter 4), 12 institutions hold women and are classified into different types; most have the dual function of being a local and resettlement prison or a training and resettlement prison. Two out of the 12 prisons are privately run; the rest are managed by HMPPS. There are two open prisons in the female estate: Askham Grange in Yorkshire and East Sutton Park in Kent. The sheer geographic spread of just these two institutions shows the challenges that women in the secure estate face in terms of geography on their journey towards resettlement. A number of the prisons in the female secure estate are what are known as 'split sites' whereby one half of the prison operates for women and the other part as a YOI for young women (those under the age of 21). Uniquely, HMP Peterborough is a privately run prison which operates as the only split-site prison in England and Wales, holding both adult men and adult women who are kept apart at all times. There are six mother and baby units located within six of the female prisons. Women who give birth in prison can keep their babies for the first 18 months if they are successful in securing a place in a mother and baby unit. Also, if they have a child under

18 months old and are sentenced to custody they can apply to bring the child to prison with them. Contrary to popular opinion, places in mother and baby units are not guaranteed and there is a clear application and assessment process.

Spotlight prison: HMP/YOI New Hall

HMP/YOI New Hall opened in 1933 as a prison to hold men who were due for release from HMP Wakefield. It has had many different functions since it was built and has held every type of prisoner population from adult men to young people and its present-day population of women. It currently operates as a women's resettlement and local prison; it can hold 425 but averages a population of 395 (HMIP, 2019c). Given the small number of female establishments, it is often the case that prisons have a mixed population with New Hall being an example; at any one time, it holds women on remand up to those women sentenced to serving life. Most of the women at New Hall are serving long-term prison sentences of four years or more. According to the most recent inspection report, New Hall was found to be a safe, respectful and purposeful prison where work to resettle and rehabilitate prisoners was improving (HMIP, 2019c). Given the age of the prison, concerns were raised about the quality of the accommodation that some of the women were living in. Interestingly, HMIP (2019c) reported that the proportion of female staff was too low and it was something that was a very stark and particular feature of the senior team.

Youth secure estate

Children, in a prison context, are those aged 10–17. For those who may be sentenced to custody there is a bespoke secure estate for them managed by the Youth Justice Board. There are three different types of institution that a child under the age of 17 can be sent to; the decision about which one depends on their age, gender and assessed level of vulnerability.

- Secure children's homes (SCHs): these are run by local councils and essentially operate like a children's home but one where the residents cannot leave. They are specifically for children aged 10–14 and are the smallest institutions in the secure estate, ranging from eight beds to 40. SCHs provide the children with 30 hours of education and training a week, following a school-day pattern.
- Secure training centres (STCs): these are purpose-built institutions that are privately run. Usually, girls aged 12–17, boys aged 12–14 and older boys who are considered vulnerable are sent to an STC. There are three STCs, each of which houses between 50 and 80 young people, usually subdivided into units of between five and eight residents. Their regime is education focused, providing the children with a timetable based on a school day.
- Young offender institutions (YOIs): these are the most like prisons in the secure estate for children; there are five dedicated YOIs for children under

17 years of age. They hold boys aged 15–17; some are split sites, holding under-17s in one half and young adults (those aged 18–21) in the other half. They are the biggest institutions in the secure estate for children, housing between 60 and 400.

> ### Spotlight prison: HMYOI Feltham A
>
> HMYOI Feltham A is a prison in west London that holds children aged 15–18. It has a partner institution, HMYOI Feltham B, which holds young adults (18–21 years). Feltham was built in 1854 as an industrial school and in 1910 was taken over by the Prison Commissioner to become a borstal. As a prison it has a notorious reputation for poor conditions and treatment of the children it holds, something that has been problematic for a considerable period. When Feltham was last fully inspected in 2019, HMIP (2019d) ranked the prison as 'poor' in three out of the four areas of the healthy prisons test. It concluded that the situation was so dire at the institution that the Chief Inspector needed to issue an Urgent Notification, the first to ever be issued to an institution that holds children (HMIP, 2019d). This notification triggers a chain of events which result in the Secretary of State for Justice being held accountable for the establishment and required to issue an action plan for improvement. The situation at Feltham was so poor, with both staff and children reported to be significantly unsafe, that the Secretary of State responded by stopping any more children from being sent there. Despite the challenges of the pandemic, in a recent scrutiny visit HMIP (2021c) reported that conditions had improved at the YOI; in part, this has been helped by a smaller population being in the institution.

Young adults

For those aged 18–21, there are designated institutions for them. Referred to as young adults within the prison system, they will be placed into a YOI which is usually attached to either an adult male prison or a split site with a YOI for young people. They operate a standard prison regime and are used as a stop-gap between youth custody and the adult estate in recognition of the vulnerability due to their age that young adults can have.

Prison privatisation

The privatisation of the Prison Service began in 1986 when the prison population had reached a record high (51,000). The Home Affairs parliamentary committee at the time, following practices that had taken place in the USA, decided to outsource the building and running of penal establishments. It was believed that the process would ultimately save the taxpayer money, speed up the building of new prisons and create more efficient establishments (Nathan, 2003). HMP

Wolds was the first privately run prison established in 1992 following amendments made to the Criminal Justice Act 1991 to allow for the contracting out of penal establishments. The Conservative government at the time went further in 1993 by amending the Criminal Justice Act 1991 again to allow for existing prisons to be privatised as well as new ones. New Labour further established processes for privatisation with the creation of the private finance initiative in 1997. The scheme covered the contracting out of prisons in all aspects from financing to design, construction and operation, with the contracts lasting for 25 years. Nathan (2003) states that in 1996 the aspiration was to have 25 per cent of the prison estate managed by the private sector; in 2022 this stands at just 11 per cent. Due to the accountability placed on private prisons in terms of targets and subsequent financial penalties if missed, they can perform better in some areas than public prisons. A key difference between public and private prisons is that the latter will only operate to the contractually agreed number of prisoners; once that number is reached the prison is officially full so the prison is less likely to be overcrowded than a public prison. Given the impact that overcrowding has on a prison (see further on), this can again contribute to somewhat better conditions inside a private prison. Yet, in more recent years this has been found not to be the case as private prisons have become overcrowded as financial profit has outweighed the imperative for safety. Whether private prisons are better than public prisons has been a consistent debate; arguably, if private prisons were better there would be more of them yet the rate of privatisation is decreasing, rather than the opposite. Crewe and Liebling (2018: 171) found in their study exploring this issue that private sector prisons appeared at both the top and bottom of the quality spectrum. When looking at scoring prisons on prisoner safety, policing and security, drugs and exploitation, decency and staff–prisoner relationships, two private prisons were rated as 'very good', two public sector prisons as 'good' and three private prisons were rated as 'poor' or 'average' (Crewe and Liebling, 2018).

The coalition government in 2012 abolished the whole prison contracting out process, replacing it with what was called public sector benchmarking. This meant that staffing levels in the public sector would be benchmarked or matched against those in the private sector. The benchmarking exercise is one viewed as a complete unmitigated disaster of government policy which resulted in the loss of many prison officer jobs. Many prison officers took voluntary redundancy or retirement with the result that significant levels of experienced officers were lost in a short space of time. The loss of such a high number of staff meant that there were fewer staff looking after more prisoners (Prison Reform Trust, 2021). HMPPS reportedly saved £900 million between 2010 and 2015 through this process but at a cost of prison conditions deteriorating and levels of violence reaching exceptionally high levels (see Chapter 6). The lack of thought by the government in this process is astounding; they did not consider the key differences between public prisons and private prisons when establishing this approach. The reasons why private prisons can operate with fewer staff than public prisons are because they are bespoke and purpose-built; they also have up-to-date IT facilities, hence their administration is more efficient. These two issues were never taken into account by the Ministry of Justice at the time of creating benchmarking, the effects of which will take years to eradicate from the prison system.

The final key issue in relation to prison privatisation poses an ethical and moral dilemma. Should private companies be allowed to profit from imprisonment? Given that it is the state that imposes prison sentences, the question has been raised as to whether the state should therefore oversee and manage those establishments which carry them out (Harrison, 2020). It appears counterproductive to create a business from imprisonment, particularly at times when charities and not-for-profit organisations such as the Howard League for Penal Reform and the Prison Reform Trust are actively campaigning for the reduction in imprisonment. While it might be a somewhat cynical view, it appears that the types of businesses the penal system attracts might not subscribe to its goals and rehabilitative aims (see Chapter 6). After all, their profit relies on the revolving door of imprisonment so it appears counterintuitive to involve them in the process of rehabilitation. As Shichor (1998: 85) has stated, large companies can sway government policy which could result in corporate influence working in favour of more and longer sentences. The future of private prisons is unclear. The government has recently announced the building of four new prisons, three of which will be privately run (MoJ, 2020g). This is somewhat surprising given the number of prisons that over recent years have been taken back into public control following significant failures (see Chapter 7), as well as the abject disaster of the government's Transforming Rehabilitation programme, which saw the probation service privatised then ultimately end up back in public control (BBC News, 2021). However, as governments of all persuasions are increasingly stressed in their efforts to provide the range of social, educational, health, welfare and justice services that citizens have come to expect (Rynne and Harding, 2016), it is hard to imagine that privatisation within the justice system and prisons more specifically will not continue to persist in some way.

Geography of the prison estate

Prison establishments are geographically spread throughout England and Wales, from Northumbria in England to the Isle of Wight in the south. Adult male prisons are divided into two geographical regions: north and south. The prison estate also has separate directorates for women, young people, the high security estate, contracted-out prisons and Wales (MoJ, 2022a). The prison an individual is sent to post-sentence will depend on the area of the country and the specific court at which the case has been heard. It is usual for a court to allocate prisoners to a prison in the area as there are normally local prisons attached to specific courts. However, on some occasions, the local prison may be full or the particulars of an individual's situation and categorisation may require that they are sent to a specific institution which may be further afield. In the case of women and young people, these institutions are sparse in numbers and geographically dispersed around the country, meaning that it is often the case that women and young people sentenced to custody will be placed a long distance from home. For instance, there is no custodial provision in Wales for women so they must be placed in an institution in England; on average women are held 64 miles away from their homes (Women in Prison, 2015). This can have a significantly detrimental effect on their ability to maintain contact with their families, which is well documented and regarded as important for rehabilitation and resettlement (see Chapter 4).

Recent and current trends in prison populations

The prison population in relation to overcrowding has been scrutinised for decades because it is one of the barometers of how successfully or unsuccessfully the Prison Service is performing. It has increased significantly in England and Wales over time, from 9,377 in 1940 to an all-time high of just over 88,000 in 2011 (see Figure 3.1). Since that peak it has remained relatively stable with around 80,000 being in the custodial estate at any one time (Sturge, 2021).

According to Sturge (2021: 7), as of the end of September 2021, the total prison population was 78,756, having fallen overall since February 2020. This is the result of fewer people being sentenced to custody because the criminal courts were operating at reduced capacity during the COVID-19 restrictions.

The rise in the prison population in the 2000s when the country was under the control of New Labour can be linked to several issues:

1. The abandonment by Charles Clarke, then-Home Secretary, of his target of keeping the upper limits of the prison population at around 80,000, largely due to an increased appetite for prison as the main form of punishment.
2. Judges and magistrates choosing to sentence more individuals to immediate custody as opposed to using alternative sentences such as community-based punishment. This is viewed to have been driven by a loss of faith in community punishment.
3. A wider policy approach of New Labour to be 'tough on crime and tough on the causes of crime' (Pratt, 2007), which built on the Conservative approach in the 1990s of 'prison works' and was continued by David Cameron in 2011 after the August riots.

Current prison population projections forecast that it will be around 98,700 by June 2026. It should be noted that older projections forecasted a much higher prison population than is currently the case: for example, the 2014–20 projections predicted that the prison population of England and Wales would have exceeded 90,000 by June 2019 whereas the true figure was below 83,000 (Sturge, 2021).

Figure 3.1: Total average daily prison population of England and Wales since 1900

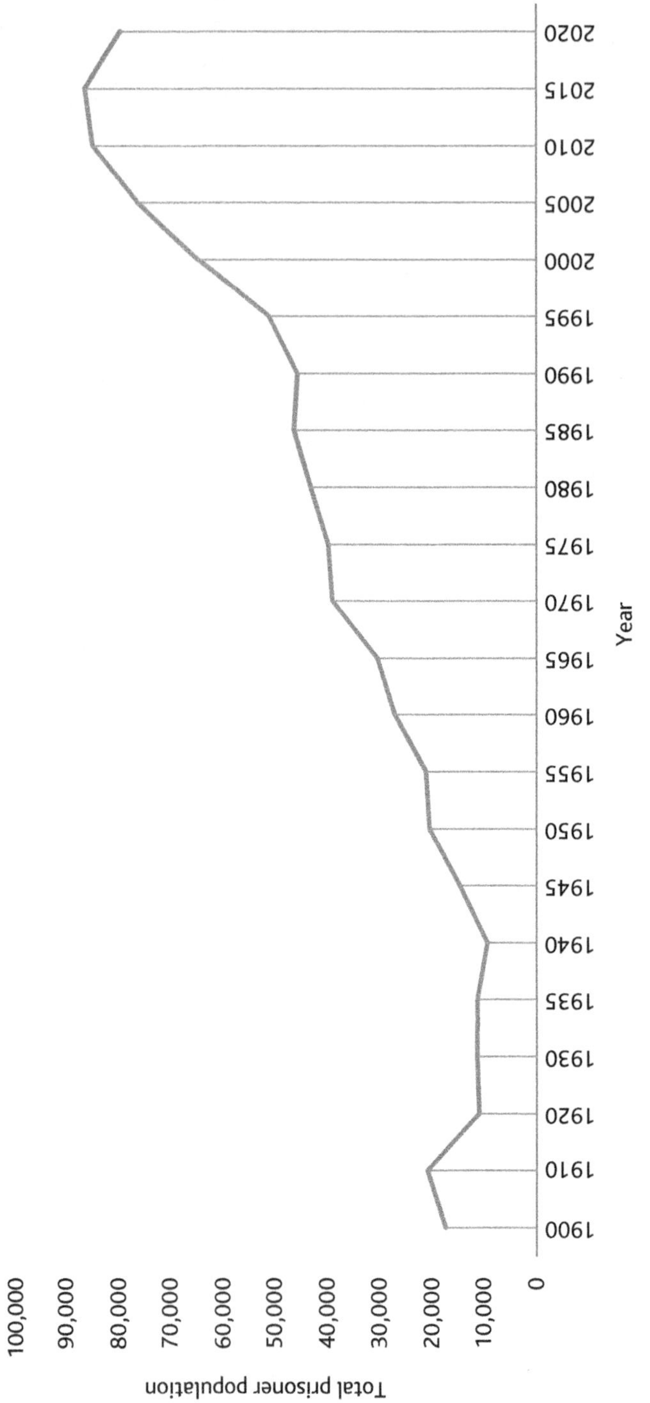

Source: Data from Sturge, 2021

Prison data trends

To provide some additional insights into prison population trends and corresponding events, it is interesting to consider the following six dates and sets of prison population figures:

- December 1992: 40,600 prisoners – the lowest recorded rate of prisoners in the last 30 years.
- May 1997: 60,131 prisoners – the number of prisoners when the New Labour government was elected.
- May 2010: 85,009 prisoners – the number of prisoners during the week in which the coalition government was formed.
- December 2011: 88,179 prisoners – the record high of the total number of prisoners in recent times, said to have been driven by the remanding and sentencing of people alleged to have been involved in the city riots which took place in August 2011 in England.
- June 2017: 85,367 – the number of prisoners during the week in which the Conservatives won the 2017 general election.
- March 2020: 83,708 – the number of prisoners during the week the first COVID-19 lockdown restrictions were announced in England.

Adapted from Scott and Flynn (2014: 137)

Prison population figures are often considered in relation to the physical capacity of the prison estate; is there enough space in the prison estate to hold the people sentenced to custody? This calculation is done in two ways: useable operational capacity (UOC) and certified normal accommodation (CNA). It is through an exploration of the relationship between the prison population, UOC and CNA that it can be determined as to whether individual prisons or more broadly the prison estate is overcrowded. In January 2022, the UOC in prison establishments in England and Wales was 81,292 (MoJ, 2022b). The operational capacity is the total number of prisoners that an establishment can hold taking into account control, security and the proper running and operation of a planned regime. Therefore, the UOC of the estate is the sum of all establishments' operational capacity minus 2,750 places. This is known as the operating margin and reflects the constraints imposed by the need to provide appropriate accommodation for different classes of prisoner: that is, by sex, age, security category, conviction status, single-cell risk assessment and also due to geographical distribution (MoJ, 2022b). Each prison has a designated operational capacity and also what is called a CNA; the CNA represents the 'good, decent standard of accommodation that the service aspires to provide all prisoners' (MoJ, 2012). Any prison establishment or cell that is operating above the CNA is officially overcrowded. Overcrowding is a well-documented fact of the prison estate; the system as a whole has been overcrowded every year since 1994 (Prison Reform Trust, 2021). Two in every three prisons in England and Wales are overcrowded (80 of the 121 prisons), with nearly 18,700 people held in overcrowded accommodation – more than a fifth of the prison population (MoJ, 2020a). Overcrowding was first highlighted in the era of John Howard and Elizabeth Fry in the 18th and 19th centuries (see Chapter 2) and has plagued the prison system ever since. There is a strong link between overcrowding and deteriorating prison conditions – HMIP regularly comments in its inspection reports on poor conditions, citing overcrowding as a key aggravating factor. Overcrowding affects whether activities, staff and other resources are available to undertake the work that prisons are meant to do such as reducing the risk of reoffending. Over 12,000 prisoners are being held two to a cell that was designed for one. Many of these cells have unscreened toilets, which fail to provide even basic human dignity. The oldest establishments in the prison estate are also among the most overcrowded and therefore are the least fit for purpose. Table 3.1 shows the top five overcrowded prisons as of January 2022; as can be seen, four out of the five prisons are either Victorian or pre-Victorian establishments.

Overcrowding is experienced most sharply in the local male prison estate. This means that cells originally designed to hold one person now contain bunk beds to allow for more people to be held in the prison. Usually, it means two individuals are sharing a cell designed for one but in some prisons this can mean three people are sharing a cell designed for one. As individuals within the prison estate do not get to choose whom they share a cell with this can result in a clash of personalities when prisoners are forced to mix. The main problem, however, is the lack of space that overcrowding results in and the subsequent lack of privacy. The proposed solution to the overcrowding problem as promised by successive governments has been to build its way out of the issue. In March 2017, the MoJ announced plans to build four new prisons: one to be sited in South Wales, one adjacent to HMP Full Sutton in Yorkshire, and to redevelop HMP/YOI Rochester in Kent and HMP/YOI Hindley in Wigan. This would have added up to 10,000 modern prison places (MoJ, 2020b). Additionally, two further new prisons have also been announced that will be built at HMP Five Wells in Wellingborough and a new prison in Glen Parva in Leicestershire (MoJ, 2021a), taking the total to six new institutions and

Table 3.1: Top five overcrowded prisons (January 2022)

Prison	CNA	Prison population	% of CNA
Leeds (built 1847)	641	1,093	171
Lincoln (built 1872)	403	664	165
Durham (built 1819)	578	945	163
Preston (built 1790)	426	675	158
Doncaster (built 1994)	738	1,144	155

Source: Howard League for Penal Reform, 2022

an increase of 20,000 prison places. Yet, they have been affected by problems which have caused significant delays including the impact of the COVID-19 pandemic, delays access to building materials caused by Britain's exit from the EU, and legal challenges from residents and local businesses who are objecting to the planning applications. So far, only two of the planned six prisons have started to be built. Building new prisons may not be the only answer to the overcrowding that plagues the prison estate. A renewed focus and drive to use alternative methods of punishment may be a better way to deal with non-dangerous, low-level offending. As Juliet Lyon (2012), previous director of the Prison Reform Trust has stated:

> Building our way out of the overcrowding problem is not the answer. The prison population can be safely reduced by curbing inflation in sentencing, calling a halt to any unnecessary use of custodial remand and investing in effective community penalties.

Categorising prisoners

When individuals are sentenced to custody there is a clear set of criteria in place. Adult males (those over 22 years old) will be assessed based on the risks they pose in terms of:

- the likelihood of escape or absconding;
- the risk of harm to the public in the event of an escape or abscondment; and
- any control issues that affect the security and good order of the prison and the safety of those within it. (Ministry of Justice, 2020c)

The individual is then assigned to the prison within the lowest security category consistent with managing those risks: category A (high security), B, C or D. The female adult estate operates in a similar manner but with significantly fewer prisons to choose from than in the adult male estate.

Who is in prison?

The vast proportion of individuals within the custodial estate are men; they dominate the estate, accounting for 96 per cent of the prison population with women making up the remaining 4 per cent (Prison Reform Trust, 2021). It is often thought that our prisons hold our country's most dangerous individuals who have committed some of the most depraved acts imaginable. In some ways this is true, but when the social backgrounds of the vast proportion of those who make up the prison population are explored a more complex picture begins to emerge. When compared with how individuals are categorised according to their supposed security risk, the administrative classification system does not show the depth and breadth of the disadvantage in the prison population.

Table 3.2: Social characteristics of adult prisoners

Characteristic	Prison population	General population
Taken into care as a child	24% (31% for women, 24% for men)	2%
Experienced abuse as a child	29% (53% for women, 27% for men)	20%
Observed violence in the home as a child	41% (50% for women, 40% for men)	14%
Regularly played truant from school	59%	5.2% (England) and 4.8% (Wales)
Expelled or permanently excluded from school	42% (32% for women, 43% for men)	In 2005 <1% of school pupils were permanently excluded (England)
No qualifications	47%	15% of working-age population
Unemployed in the four weeks before custody	68% (81% for women, 67% for men)	7.7% of the economically active population are unemployed
Never had a job	13%	3.9%
Homeless before entering custody	15%	4% have been homeless or in temporary accommodation
Have children under the age of 18	54%	c.27% of the over-18 population
Are young fathers (aged 18–20)	19%	4%
Identified as suffering from both anxiety and depression	25% (49% for women, 23% for men)	15%
Have attempted suicide at some point	46% for women, 21% for men	6%
Have ever used Class A drug	64%	13%
Drank alcohol every day in the four weeks before custody	22%	16% of men and 10% of women reported drinking on a daily basis

Source: Prison Reform Trust, 2021

Table 3.2 shows some of the complex and intertwined economic, health- and social-related problems experienced by adult prisoners.

As the substantial evidence indicates, there are enormously high levels of disadvantage among those in prison. This is not simply that those who receive custodial sentences are predominately drawn from the poorer and more marginal sections of our society, though this is very much the case – research evidence points to a problem of multiple disadvantage among those in our prisons. It is the complexity of the multiple disadvantage, the effects of the prison environment and the fact that prison often cannot fix the issues that individuals present with because the solutions often lie in broader areas of social policy than the prison system has influence over which result in questions over whether prison works or not.

What are people in prison for and for how long?

Prison sentences are continuing to get longer. The average prison sentence is now over four months longer than a decade ago at 16.4 months. For more serious, indictable offences, the average is now 58 months (over four years) – over two years longer than ten years ago (MoJ, 2021b).

Evidence has shown that short sentences are less effective than community sentences at reducing reoffending yet nearly half (47 per cent) of all people entering prison are serving a sentence of six months or less (MoJ, 2020d). The majority of people who are imprisoned are convicted of non-violent offences. Despite media representations, only 6 per cent of those sentenced to custody had been convicted of a sexual offence.

There are several different types of sentences that can result in individuals being imprisoned. These are:

- suspended sentences
- determinate sentences
- extended sentences
- life sentences

When an individual will be released depends on the type of sentence the judge or magistrates give them at their sentencing hearing. In 2020, 76,000 defendants were given an immediate custodial sentence, representing 6 per cent of offenders sentenced that year (MoJ, 2021b).

Determinate sentences are the most common type of prison sentence used in the CJS. When an individual is sentenced to a period in custody – for instance, four years – that is the maximum amount of time they can spend in prison but it does not necessarily mean they will spend the whole of those four years in prison. The length of the sentence is key in determining when an individual is released and what subsequently happens after release:

- Individuals who are sentenced to **less than two years** will be released at the halfway point of their sentence and will be placed on licence and subject to licence conditions for the remainder of their sentence (which will be served in the community). According to current approaches, the individual will be subject to supervision. Table 3.3 shows a series of examples as to how this works.
- Those who are sentenced to **two years or more** will usually serve half their sentence in prison and serve the remainder on licence in the community. The

Table 3.3: Examples of periods of supervision for sentences of less than two years

Sentence imposed by court	Period in custody before release	Arrangements on release
6 months	3 months	3 months' licence and 9 months' post-sentence supervision. Total supervision 12 months
10 months	5 months	5 months' licence and 7 months' post-sentence supervision. Total supervision 12 months
18 months	9 months	9 months' licence and 3 months' post-sentence supervision. Total supervision 12 months

Source: Sentencing Council, 2022

individual will have conditions attached to their licence; if they breach those conditions, they may be recalled to prison. Where an individual has been convicted of a serious violent or sexual offence and sentenced to seven years or more, then the individual will be released at the two-thirds point. Equally, for individuals convicted of terrorist offences, the release arrangements are different and they are likely to serve two thirds or more of their sentence in custody.

In 2021, 63,540 individuals were given a determinate sentence, representing 7 per cent of the total offenders sentenced and 99 per cent of total immediate custodial sentence outcomes (MoJ, 2021b).

Extended determinate sentences can be given to anyone aged 18 or over when:

- the individual is found guilty of a specified violent, sexual or terrorist offence (as listed in Schedule 18 of the Sentencing Code);
- the court determines that the individual poses a significant risk of committing further specified offences to the public;
- a sentence of life imprisonment is not available or justified;
- the individual has a previous conviction for an offence listed in Schedule 14 of the Sentencing Code or the current offence justifies an appropriate custodial term of at least four years.

Such sentences are imposed where the court determines that an individual is dangerous and that an extended determinate sentence is required; it means that the individual will also have an extended licence period so that the public is protected from risk of serious harm. It is the judge who determines how long the individual should stay in prison and fixes the extended licence period up to a maximum of eight years. In a similar way to individuals sentenced to a determinate sentence of four years or more for serious violent or sexual offences, those on an extended determinate sentence can apply for parole two thirds of the way through their custodial term. If they are not granted parole then they will be automatically released at the end of their custodial term.

Life sentences are, according to the Sentencing Council (2022), the only sentence that lasts for life. When a judge pronounces a life sentence they must determine the minimum term the individual will spend in prison before becoming eligible to apply for parole, often referred to as a tariff. The only exception to this is when a judge passes a 'whole-life order'; this sentence means that the individual will spend the rest of their life in prison – they will never be released. Contrary to popular belief, there are three different versions of the life sentence that can be used by the court. Mandatory life sentences are required to be given in all cases of murder; there is no alternative sentence. If an individual is convicted of murder, they will be sentenced to a mandatory life sentence with the minimum term they will serve set by the judge at their trial. There is guidance available to the judge to determine the tariff; it sets out different types of cases and starting points that judges can refer to. For example, where a murder is committed with a knife or other weapon that the person took to the scene intending to commit an offence, the starting point for the minimum term would be 25 years. Once the individual has served the minimum tariff and they have satisfied the Parole Board that they are no longer a risk to the public they will be released but placed on a life licence which is monitored by the Probation Service. They may be recalled to prison at any time if they are considered to be a risk to the public regardless of whether they have committed a further offence.

One of the most controversial sentences in operation in the CJS is the whole-life order. This sentence is used in the most serious cases of murder; this means that the crime committed is so serious that the offender will never be released from prison. As of January 2022, 63 whole-life prisoners were serving their sentence in the prison estate. The list of individuals serving such a sentence includes Rosemary West (convicted in November 1995 of the murder of ten women and girls at her home alongside her husband), Dale Cregan (convicted in June 2013 of killing two Greater Manchester police officers in a gun and grenade attack) and Khairi Saadallah (sentenced to a whole-life order in January 2021 for murdering three people in a park in Reading in 2020).

Finally, there are discretionary life sentences which allow judges to hand out a life sentence for a number of different crimes including rape or robbery should they consider that the individual and the offence warrant one. There are specific criteria that must be met for such a sentence to be handed out.

Summary

This chapter has presented the modern context of the prison estate in England and Wales. It has described the different functions of the prisons within the estate as well as how prisoners are categorised. The recent and current trends regarding the prison population provide key insights into the challenges that prisons currently face in terms of overcrowding. The impact of this will be discussed in future chapters.

Questions to consider

1. What is the current organisational structure of the prison system in England and Wales and what impact does this have on the aims of imprisonment?
2. How many prisoners are currently in prison and what for? Can you update the statistics presented?
3. Do short-term prison sentences work better than long-term prison sentences? What is the impact of length of sentence on a prisoner?

TAKING IT FURTHER

There are several texts that explore the issues presented in this chapter, which you might wish to consult for further detail:

- Cavadino, M., Dignan, J. and Mair, G. (2013). *The Penal System: An Introduction*. 5th edn. London: Sage.

- Jewkes, Y., Bennett, J. and Crewe, B. (eds) (2016). *Handbook on Prisons*. 2nd edn. London: Routledge.

- Owens, F. (2012). *The Little Book of Prison: A Beginner's Guide*. Hampshire: Waterside Press. This is a guide written for prisoners by a serving prisoner about what to expect when in prison.

It is also worth consulting the various government websites for the organisations mentioned in the chapter as they are often the most up-to-date sources for contextual information:

- His Majesty's Prison and Probation Service: https://www.gov.uk/government/organisations/hm-prison-and-probation-service

- His Majesty's Chief Inspectorate of Prisons: https://www.justiceinspectorates.gov.uk/hmiprisons

- Ministry of Justice: https://www.gov.uk/government/organisations/ministry-of-justice

4

Doing time: how different groups experience prison differently

Key learning outcomes

By the end of this chapter, you should be able to:

- Explain the key differences in how women, ethnically minoritised people and older people experience prison differently

- Describe the key issues for each group

- Understand how the prison system caters for and meets the needs of different prisoner populations

Introduction

The focus of this chapter is to think critically about specific groups in the prison system and how they experience prison differently. While this is not an exhaustive exploration of all the different groups who are recognised under diversity legislation, the focus is on three specific groups to show how, depending on factors including age, gender, race and ethnicity, individuals experience prison differently. Each of these groups is interesting to explore for different reasons. Women make up approximately 4 per cent of the prison population and are housed in only 12 establishments across the prison estate, yet they are one of the most vulnerable groups for reasons of their poor mental health and experiences of trauma (Women in Prison, 2017). There is now a greater disproportionality in the number of Black people in prison in England and Wales than in the USA (Lammy, 2017). People aged 60 and over are the fastest-growing age group in the prison estate (Sturge, 2021). These three observations indicate why it is important to explore these three groups, the reasons behind the increases and what it means for their prison experience. This chapter will outline how these groups experience prison differently and discuss, critically, the extent to which the prison system caters for and meets the needs of different prisoner populations.

Women in custody

Women are considered a minority in the context of the CJS, accounting for around 10 per cent of the probation caseload and only 4 per cent of the prison population (PRT, 2021). It is well documented across waves of academic-, policy- and practice-based research that women's routes into offending are as different from men's as are their routes out of it. It is also known that as a population within the context of the CJS they are more likely to have complex needs, hence research has consistently called for a different approach to be taken to women in the CJS, specifically in the context of prison (Corston, 2007; Women in Prison, 2017).

The female adult prison population has increased over time from 841 women being in custody in 1965 to 3,225 in January 2022 (MoJ, 2022b) but at a slower rate than the male prison population increase. There are 12 prisons in England and Wales that house adult female offenders; two of the 12 operate as open prisons (Askham Grange and East Sutton Park). To understand the nature of female imprisonment, it is worth considering the following statistical information:

- Most women entering prison to serve a sentence (77 per cent) have committed a non-violent offence.
- More women are sent to prison to serve a sentence for theft than for violence, robbery, sexual offences, fraud, drugs and motoring offences combined.
- The proportion of women being sent to prison to serve very short prison sentences has risen sharply. In 1993 only a third of custodial sentences given to women were for less than six months – in 2019 it was nearly double this (62 per cent). (MoJ, 2020b)

The nature of female offending is different from male offending, as these statistics demonstrate. A series of inquiries and reports in recent decades have all concluded that prison is rarely a necessary, appropriate or proportionate response to women who offend. Historically, women who have been labelled as criminals have been considered 'more depraved and morally corrupt' than men (Welch, 2011). Women's behaviour has been scrutinised for a long time, with many original theories on female offending considering them to be 'mad or bad' as opposed to having other more social or economic reasons for offending. The history of women's imprisonment is considered to be 'shadowy' (Medlicott, 2007: 246), with their needs seen through the lens of male-focused institutional policies and practices. Given that the prison estate in England and Wales was built by men to house men, the facilities and provisions are therefore not gender specific and fail to recognise even in the very infrastructure of the prison estate that women's needs are different (Corston, 2007). Women's needs are often ignored, in part because of the perpetual crisis in the male estate which always appears to take precedence because it dominates the discourse about imprisonment.

The female prison population has complex needs. Women in custody have low self-esteem, poor mental health and high levels of addiction, have disproportionally suffered domestic violence and other forms of abuse, and are at significant risk of self-harm and suicide (HMCIP, 2020). Furthermore, the lives of women in prison are blighted by poverty, unemployment, insecure accommodation, homelessness, debt and education shortfalls (SEU, 2002; Corston, 2007; Cabinet

Office Social Exclusion Unit, 2009). Corston (2007: 3) found in her landmark review that women's pathways into crime are framed by exploitation and violence within relationships, with them often being coerced into offending by men and suffering physical, emotional and sexual abuse. Despite these well-documented and evidenced vulnerabilities, women are often viewed, still, within the CJS as having 'attitudinal issues' or 'pro-criminal views' resulting in overly harsh sentences and overt criminalisation (Cabinet Office Social Exclusion Unit, 2009).

Salient issues

Women's experiences in prison are significantly gendered with services and opportunities being much more limited than men's (Carlen, 1983). They have essential care needs such as the need for sanitary products, which are regulated in their provision. They are vulnerable to sexual abuse and exploitation by male and female prison officers while in custody. All female and male prisons operate under the same policies but all women's prisons are additionally required to comply with gender-specific standards for working with women prisoners, which are set out in Prison Service Order 4800. Some of that has been superseded by the Female Offender Strategy, which will be discussed later in this chapter. What this means in theory, at least, is that staff in women's prisons should be aware of the gender-specific issues that affect female prisoners and respond appropriately.

Family contact

Due to the small number of women who are sentenced to custody each year, the prison estate for women is equally small, with just 12 institutions. Unlike the male prison estate, however, these institutions are not equally dispersed across the country; there are no institutions for women sentenced to custody in Wales or London, for example. In a different manner to men, women are not assigned a security category; rather, it is decided whether they need open or closed conditions. Due to the geographic spread of institutions for women, one of the most perennial problems women can face in the prison estate is being detained a long way from home. It is well documented that family contact can help address the causes of reoffending on release. However, the average distance for women to be housed from home is 64 miles, but it is often significantly more. For instance, in 2009, 753 women were held in prisons over 100 miles from home, making visits from family members including their children nearly impossible (HMIP, 2010). This can have a damaging impact on family relationships and resettlement following release.

It is estimated that thousands of children are separated from their mothers by imprisonment each year. The caring responsibilities of women in prison is not information that is collected centrally by the government, hence there is a gap in knowledge in this area. There are six mother and baby units (MBUs) attached to six prisons in England; these comprise separate living accommodation for mothers and their children meaning that some mothers are allowed to have their children with them while they serve their custodial sentence. Places on these units are competitive; in the application process women must demonstrate their suitability for the unit and that it is in their child's best interests to be there. The mothers must also show that their presence on the unit will not be detrimental to the wellbeing of other children on the unit; they must continue to behave themselves and demonstrate appropriate behaviour. The application process is often criticised because of the very high level of scrutiny of someone who is trying to look after a child within a difficult environment. The national capacity of these units collectively is 75 and they are dispersed around the female secure estate. Thirty babies were held in prison in an MBU in March 2020 (MoJ, 2020a). Applications for admission to an MBU were successful in only three out of four cases where the assessment board processed the case and made a decision; this resulted in 49 women moving into a unit in 2019–20 (MoJ, 2020a). Babies and children can remain with their mothers on an MBU up to 18 months of age. MBUs have been sources of great controversy regarding their overall appropriateness. On the one hand, it is argued there is nothing better for a young baby than to be cared for by their mother when the alternative is very likely to be that the infant will be taken into care while their mother is in custody. On the other hand, it has been argued that because we have these units, sentencers – that is, judges and magistrates – can send pregnant women to prison with the view that at some point they could be in an MBU. This leads to the debate as to whether it is ever appropriate to send a pregnant woman to prison. It is also questionable how well children thrive on MBUs (Dolan et al, 2019). Evidence shows that separation from their children is highly damaging for women prisoners and the most painful consequence for them to bear. We also know from the evidence about the impact of separation due to the high rates of self-harm and self-inflicted deaths, which are often attributed to issues of maintaining relationships with children while in prison. Given that parental imprisonment, both male and female, is a known risk factor for the onset of criminal behaviour in young people (Farrington et al, 2012) it follows that women going to prison can have a generational impact. This suggests the next generation could be affected by even short-term sentences.

Women's mental health

Women in prison are more likely than men to report a mental health problem: more than seven in ten women (71 per cent) compared with 47 per cent of men (HMCIP, 2020). It is also well documented that self-harm among women in custody is a particularly challenging issue. While it has also increased among male prisoners (see Chapter 6) in recent years, the number of females known to self-harm is seven times the rate than it is among men. This is thought to potentially represent a different reaction to prison by women whereby their violence is internalised against themselves rather than being violent towards other prisoners or prison officers. Due to the prolific nature of self-harm in women's prisons, it has almost, in a shocking way, become accepted that this is the norm in the women's estate (Corston, 2007).

The requirement that prison staff take on the management of these women, despite insufficient training and a lack of empathy and awareness of the reasons why they injure themselves has been a long-standing concern regarding the management and staffing of female prisons (Corston, 2007). Indeed, Corston (2007) argued that prison cannot be the right place for managing this type of behaviour, which stems from deep-rooted, long-term, complex life experiences such as violence and/or sexual abuse, lack of care and/or post-traumatic stress disorder, and perhaps from having a personality disorder. Such problems, Corston (2007) argued, are created within the community, which is where they should be addressed; the Prison Service cannot and should not be expected to solve social problems.

The seminal Corston (2007) report was a review led by Baroness Corston of women with particular vulnerabilities in the CJS and was commissioned by the Home Secretary following the deaths of six women within 13 months in HMP Styal in Manchester. The report was a reaction to public concerns and campaigns following the deaths in custody and the particular concern about the suitability of women's prisons for women with serious mental health issues and/or drug addictions. The report called for a radical change in how the women's estate was set up and how the CJS manages women offenders (Corston, 2007). In particular, Corston (2007) called for a holistic, women–centred approach within the CJS that was sensitive to the complex needs of the majority of women offenders. She also called for an emphasis on appropriate punishment in the community for low-risk, non-violent women and the abolition of large prisons in favour of small custodial units geographically dispersed widely around the country (Corston, 2007). The aim of such units would be to help make prison visits and maintaining relationships with children easier and to also allow for better-quality resettlement work. Corston (2007) proposed that these units replace the existing women's prisons within ten years along with transferring governance from the Prison Service to a new Commission for Women, which would be responsible for women 'at risk of offending or who have offended'. New Labour, represented by Jack Straw, then-Secretary of State for Justice, accepted most of the recommendations made by Corston, announcing substantial financial support for community projects for women. Yet, Corston's most significant recommendation about restructuring the female prison estate was limited to a commitment to review the existing provision. There is no doubt that the Corston (2007) report was significant in terms of what it did to raise political awareness of women prisoners' issues. Yet, the issues it raised and addressed were well known in academic and campaigning spaces for decades before the report came out. It has been well established that the vast majority of women in prison have highly complex needs, suffer from multiple disadvantages and that their offending is often directly caused by the impoverished and difficult social circumstances in which they find themselves. This is further exacerbated by substance misuse, mental health issues and experiences of abuse and trauma.

- The 'same social histories of poverty, abuse, lone parenthood, homelessness and poor mental health as they had 30 years ago' (Carlen and Tombs, 2006: 338).

- The 'vicious circle of victimisation and criminal activity … worsened by poverty, substance dependency or poor mental health' (Prison Reform Trust, 2013: 337).
- The 'adverse social and economic circumstances of women who are at risk of offending … remains unchanged' (Gelsthorpe and Morris, 2002: 278).

It seems that despite greater acknowledgement of these facts within criminal justice policy and practice in recent times, nothing much has changed or progressed regarding the treatment of women who offend and their experiences in prison. There is certainly clear agreement among academics and campaigners that prisons are not the best places to help women, or indeed men, overcome their difficult life experiences both as victims and offenders and try to move on to happier and more fulfilling lives – free from drug and alcohol use, abuse and crime. Indeed, it has been argued strongly that time in prison just exacerbates women's problems to the extent that they return to the community in far worse positions than they were in before their sentence.

There is, however, potential hope for the future. Following a review of the Corston Report ten years on (Women in Prison, 2017), in which the 43 recommendations originally made by Corston (2007) were assessed to see how much they had been implemented, the MoJ published its long-awaited Female Offender Strategy (MoJ, 2018). The strategy aims 'to improve our collective approach to female offenders and make society safer by tackling the underlying causes of offending and reoffending' (MoJ, 2018). It shows that the government recognises the evidence for a distinct approach to women and for a local 'whole systems approach' to women who offend (MoJ, 2018). Later in 2018, the Victims Strategy was also published, with this cross-government policy document promising to 'use trauma-informed approaches to support female offenders who are also victims' (HM Government, 2018). Finally, in 2018, the government also commissioned Lord Farmer to look at women in the CJS through the lens of family and other relational ties. His report made a number of recommendations regarding women in custody and reiterated the need to restructure the female secure estate (Farmer, 2019). He noted that 'investment, from both national and local budgets in women's centres, domestic abuse and other community services and inside prisons was needed … a relatively modest investment will go a long way' (Farmer, 2019). Following the publication of all these reports, ministers in England and Wales have reiterated their commitment to reducing women's imprisonment. However, how this vision will be realised is yet to be seen in the sphere of the female prison estate.

Ethnically minoritised populations in custody

To understand the experiences that ethnically minoritised populations have in custody they must be understood in the wider context of the experiences they have in the CJS overall. The term Black and minority ethnic groups, or BAME as it is commonly abbreviated, has dominated the literature and public discourse when talking about individuals from a non-White ethnicity. However, since

2020 and the significant death of George Floyd who was killed by a police officer in Minneapolis, USA, which triggered in part the Black Lives Matter (BLM) movement, the term BAME has started to be viewed as inappropriate. This is largely because it is seen to focus on skin colour and potentially alienates those it is meant to include. Instead, the term 'ethnically minoritised' or 'racially minoritised' is preferred, as Milner and Jumbe (2020) explain:

> Race refers to perceived biological differences linked with physical characteristics such as skin colour and hair texture, whereas ethnicity refers to perceived cultural differences between groups. Although some groups are perceived as primarily racial (e.g., Black people), or primarily ethnic (e.g., Asian people), and some race-ethnic (e.g., Black Caribbean people), a racialised component exists in all these groups' perceived differentiation to other racial groups. (Milner and Jumbe, 2020)

'Minoritised' is also the preferred term when talking about individuals who are non-White as it recognises that minoritisation is an active process which is socially constructed out of power imbalances (Gunaratnam, 2003). People do not choose their minority status nor do people exist as a predetermined minority within society. Therefore, throughout the following section and the book, the term ethnically minoritised is used when addressing issues of race and ethnicity within the prison system. Ethnically minoritised individuals are significantly more likely to be sentenced to custody than their White counterparts. Compared with the population as a whole, those who are ethnically minoritised are overrepresented within the prison population: 28 per cent in the prison population in contrast to 13 per cent in the general population (Sturge, 2021). Not only is this population group overrepresented, but they serve longer sentences and are less likely to be released (Lammy, 2017). The discrimination within our prison population is so stark that in his review of the treatment and outcomes for ethnically minoritised individuals in the CJS, MP David Lammy (2017: 3) argued that 'if our prison population reflected the make-up of England and Wales, we would have over 9,000 fewer people in prison, the equivalent of 12 average-sized prisons'. Kneen (2017) reports that the estimated cost associated with the overrepresentation of ethnically minoritised groups within the prison system is £234 million (£26 million attributable to youths and £208 million attributable to adults). The disparity in the numbers of ethnically minoritised groups within the prison system is shocking but it is only part of the problem; it is the experience they have within the prison system that compounds the issue.

Salient issues

Placement in prison

Ethnically minoritised individuals are more likely than their White counterparts to be placed in the high security estate. According to official statistics, Black and Asian men were more likely than White men to be housed in high security prisons for public order offences: specifically, just over four times more likely for Black men and more than six times more likely for Asian men (Uhrig, 2016). Other areas of disproportionality emerged when the statistics were analysed: Black men who had committed theft (1.9 times more likely), possession of weapons (1.8 times more likely) and violence against the person (1.6 times more likely); and Asian men who committed criminal damage (1.9 times more likely) (Uhrig, 2016). The reason this is important is because the regime in a high security prison is predominately focused on preventing escape (see Chapter 3), meaning that there is less freedom of movement. The restriction on freedom of movement has implications for the amount of rehabilitation-focused work that can be offered. This in turn will have a long-term impact on the chances of an individual being released and, ultimately, not reoffending. Given that ethnically minoritised groups face discrimination in other areas such as access to healthcare, education and employment, an unnecessary placement in the secure estate creates further barriers to successful post-prison life.

Adjudications in prison

Ethnically minoritised groups experience prison more harshly than their White counterparts; this is illustrated through an exploration of adjudication figures. If someone breaks the prison rules they must attend an adjudication hearing. This is where the facts of the offence are discussed and if a prisoner is found guilty of the offence they will be punished; the hearing is usually conducted by a governor (see Chapter 5). Statistics show that more adjudications are brought against ethnically minoritised prisoners but, interestingly, fewer are proven at the hearing (Uhrig, 2016). What this potentially implies is that ethnically minoritised groups in prison have their behaviour more scrutinised and acted against than their White counterparts. But clearly, this is done on less evidential grounds because otherwise the proven adjudication rate would be higher. So, in other words, the scrutiny might not be fair and the interpretation of behaviour by prison officers appears to be faulty, potentially driven by, at best, cultural insensitivity and, at worst, racism. This is more troubling when it is considered alongside the fact that ethnically minoritised people in prison often report more negatively about their experiences and relationships with staff. According to the Prisons and Probation Ombudsman (2018), fewer individuals said they felt safe, fewer had a member of staff they could turn to for help, fewer said staff treated them with respect, and more said they had been bullied or victimised by staff.

Release on temporary licence

One of the other key issues regarding ethnically minoritised prisoners and their experience of prison and how it is different can be seen through the release on temporary licence process (ROTL). Statistics show that ethnically minoritised groups are less likely to be granted ROTL (Uhrig, 2016). In a similar way to their overrepresentation in the high security estate, this can have significant impacts on their prospects for rehabilitation and resettlement. The process of ROTL is key in allowing prisoners the opportunity to gradually reintegrate into the community and also to engage in key education, training and employment opportunities, which have been shown to be a vital protective factor against the likelihood of reoffending. By denying ethnically minoritised individuals the opportunity to do this, they face a significant impediment to a successful release from custody (HMIP, 2020c).

Racism within prisons

The tragic events surrounding the death of George Floyd in the USA in May 2020 have led to increased emphasis on concerns worldwide about racism and inequality faced by ethnically minoritised individuals. Floyd's death during the process of his arrest (BBC News, 2020a) sparked widespread protests led by the BLM movement against the treatment of ethnically minoritised individuals by police forces in both the USA and the UK. The BLM movement prompted many organisations to commit to addressing the systemic racism and racial inequality experienced by ethnically minoritised individuals across all areas of social policy, not just within the CJS. Yet, despite the catapulting of these significant and powerful issues into the mainstream news, they are not new to the USA or the UK. As Thompson (2021: 6) states, 'It is questionable that any organisation in the criminal justice system would have no knowledge of the pervasive nature of systemic racism or inequality, or what they should be doing to address it.' The publication of the MacPherson report (1999) following the inquiry into the death of Stephen Lawrence prompted significant efforts to improve policing practices.

One of the most disturbing and shocking cases that continues to have a profound impact on the prison system today is the death of Zahid Mubarek. Zahid, a 19-year-old British Pakistani boy, was battered to death on the morning of his release from prison by his White cell mate in a racially motivated attack in Feltham Young Offender Institution in 2000. He had been sentenced to 90 days in custody following a conviction of shoplifting £6 worth of goods. He was placed in a cell with a known racist; the prison service knew that Robert Stewart was volatile and dangerous yet placed Zahid in a cell with him. Following his death and the conviction of Stewart for Zahid's murder, Zahid's family actively campaigned for a public inquiry into his death, particularly after the Prison Service accepted their failure to fulfil their responsibilities to care for Zahid, describing it as a 'wholly preventable death' after their internal inquiry. The subsequent public inquiry led by Lord Keith (2006), reporting in 2006, reached damning conclusions about the Prison Service and its treatment of ethnically minoritised prisoners. In a similar timeframe, the Commission for Racial Equality (CRE) also reported on its investigations into the Prison Service, triggered by reports of racism in several prisons. In response to both reports, (CRE, 2003a, 2003b; Keith,

2006), the CRE and the Prison Service agreed on a plan to address the findings of both investigations. The plan, implemented by HMPPS, was underpinned by an approach to managing race equality through high-level management structures, a Prison Service Standard on race equality and the development of a comprehensive ethnic monitoring tool, the Systematic Monitoring and Analysing of Race Equality Template (Earle, 2016: 573). Following the implementation of the plan, the *Race Review 2008* (Race and Equalities Action Group, 2008) concluded that while substantial progress had been made, the experience of ethnically minoritised prisoners and staff had not been transformed and that a refreshed programme of activity was required in order to consolidate progress and go further (Thompson, 2021: 9). Hence, when David Lammy published his review in 2017 into the treatment of and outcomes for ethnically minoritised individuals in the CJS, it made for somewhat sad reading, in that some of the findings still echoed those found after the Mubarek inquiry (Keith, 2006) and the CRE reports (2003a, 2003b). Worryingly, there have been several incidents and tragedies since the deaths of Stephen Lawrence and Zahid Mubarek, which continue to show, at best, institutional failures and, at worst, institutional racism towards ethnically minoritised individuals in contact with the CJS. For instance, a Black Muslim prisoner, Mohamed Sharif, was left severely brain damaged following an attack by a White prisoner at HMP Bristol in 2014. Ryan Guest had previously told staff he would "only share a cell with a White person who was not homosexual", yet these comments were not investigated (Taylor, 2020); the case shares striking similarities with the murder of Zahid Mubarek. Arguably, some of the drive and ambition to tackle racial inequality that the Prison Service had in the 2000s has been lost; perhaps the BLM movement offers a further catalyst for change. Yet, in some ways, irrespective of what the Prison Service does to tackle racial inequality, broader social inequalities in which race plays such a significant role need to be addressed first. As a service, it cannot tackle racial inequality alone but it can improve the treatment of ethnically minoritised individuals in prison in the first instance.

Older people

The older age group of prisoners has seen the largest growth in recent years, with the proportion of prisoners aged 50 and over having gone from 10 per cent of the prison population in 2011 to 17 per cent in 2021 (Sturge, 2021). The prison estate is facing a new and emerging challenge in how it manages an ageing population. The older population is made up of several different types of prisoners:

- Repeat prisoners: people in and out of prison for less serious offences who have returned to prison at an older age.
- Grown old in prison: people sentenced to a long sentence before the age of 50 who have grown old in prison.

- Short-term, first-time prisoners: people sentenced to prison for the first time for a short sentence.
- Long-term, first-time prisoners: people sentenced to prison for the first time for a long sentence, possibly for historic sexual or violent offences.

It is the drive within the last five years to prosecute those responsible for historic child sexual offences which has caused the older prisoner population boom, resulting in a significant increase in those entering prison in their later years (that is, aged 65 or over). According to the MoJ (2022c), 17 per cent of the prison population are aged 50 or over – 13,212 people; of these 3,263 are in their 60s and a further 1,693 people are aged 70 or older. The majority of men in prison aged 50 or older are in prison for sex offences (MoJ, 2022c). Various organisations including the Prison Reform Trust and Age UK have called for a national strategy for working with older people in prison in recognition of the significant challenges they pose for prison management. The House of Commons Justice Committee (2020: 41) has supported the call, stating that it is inconsistent for the MoJ to recognise both the growth in the older prisoner population and the severity of their needs and not to articulate a strategy to properly account for this. The government accepted the initial call for a strategy in 2020 but a clear approach has yet to be announced.

Salient issues

Caring for an ageing population

Prisons were designed for young men; they were not designed for individuals to age in them. Much of the prison estate in current use is not fit for purpose and certainly does not cater for an ageing population. This is particularly so for many of the prisons built in the Victorian era that are still in use today; filled with spiral staircases, wings and landings on numerous levels, and great distances between buildings, these institutions are particularly challenging for the older prisoner to physically navigate due to the general health challenges that ageing can bring. It is well known that prison ages one due to the psychological strains and stresses that it places on the mind and body (see Chapter 6); entering prison at an older age can only compound this further. Older prisoners tend to have increasingly failing health; six out of ten older people in prison (59 per cent) reported having a long-standing illness or disability, compared with just over a quarter (27 per cent) of younger people in prison (Omolade, 2014). This can place considerable strains on the prison healthcare system to manage and support these individuals with complex health conditions. As this group has greater health-related needs, they are disproportionately affected by the problems faced by prison healthcare (House of Commons Justice Committee, 2020). A particular issue is the cancellation of external medical appointments to escort prisoners to hospital or doctors' surgeries due to shortages of staff. The ageing population also poses challenges for prison staff as to where the boundaries of their role lie. Prison staff are there to manage prisoners and maintain the order of the prison (see Chapter 7) but the ageing prisoner population raises the issue of just how far this is possible when you are looking after older people who may require more care than control. There is a lack of training and awareness among prison staff of conditions such as dementia; the prison estate does not have a clear approach or policy for how best to manage prisoners with such conditions, which will be aggravated by the prison experience. The House of Commons Justice Committee (2020) has raised concerns regarding this and recommended that for cases where the prisoner is living with dementia alternative forms of custody should be considered.

Provision for older prisoners

Many prisons have struggled to keep pace with the growing age of their prison population, meaning there is often little specialised provision available for this group. HMCIP (2020) found that while some prisons did have good provision for older people, most did not and in some cases prisoners who were aged 65 or over spent most of their days locked in their cells as there was little for them to do. This is largely due to prisons catering for the younger age group because the major part of education and training is centred on upskilling younger individuals who are expected to enter the labour market on release. This is also true in regard to resettlement provision being inadvertently centred on younger people. It is likely that older prisoners will face different challenges from their younger counterparts on release, which can pose real difficulties for the Probation Service. For instance, it can be difficult to find suitable post-release accommodation for those with disabilities, reduced mobility or complex health conditions (House of Commons Justice Committee, 2020). Senior et al (2013) found that release planning for older people in prison was frequently non-existent, with the lack of information in preparation for release causing high levels of anxiety. Many reported minimal or no contact from probation workers or offender managers during their time in custody (Senior et al, 2013). The Care Act 2014 states that local authorities have a duty to assess and give care and support to those who meet the threshold and are in prisons within their locality. There is, however, a general lack of multi-agency working in this area; this is a considerable hindrance to any form of progress in improving the release prospects of older prisoners.

Summary

This chapter has shown that different groups experience prison differently depending on the social characteristics that they possess. For women, ethnically minoritised groups and those who are older, prison can be a particularly challenging place, with various specific and salient issues faced by each group. When different social characteristics intersect, it should be noted that they will coalesce to make the prison experience even more difficult. For instance, one of the most challenging issues facing prisons today is that of individuals who identify as transgender and/or non-binary. Given that prisons operate on distinct biological sex boundaries, for individuals who are transgender the Prison Service struggles to provide adequate support and safe accommodation for them; they are at a heightened risk of being discriminated against. Prisons, as has been illustrated, are places designed by men for young White men and struggle to meet the needs of the diverse populations that go through their gates. The failure of prisons to recognise the diversity of their population and to cater for their different needs compounds the discrimination faced by these groups throughout the CJS.

Questions to consider

1. How do we reduce discrimination in the prison system?
2. Is now the right time to stop the use of imprisonment for women and to focus on alternatives to custody?
3. Should older people be sentenced to custody? Should prison have an age cut-off point?

TAKING IT FURTHER

There are several texts that explore the issues presented in this chapter, which you might wish to consult for further detail:

- Codd, H. (2018). Ageing in prison. In Westwood, S. (ed.) *Ageing, Diversity and Equality: Social Justice Perspectives*. London: Routledge, p 345–346.

- Earle, R. (2016). Race, ethnicity, multiculture and prison life. In Jewkes, Y., Bennett, J. and Crewe, B. (eds) *Handbook on Prisons*. (2nd edn). Abingdon: Routledge, pp. 568–585.

- Grace, S., O'Neill, M., Walker, T., King, H., Baldwin, L., Jobe, A., Lynch, O., Measham, F., O'Brien, K. and Seaman, V. (2022). *Criminal Women: Gender Matters*. Bristol: Bristol University Press.

It is well worth exploring the following sources for further information about the topics discussed in this chapter:

- HMPPS has clear equality and diversity policies and provides details of how equality and diversity are monitored across the CJS: https://www.gov.uk/government/organisations/hm-prison-and-probation-service/about/equality-and-diversity

- The Lammy Review: all the information including the evidence submitted to the review can be found on the website: https://www.gov.uk/government/organisations/lammy-review

- The Zahid Mubarek Trust: to explore more about the legacy of Zahid Mubarek and the impact that his family are trying to have on the prison system visit: https://thezmt.org

- LSE Events | Women in Prison: more troubled than troublesome – Jean Corston revisits her groundbreaking 2007 report on vulnerable women in prison and discusses subsequent developments: https://www.youtube.com/watch?v=-vnyRX98whE&t=1s

5

Prison life

Key learning outcomes

By the end of this chapter, you should be able to:

- Explain what a typical prison regime is like
- Describe what prisoners do with their time in prison
- Understand some of the challenges of being a prisoner

Introduction

This chapter will introduce what life in prison is like. There will be an exploration of what exactly prisoners do while 'doing time'; such an exploration is important if we are to explore whether the prison system is working and meeting its aim of 'helping prisoners lead law abiding and useful lives' (HMPPS, 2021a). This chapter provides a snapshot of the routine nature of life in custody via an exploration of prison regimes. It explores different types of activity offered to prisoners, such as work, education and training, and provides examples of innovative practice across the prison estate within this area. How prisoners are rewarded for good behaviour and engagement with these activities is discussed. The chapter also explores prison healthcare systems and discusses the challenges of accessing support both from a physical and mental perspective. An exploration of how individuals practise their religion and/or faith is provided as well as a look at what prisoners do in prison during their free time. The chapter also explores some of the more negative aspects of prison life including the issues of radicalisation and extremism, and punishment for non-compliance with the rules. It is highly recommended that this chapter is read in conjunction with Chapter 6 so that a fully rounded view of what life inside is like can be realised. Overall, this chapter demonstrates that the everyday lives of prisoners are largely mundane and boring because they are stuck between the prisons' careful balancing act of maintaining security (power), control (legitimacy) and the desire for change (rehabilitation).

Regimes

One of the key features of prison life is the overwhelming routine and mundane nature of it. Prisons run on a regime, the prison routine, which determines when individuals will be unlocked from their cells for work, association, meals and access to other services. Regimes are different at different prisons largely because the available services and opportunities vary at each institution. Prisons run on a timetable, similar to the structure of a school, but with an emphasis on controlling prisoners' movements around the establishment. There are few established rules determining how long they can be kept in their cells and it is not unlawful for individuals to be kept in their cells for long periods. According to prison service instruction (PSI) 75/2011, 'prisoners must be afforded time out of their living accommodation, time in the open air and the opportunity for family contact (through phone calls)' (HMPPS, 2020a). What the instruction does not do, however, is set any minimum standards apart from time in the open air. HMPPS (2020a) defines time in the open air as 'time spent in a situation where the prisoner is able to benefit from fresh air and natural light'. It goes on to clarify that individuals should get a minimum of 30 minutes in the open air daily, though this is subject to weather conditions and the need to maintain good order and discipline (HMPPS, 2020a). The PSI (HMPPS, 2020a) states that time outdoors as part of work, watching or participating in sports counts, as does time in the open air moving between activities.

While there is no specific guidance provided by the government as to the timings of a regime, the average prison regime runs on what is akin to a four-day working week, with a different regime format operating on a Friday, Saturday and Sunday. The average prison regime operates as follows:

- 08:15 Most individuals will start their day at 08:15, having been up earlier than that to get ready for movement. Once movement commences, they will move from their cells to attend work or education.
- 11:45 They will return to the wing to collect their lunch from the servery and eat it. They will then largely be locked back in their cells.
- 13:35 They will be unlocked and move again to education or work.
- 17:00 They will return to the wing for their evening meal and association.
- 19:45 They will be locked in their cells until the following morning.

On a Friday, Saturday and Sunday the regime operates on the pattern of two blocks, morning and afternoon. Most individuals will use the time out of their cell to engage in key aspects of prison life such as attending work or education, having visits from family and friends, attending appointments for healthcare or meeting with probation officers and legal representatives. They may also use the time to practise their faith or go to the gym. One of the most persistent criticisms of prisons is the amount of time individuals spend locked up in their cells rather than being unlocked and engaging with the full regime. Inspectors in 2019–20 found that people continue to spend too long locked up in their cells – around a fifth (19 per cent) were routinely locked up during the working day in most prisons; this is an improvement on 2018–19 when around a quarter were locked up during the working day (HMCIP, 2020). You are more likely to be locked up for longer periods in local and young adult prisons; around a third of people in local prisons (32 per cent) and young adult prisons (35 per cent) said they spent less than two hours a day out of their cells (HMCIP, 2020). This is potentially due to these two types of institutions being the most volatile in the estate as well as having the most regular turnover of population, making sustained engagement with work and education, for instance, difficult to manage. What is disappointing, however, are the training prisons. Their role is to provide education and training with the goal of reducing individuals' risk of reoffending, yet almost one in eight people in category C prisons and one in six (16 per cent) in category B prisons said they were locked up for more than 22 hours a day (HMCIP, 2020).

A significant amount of attention is paid both by the media, including factual and fictional media, and politicians on life in prison being full of violence, contraband and drugs. While this is sadly somewhat the case, often it is the routine and monotonous nature of prison life which is at the root of some of the difficulties individuals face in adapting to life inside. The following quotes are taken from the Howard League for Penal Reform's 150th birthday celebrations project, whereby prisoners were asked to write about what life in prison is really like by keeping a diary for a day:

Extracts from prisoner diaries

Lights out – sleep. Hours out of cell: 5. Purposeful activity: none. Cups of tea: 6. Days left of sentence: one fewer. – **Prisoner, 46, Elmley**

The morning is unusual due to no work – whilst pay is dismal, work is preferable to sitting in cell. There is no exercise or activity out of cell in the a.m. Time could be used better in prison. Unable to shower due to the lack of privacy over lunchtimes. – **Prisoner, 55, Oakwood**

Bang up is early here on a Friday due to a regime change so now banging up at 5:15 for the night, unlock isn't till 11:30 a.m. tomorrow. ... That's another Friday done, another slow weekend to come then start all over again next week. – **Prisoner, 29, Norwich**

(Howard League for Penal Reform, 2016a)

What the quotes illustrate is the sheer boredom and lack of stimulation faced by most individuals behind bars. In recent years, to create some innovation in prison regimes and provide an opportunity for individuals who are excluded from open conditions to demonstrate their suitability for open conditions, a number of 'progression regimes' (PR) have been developed. Four prisons are operating a PR: Warren Hill, Buckley Hall, Humber and Erlestoke. The purpose of a PR is to reintroduce the responsibilities, tasks and routines associated with daily life in the community, to test prisoners' readiness to respond appropriately to the trust placed in them, and to actively pursue activities and relations which support rehabilitation (MoJ, 2021c). The PR regime aims to empower the individual in their sentence planning and offers them an opportunity to engage in a regime focused on life post-prison. Under a PR, there are no lock-ups, there is a different pattern for the core day in terms of timings, individuals are allowed to cook their food and eat together and they are encouraged to manage a budget and shop for items they need to prepare meals. HMP Warren Hill has been a huge success in implementing this regime, with it having a significant impact on the prison environment: incidents of violence are extremely low, better relationships between staff and prisoners are reported and there are more successful releases into the community or to category D prisons. It is viewed as the gold standard in terms of a category C prison within the estate and recommendations have been made to encourage emulation of the practices elsewhere (HMIP, 2020d).

Education and work

The importance of prisoners engaging in education and/or work while serving their time in prison is well known. Receiving education or pursuing training or work opportunities while in prison is a fundamental feature of prison life, and has been since late Victorian times. The quality of education and purposeful activity is one of the main ways by which prisons are inspected and measured in terms of performance (HMIP, 2022). The discussion that follows refers to the period before the COVID-19 pandemic unless otherwise stated. This is because from April 2020 to November 2021 almost all purposeful activity had stopped or was sporadic in the prison estate; there was also a delay in the publication of statistics and other such information.

Education and training

Engagement with education within prison can have a significant impact on an individual's likelihood of reoffending; the proven one-year reoffending rate is 34 per cent for prisoner learners, compared with 43 per cent for those who do not engage in any form of learning (MoJ/DfE, 2017). The education provided in prisons is largely outsourced to private companies. It was considered the biggest shake-up in prison education for many years when in April 2019 the government, as part of its agenda to increase governor autonomy (to give prison governors more control over their establishments), allocated the responsibility for managing education to each governor. This process only applied to prisons in England that were publicly run. The MoJ through a procurement process found a group of new education providers known as the Prison Education Framework (PEF); these were grouped into 'lots' of 17 mainly geographical areas to provide education in groups of prisons for four years. The four providers (Milton Keynes College, Novus, People Plus and Weston College) of the new PEF contracts were already the current education providers in the secure estate but each provider lost or gained prisons under the new arrangements. The idea of the new system was to increase flexibility regarding which education courses were being provided so they were more tailored to the prison population in each establishment and there was more accountability for poor performance. Whether this is the case is yet to be seen.

Prison education serves some of the most educationally disadvantaged in our society. The Prisoner Learning Alliance (2020) has reported that, on entering custody, 47 per cent of prisoners have no formal qualifications. Similarly, the MoJ (2014) also reports that 42 per cent have previously been expelled or permanently excluded from school. Prisoners have much lower levels of literacy than the general population with the most recent data published by the MoJ (2021d) showing that 57 per cent of adult prisoners taking initial assessments had literacy levels below that expected of an 11-year-old. There is a requirement placed on prisons that all those within them should leave with a basic qualification in English and maths. It is a requirement therefore that those in prison must complete; they must achieve these qualifications before being allowed to study or engage in other areas of work. There has been a decline in the number of people achieving these qualifications; the number of English and maths qualifications achieved has fallen by 29 per cent between the 2011–12 and 2017–18 academic years (Skills Funding Agency, 2018). The compulsory nature of these qualifications often creates tensions in the prison classroom between those who want to study and those who are being forced to.

There are other issues regarding prison education such as the fact that it is basic and limited; it is also often gendered in its provision in that men's prisons teach bricklaying and plumbing while women's prisons teach hairdressing and beauty, although there has been some movement around this in recent years. Wainwright et al (2019) found that 'prisoners want education that stretches the mind and delves deep, training that bestows industry recognised qualifications, the opportunity to use the skills they came into prison with, and work experience that makes them attractive to future employers'. A persistent critique of prison education has been the 'one-size fits all' approach, which does not work in an environment full of people with individual learning needs. In no other context would education be provided on a mass scale; elsewhere, in schools, colleges and universities there is recognition of the need to cater for individual learning needs by adapting styles of teaching, modes of teaching and assessments. Prison classrooms are not like those in schools where students are required to attend, and everyone in the class is the same age and learning a core curriculum. The diversity of the prison classroom is unparalleled in terms of the complexity teachers must cater for in the lessons and learning they provide, meaning that it is important to have a clear induction and learning plan created for each individual learner. Yet this is not often the case in the prison environment (Coates, 2016), largely due to the focus being on 'getting bums on seats' as education contractors get paid per learner in attendance, not for the quality of the course or success of the learner.

There is a lack of opportunity for those who want to pursue higher education. Those who want to study at higher levels often have to fight to do so, and there has been a considerable decline over recent years in the number of people studying at degree level or above (Coates, 2016). The Open University continues to be the main route for individuals in prison to undertake degree study. In recent years, universities have partnered with prisons to help facilitate wider access to higher education and to deliver on-site learning opportunities. Durham University has developed the Inside-Out partnership with HMP Frankland whereby students and academics deliver criminology courses to prison learners. The University of York via the Department of Social Policy and Social Work has partnered with HMP Buckley Hall to deliver a module that takes students from York to the prison to learn alongside fellow prison-based learners about issues of social policy. Students from both groups of learners have spoken powerfully about the benefits achieved by breaking down barriers, challenging perceptions and learning from each other.

One of the main barriers to education in prison is the lack of infrastructure and investment in IT facilities. Digital literacy is crucial if individuals are going to be able to engage in successful rehabilitation. If prisoners are to secure employment, continue to study or otherwise contribute to society on release, they must be given the opportunity to use and improve their digital skills while in prison (Coates, 2016). IT facilities within prisons are often dated and do not match up to the modern technology on the outside; for instance, several prisons that the author has visited are still running computers on Windows 98. Currently, digital learning on offer in prisons is comprised of basic digital skills training provided by Virtual Campus, a secure, web-based intranet system. It offers a range of skills (examinations and courses) and employment-focused material (job searches, submitting job applications, CV building and secure relay messaging), yet it is often underutilised, does not work properly or is hosted in rooms that prisoners seldom have access to. Part of the barrier to successful digital literacy training is the ongoing security risks associated with potentially giving prisoners access to computers, especially ones that are connected to the internet. Internet use is part of everyone's daily lives on the outside and now more than ever is used for most basic household tasks such as banking, organising utility bills and accessing healthcare services; prohibiting prisoners' access to the internet through a blanket ban does not support their prospects of rehabilitation. As Nick Hardwick (2013), a former Chief Inspector of Prisons, has said:

> We can't go on with prisons in a pre-internet dark age: inefficient, wasteful and leaving prisoners woefully unprepared for the real world they will face on release. I have not met one prison professional who does not think drastic change is needed.

One of the main recommendations from the Coates (2016) review of prison education was that the security arrangements that currently underpin the use of IT in the prison estate should be reviewed. She argued that governors should be allowed to develop an approach that allows suitably risk-assessed prison learners to have controlled access to the internet to support their studies and enable applications for jobs on release (Coates, 2016).

Often, one of the main issues with prison education is the tension between education and work. This is due to the significant differences in pay that prisoners earn between being in education and working within the prison environment; those in education are in the lowest-paid position in the prison with most earning just £1 a day for undertaking studying in comparison with those in workshops who can earn over £5 a day. This is important in terms of being able to fund the additional things that prisoners need to buy such as additional food, toiletries and phone cards. This means that individuals often choose to work rather than educate themselves despite education placing people in better positions post-release. For those required to be in education because they do not have a basic English or maths qualification and so are being forced to learn, it can often be a disruptive influence and cause issues in the classroom because they do not want to be there nor do they get paid enough to make it worthwhile to be there (Nichols, 2021). Coates (2016) argued that prisoners should be paid at least the same for education, if not more than for their other activities, because paying more shows that this is what is valued, and creates additional incentives for prisoners to attend classes.

Work and earning money inside

An average of 10,500 prisoners are working in the public prison estate, and a further 2,000 are working in private prisons; they worked for over 17 million hours in total in 2019–20 (MoJ, 2020a). Work in prison is the other main route by which prisoners can earn money if they are not in education but it is also how they can combat the boredom of prison life. Since 1964, Prison Service rules have indicated that prisoners may be paid for the purposeful activity they take part in, which includes education, training and work. The current minimum rate of pay in England and Wales was set in Prison Service Order 4460, issued in 2002 but last updated in January 2020; it sets out that all prisoners who are in some form of employment have to earn a minimum of £4 a week (MoJ, 2002). Prisoners can earn more than £4 a week; in 2020, the average working prisoner earned £10 a week. Although prison wages are low, prisoners do not have to pay for accommodation, meals, basic toiletries or clothing. Some may be able to bring some approved items into prison with them or have them sent in by families or friends. Prisoners must provide for everything else themselves. They must purchase phone credit themselves and pay rent for a TV. Everything else must be purchased from the prison shop or canteen. In public sector prisons, this consists of a list of items, such as vape liquid, non-prescribed medication, additional food and toiletries, hobby materials and stationery, chosen to meet the needs of prison populations from a national product list of approved items. Prisoners may also purchase other items such as clothing or religious artefacts from approved retail catalogues, for which prisons charge an administration fee. Private sector prisons have their own canteen arrangements. The three things that most prisoners spend their money on are contacting family, television rental and buying items from the canteen. The governor also has the autonomy to set local pay rates above the minimum as set out in the Incentives Policy Framework (MoJ, 2020e) to 'encourage and reward prisoner's constructive participation in the regime'. In practice, this means that those with enhanced status through the Incentives and Earned Privileges scheme can earn a higher rate of pay; prisoners doing the same job may earn different wages.

In terms of the nature of prison work, it suffers similar critiques in part to that of education in that HM Inspectors have found that, in too many prisons, work remains mundane, unskilled and repetitive (HMCIP, 2020). Classic examples of work in prison include packing boxes of teabags, removing labels from clothing and breaking down pallets. Where prisoners do develop work skills, they are often not recorded, recognised or accredited, leaving them unable to demonstrate their abilities to prospective employers. The nature of prison work does not necessarily correlate to work on the outside, meaning that there is little value in prison work to aid future rehabilitation. Prisons have tried to combat this in recent years by making sure that some of the jobs which are essential to the good running of a prison, such as wing cleaners, require training qualifications to do them; in this way, they are trying to bridge the divide between work and education. Some of the most sought-after jobs within the prison system are ones which on the outside are considered low status or 'dirty work' (Ashforth and Kreiner, 1999); for instance, being a cleaner outside prison has a stigma attached to it but inside prison it is one of the most sought-after jobs largely because of the freedom of movement that comes with it around the prison site.

Prisons have also become more innovative over time through selling products made or grown by prisoners to the public; for instance, HMP Buckley Hall often sells wooden products made in the workshop and HMP Askham Grange has an on-site garden centre and cafe, which is run by some of the women at the prison. The aim is to proactively bridge the gap between working in prison and working post-release, to develop prisoners' employability skills and subsequently improve their chances of employment. A big innovation in this area in recent years is the partnerships that have developed between businesses and prisons. These have been encouraged and supported by the MoJ which has tried to support prisons through the governor autonomy agenda to have more control and subsequently more opportunities to develop local partnerships. This embeds the prison into the local economy, so it is not as isolated as perhaps it once was. There are several examples which could be cited as showing innovation in this area:

Innovative practice in the employment of prisoners

- **Timpson actively recruits people with convictions to work for the company, and currently employs around 650 colleagues.** There are seven prison training academies, including at HMPs Downview, New Hall, Blantyre House and Whitemoor. In addition, at HMP Thorn Cross there are three workshops where shoe repairs and specialist photo production take place. Thorn Cross also deploys people on ROTL who work by day in other parts of the business and return to prison each evening.

- **The Clink Charity operates restaurants that are open to the public at HMPs High Down, Brixton, the women's prison HMP Styal and a cafe in central Manchester, in partnership with the Prison Service.** It offers prisoners the chance to gain experience and qualifications in the food and hospitality industry, with mentoring and guidance to find full-time employment, and provides resettlement support on release. Research by the MoJ showed a 50 per cent reduction in the likelihood of reoffending and a lower frequency of reoffences.
- **Lendlease's not-for-profit subsidiary BeOnsite provides training and employment opportunities in the construction industry.** Their Mind the Gap programme works with people on ROTL and at the end of their sentence, with the aim of reducing construction industry skills gaps and reoffending. It is tackling the challenges of sustainable job creation and reducing reoffending by developing an infrastructure to deliver long-term construction training and support for 400 businesses and 60 sustainable job outcomes.
- **Recycling Lives is a social business which enables prisoners to gain skills and qualifications to help them reduce their risk of reoffending on release.** It works in 11 prisons in the UK and engages up to 250 men and women at a time in its HMP Academies programme, which employs prisoners in either recycling or fabrication work.

Prison Reform Trust (2021)

Rewarding and punishing behaviour

The management of prisoners is framed by the incentives and earned privileges (IEP) scheme, which was introduced in 1995. The system of privileges is a key tool for incentivising prisoners to abide by the rules and engage in the prison regime. It encourages prisoners to participate in rehabilitation activities such as education, work and offending behaviour programmes while facilitating the removal of privileges from those who behave poorly or refuse to engage. Incentives and rewards for good behaviour had been key to the prison system throughout the 20th century; the IEP scheme formalised this notion into a clear policy. At the launch of the IEP scheme, Michael Howard, Home Secretary at the time, said:

> Privileges should be earned, not enjoyed as of right. Prisoners who behave well should benefit and those who behave badly should face sanction. Once earned, privileges should not necessarily be permanent. They will be lost if a prisoner's behaviour deteriorates. The new system is transparently fair. This means real progress towards meeting public expectations about what kind of place prisons should be. (Liebling, 2008)

The policy is guided by the assumption that prisoners when faced with the addition or removal of material benefits will comply with prison rules. However, as Crewe

(2016: 94) argues, such a rational choice model of prisoner behaviour is flawed: many prisoners are not 'rational choice' thinkers, and resent being managed by a 'carrot and stick' approach to behaviour modification, especially if it is implemented unfairly. The IEP scheme operates at three incentive levels: basic, standard and enhanced:

IEP incentives

- Basic: prisoners who have not abided by the behaviour principles.
- Standard: prisoners who adequately abide by the behaviour principles, demonstrating the types of behaviour required.
- Enhanced: prisoners who exceed the standard level by abiding by the behaviour principles, demonstrating the required types of behaviour to a consistently high standard, including good attendance and attitude at activities and education/work and interventions.

Prisoners' Advice Service (2020)

The principles of what constitutes good behaviour are laid out in the IEP framework (HMPPS, 2020b); among others, they include being respectful to staff and other prisoners, complying with prison rules, making progress on personal goals and sentence plans, and refraining from drug and alcohol use. All prisoners enter prison at standard level; this should be reviewed within at least three months of arrival to prison. More broadly, an incentive-level review can occur at any time but all prisoners must be given a review at least once a year. Those who find themselves on basic level must have a review initially after seven days and then at least every 28 days after that; they must be told clearly, in accordance with the IEP framework (HMPPS, 2020b), what they need to do to progress to standard level. Compliance with the prison rules alongside engagement with opportunities for rehabilitation can have a significant impact on the nature of a prisoner's time in prison. Essentially, the further up the IEP scheme they can get, the more 'comfortable' their prison stay can be. The IEP framework has the flexibility to allow governors to design their own local incentive schemes according to their understanding of what will incentivise their population and what facilities and opportunities are available (HMPPS, 2020b). Additionally, core incentives are offered across the prison estate to provide consistency; this is key given that prisoners can move around. The six designated earnable incentives that must be included in all localised prison incentive schemes are:

- access to private cash
- eligibility to earn higher rates of pay
- access to in-cell television (having a TV in one's cell, for which prisoners must then pay to use – having a TV is not guaranteed in prison)

- opportunity to wear own clothes
- additional time out of cell
- extra and improved visits (HMPPS, 2020b: 11)

Prisons can add to this list to personalise the privileges at their institution, which are often dependent on local facilities and staffing. For instance, HMP Buckley Hall has an enhanced wing to which all prisoners on enhanced level can apply to be housed. The benefits of the enhanced wing are that each cell is single occupancy and has an en-suite toilet and shower. The atmosphere on the wing is also one of calm and trust, with prisoners being afforded more time out of their cells: for instance, to use the exercise equipment on the wing or to engage in other leisure activities like playing chess. In, HMP Full Sutton, a category A prison in York, for those on enhanced level, a self-catering option is available whereby prisoners can access a kitchen to cook their own food (HMIP, 2020a). Engaging with the prison regime and demonstrating the behaviour that is expected by the IEP scheme can, therefore, open up opportunities for prisoners to make their prison experience more comfortable. However, the scheme has repeatedly faced criticism largely regarding a perceived lack of fairness in how it works. The staff–prisoner relationship is central in shaping the IEP experience of a prisoner; according to Khan's (2020) study, prisoners who had built rapport with officers were more likely to have prison rules altered for them in a way that meant they moved up the IEP categories quicker than those who did not. Khan (2020) also found that for those prisoners who did not comply, the IEP scheme was used by staff as a mode of punishment rather than having the desired therapeutic or rehabilitative effect as indicated by the framework (HMPPS, 2020b). The scheme is meant to be separate from the disciplinary system of prisons. A change in IEP status cannot be given as a punishment at an adjudication hearing and being placed on report must not automatically result in a change to a prisoner's IEP level. Yet, this is a contradiction as IEP levels are based on behaviour, so even an unproven adjudication can prompt an IEP review and lead to a downgrade in IEP status, meaning that the two systems are intertwined. The IEP policy has also incurred criticism as it has been found to fuel disproportionality within prisons. HMIP (2020c) reported that ethnically minoritised prisoners are more likely to be on the basic level of the IEP scheme with a lower proportion of ethnically minoritised males than White male prisoners (32 per cent compared with 45 per cent) feeling that they were treated fairly under the IEP scheme. Moreover, Hutton (2017) has argued that gaining enhanced status requires an element of performance management that some prisoners may be more capable of than others; those with learning disabilities or mental health issues may not be able to self–regulate behaviour to align with IEP requirements. This can result in behaviour being viewed as non-compliance or as a reluctance to engage with the regime (Hutton, 2017), which could affect an individual's IEP status, whereas the behaviour has resulted from a disability or illness and is therefore not in the control of the individual. There is also a particular challenge posed by the IEP scheme for those serving long-term prison sentences: once the enhanced level is reached, where do prisoners serving long sentences move to next to reward their continued engagement and 'active' commitment to rehabilitation as required by the IEP framework (HMPPS, 2020b)?

Despite HMPPS stating that the IEP scheme is separate from the disciplinary system within prisons, it is difficult to distinguish between the two; nonetheless, it is important to try to do so, to understand the consequences of poor behaviour in prison. As previously stated, The Prison Rules (1999) apply to every prison; on top of these, a governor can impose local rules as well. The Prison Rules (1999) is legislation which governs how prisons are run. They dictate the treatment of prisoners, the conduct of prison officers and the powers and duties of the state towards prisoners. Significantly, they also provide the legislative framework for offences against discipline within prison. When a prisoner breaks The Prison Rules (1999) it is called an offence; these offences are listed in Prison Rule 51 and Young Offender Institution Rule 55. A wide range of offences are listed under the headings: behaving in a way that could offend, threaten or hurt someone else; stopping prison staff from doing their jobs; escaping from prison; possession of contraband; causing damage to the prison and not doing what prison staff tell you to do (The Prison Rules, 1999). When a prisoner breaks the rules, they will be put on report; a prison officer will tell the prisoner what offence they believe has been committed and give the prisoner a DIS 1 form, also colloquially known as a 'nicking sheet'. The sheet will explain what the prisoner is accused of and that they must attend a hearing, also known as an adjudication. The adjudication will be run by the prison governor or in some instances an independent adjudicator (a district judge); the aim of it is to establish what happened and whether the prisoner is guilty or not. They usually take place the day after the report has been issued. The prisoner will be asked to state if they are guilty or not but the governor or the independent adjudicator will ultimately decide after listening to the prisoner and other people including staff as to what happened. Prisoners are allowed to seek legal advice regarding adjudications, which can be via telephone, letter or a legal visit; however, they are not usually, unless there are concerns that the prisoner does not understand the process, allowed legal representation at the adjudication. Should a prisoner be found guilty of an offence there are clear punishments explained in Prison Rules 55 and 55A (The Prison Rules, 1999). The punishment, as with a criminal sentencing hearing, depends on how serious the offence is. If an offence is deemed serious the prison can involve the police so that criminal proceedings can take place. A governor can issue any punishment apart from giving a prisoner extra days on their sentence; should the offence warrant it an independent adjudicator has to be brought in to do this. The punishments that can be issued range from:

- Receiving a caution.
- Removal of privileges (like having a TV in their cell) for up to 42 days. Or up to 21 days for young offenders.
- Stopping prisoners from earning for up to 84 days. Or up to 42 days for young offenders.

- Locking a prisoner in a cell by themselves away from other prisoners for up to 35 days. Or for up to 16 days for young offenders over 18. This is called cellular confinement.
- Stopping a prisoner from doing work with other prisoners for up to 21 days.
- Being placed in the segregation unit for 28 days. Or for up to 21 days for young offenders.

One of the most serious punishments is the addition of extra days in prison; the independent adjudicator can impose up to 42 days of additional imprisonment for an offence. These days are added to the end of the custodial part of a person's sentence with some prisoners ending up with hundreds of extra days added (see Chapter 8). There are other ways in which behaviour in prison is managed, which include the use of force by prison officers and the use of segregation. Prison-issued guidance dictates that where possible the use of de-escalation and communication techniques should be used before the use of force. Should such techniques not work then prison officers are permitted to use force if it is deemed reasonable or necessary. Prison officers receive training in different techniques of control and restraint which are to be deployed during incidents as a last resort; there is also guidance on specific techniques to minimise and manage physical restraints, which are used in the youth custodial estate. Some prison officers are also equipped with batons and more recently PAVA spray has been rolled out for use across the prison estate (see Chapter 7 for more information). The use of force against prisoners has increased over the past decade, arguably driven by the loss of experienced prison staff, overcrowding and subsequent growth in violence against both prisoners and staff. Force was used 49,111 times in England and Wales in the 12 months before the COVID-19 pandemic began; according to data obtained by the *Observer*, force was used 59.1 times per 100 inmates in the year from April 2019 (Savage, 2021). What this shows is that regardless of who orchestrates the violence, prisons are inherently violent places.

Food

Food plays a critical role regarding our physical, mental and emotional wellbeing. A significant amount of human interaction is centred on food; the iconic Sunday roast, for example, or going for a meal at a restaurant or pub is very much something that is associated with British culture. Food is also significant in that we use the food choices we make to construct our identity on gender, ethnic, cultural and ethical levels (de Graaf and Kilty, 2016). Food can also represent an opportunity to indulge, communicate affection, and experience or express religious or traditional values and practices (Godderis, 2006). In a similar way to hospitals and schools, mealtimes are a focal point of the day in prisons; they break up the boredom of daily life in custody and provide opportunities for association with others. Most of what prisoners eat in prison is determined for them. Unlike in the community, prisoners do not have the freedom to decide what or how much they want to eat, nor are they able to choose when they eat their meals (HMIP, 2016). Having a limited ability to determine what, when, where or how much they eat means that prisoners lose control over aspects of their health as well as this important part of their social autonomy (HMIP, 2016). For these reasons, food is a considerable source of frustration and anxiety among prisoners, and thus extremely important to understanding life in custody (de Graaf and Kilty, 2016). While there is some variation across the prison estate, The Prison Rules and PSIs set certain requirements for meal provision, to be followed by every establishment. Prison Rule 24 states that prisoners must be provided with three meals a day, and these should be 'wholesome, nutritious, well prepared and served, reasonably varied and sufficient in quantity' (The Prison Rules, 1999). HMPPS has a responsibility to meet cultural and diversity needs; this means providing meals that meet medical as well as religious or ethical dietary requirements, such as halal, kosher, vegetarian and vegan meals. Prisoners usually select their meal options in advance on a menu system that is operated on a four weekly cycle to try to provide variety. All prison food is prepared and cooked on site, usually by prisoners who are working in the servery and kitchens under the guidance of the prison chef. The quality and quantity of the food in prison has often been a source of critique, especially when it is considered that £2.02 per prisoner per day is spent on food by public sector prisons, compared with £9.88 in hospitals (HMIP, 2016). Poor nutrition can have an impact on an individual's physical and mental wellbeing. Several medical conditions can be linked to poor nutrition such as heart disease, diabetes and high cholesterol, and poor management of these can further burden already stretched prison health resources. Moreover, a number of studies (Eves and Gesch, 2003; Ramsbotham and Gesch, 2009; Zaalberg et al, 2010) have found that there are links between food, security and safety within prisons as frustration over food can be a trigger point for aggression and violence, particularly as food is often served by prisoners to prisoners. There have been attempts to improve the food situation in prisons over recent years but good practice is sketchy and often centres on individual institutions rather than across the whole estate.

Healthcare

The National Health Service (NHS) provides healthcare to prisoners while they are in prison; it is based on the principles of equivalence. The government and NHS England (2019) have set out what equivalence means at a strategic level:

> that people detained in prisons in England are afforded provision of and access to appropriate services or treatment (based on assessed population need and in line with current national or evidence-based guidelines) and that this is considered to be at least consistent in range and quality (availability, accessibility and acceptability) with that available to the wider community, in order to achieve equitable

health outcomes and to reduce health inequalities between people in prison and in the wider community. (HM Government and NHS England, 2019: 2)

Despite this, prisoners frequently report long delays in having their health concerns acted on with access to general practitioners and dentists being some of the most frequently complained about issues across the prison estate. The physical prison environment is important to ensuring the mental health and wellbeing of prisoners and that services designed to support this are delivered. This is made more difficult by the fact that much of the prison estate was not built to provide healthcare. As we know, over a quarter of the prison estate was built before 1900 and some of the older buildings were not designed with modern healthcare in mind. All prisons have some on-site healthcare services (such as primary care and mental health support); some also have dedicated healthcare wings where people can go to receive care and treatment. The exact setup depends on the characteristics of the prison itself; there is wide variation in the services available across the prison estate.

Prisoners can experience delays in getting access to medicines, including medicines they have been prescribed before they enter prison or when they are transferred to another prison. The Prisoner Advisory Service (2018) reported that prisoners can be left without vital medication including 'beta blockers, insulin, mental health medication and pain relief' and that this problem is 'endemic in certain prisons' and has resulted in hospitalisation on occasions (Prisoner Advisory Service, 2018). Unlike on the outside, prisoners are not allowed to manage their own physical health in many ways. If we have a headache, for instance, we may take some paracetamol to help with the pain; this is not possible in a prison environment as the prisoner has to request the painkillers and by the time they receive them the pain may have passed or become worse.

It is also commonly reported that individuals in prison face long delays for external appointments for investigative work or further treatment that can only take place in a hospital. Getting an appointment can be difficult in the first place. For example, it is common for prison staff to fail to pass on messages or for applications made electronically to go missing. Waiting times can sometimes be excessive, according to HMCIP (2020). For example, waiting times to see a doctor ranged from eight to 12 weeks in one prison (HMCIP, 2020). This is due to staff shortages, high demand, high rates of non-attendance, prisoners not being unlocked for or escorted to appointments, or prisoners choosing to use the time for other activities if there is only limited time out of their cells. This is also related to the fact that many prisoners move in and out of prison, or between prisons, which makes the job of providing healthcare more difficult. The sharing of a patient's medical history among those involved in treating them is crucial to ensuring that they receive the treatment that they need. Despite this, there is a clear problem between the information available to healthcare providers about the care patients have received before, during and after their time in prison. Many people arrive in prison without an accompanying medical history, which slows down and reduces the accuracy of their initial assessments, meaning that this first opportunity to provide someone with the type of support they need may be missed.

Mental health

People in prison are more likely to suffer from mental health problems than those in the community; 71 per cent of women and 47 per cent of men surveyed by inspectors in prison reported having mental health problems (HMCIP, 2020). Yet, prisoners are less able to manage their mental health conditions because most aspects of their day-to-day life are controlled by the prison. These difficulties are exacerbated by a deteriorating prison estate, a long-standing lack of prison staff and the increased prevalence of drugs.

A lack of staff within the prison system has meant that the prison regime has become more restrictive and staff are less likely and able to identify prisoners with mental health issues and prisoners are less able to self-refer. Establishing proper one-to-one engagement between prisoners and prison officers is vitally important to maintaining the mental health of prisoners, partly because prison staff can identify problems and partly because it can prevent prisoners from feeling so isolated and alone. But existing staffing levels have meant that prisoners have less regular contact with prison staff. HMIP (2019b) reported on a visit to HMP Wormwood Scrubs that just seven prison officers were responsible for 300 prisoners across four floors. Prisoners miss an average of 15 per cent of medical appointments, in large part because of a lack of prison staff to move them from the wing to healthcare appointments. In Wormwood Scrubs, it was reported that a lack of prison staff means that more than 40 per cent of medical appointments are missed (HMIP, 2019b). It has also been reported that a third of prisons inspected in 2019 had officers who had not undergone adequate mental health awareness training, despite repeated recommendations (HMCIP, 2020), meaning that a high proportion of officers are unaware of the signs to look out for when a person in prison might be having a mental health crisis. The Prison Officers Association (2021) have acknowledged that the prevalence of mental illness is increasing in prisons and have called for better training for prison officers:

> The crisis of mental health in our prisons has intensified in recent years, with rising numbers of prisoners suffering from a variety of conditions, ranging from depression to serious personality disorders. An aging prison population is also causing an increase in dementia. With mental health problems getting worse, it is more important than ever that prison officers receive adequate training to support the mental health of all those in their care. (Prison Officers Association, 2021)

The consequence of individuals suffering from a mental health crisis in prison can be severe and is reflected in the persistently high levels of self-harm that are recorded across the prison estate, and often a significant contributing cause to the high number of self-inflicted deaths that occur across the prison estate each year (see Chapter 6 for more information).

Association

When prisoners are not engaging in work or education, they can engage in other activities which are synonymous with prison life. Association is the term given to when prisoners are unlocked from their cells and allowed to move freely on the wing where they reside. Prisoners often take this opportunity to perform tasks such as laundry, contact family and friends, have a shower and socialise with one another. Pool tables, table football, chess and other board games are all staple features of prison life that prisoners can choose to engage with during this free time. During the summer, prisoners may be allowed to associate outside in the prison yard. Other opportunities that some establishments provide come in the form of evening classes such as art, music and creative writing groups. Prisoners may also use this time to access the prison gym. The gym within the prison is one of the main ways in which prisoners try to maintain health and fitness, both physically and mentally. It also provides a secondary function in that prison staff can also use it when on their lunch break or off duty. As previously detailed, The Prison Rules (1999) state that all prisoners should be given the opportunity to take at least an hour of exercise in the open air each day, 'weather permitting'. Accessing the gym is on top of this opportunity and can be an important place for prisoners, both male and female, to let off steam and exercise. Often it is one of the few places where individuals can exert some control over their lives through the choice of what they choose to do and how they do it. In some prisons, the gym is a place where prisoners and staff interact differently, with prison officers often engaging in healthy competition with prisoners over their fitness. Some prisons hold annual sports days, where staff and prisoners compete on the same teams to win prizes for their wing; it is opportunities like this that can improve prisoner–staff relationships and significantly pass the time within the prison walls. Most prisoners will also have access to the prison library at some point during an association session whereby they can access books to read for pleasure or for studying purposes. There are many opportunities available across the prison estate for prisoners to engage in to pass their free time; it should be noted, however, that these can vary significantly from institution to institution, meaning that some prisoners, depending on where they are placed, can have a more varied range of opportunities to engage in than others.

Religious practice

According to The Prison Rules (1999), the Prison Service has the responsibility to recognise and respect the rights of prisoners to register and practise their faith while in custody. When an individual is received into custody, their details are taken which will include being asked what religion they are; this will be recorded on their file and the prison information system, including if the person states they have no religion. All prisons have a chaplaincy team and most have a multi-faith centre or unit whereby individuals can practise their faith. The chaplains and chaplaincy team must be appointed to meet the needs and reflect the faith make-up of the prison population according to PSI 05/2016 (HMPPS, 2016) which means that it can vary from prison to prison but usually there will be chaplains available from the following religions and faiths:

- Christianity – including Anglicanism, Roman Catholicism, Methodism and free churches
- Islam
- Judaism
- Hinduism
- Sikhism
- Buddhism

If an individual practises a religion that is not represented, they can request to have a person come to the prison to practise their religion with, should it be necessary. On arrival to custody, individuals should be seen by a member of the chaplaincy team within 24 hours; the chaplaincy member might not be of that individual's registered faith and should explain to them more about their team's work and provide guidance on who the appropriate chaplain is and when they will be available. Prisons must facilitate the wearing of religious clothing including headdresses where required by an individual's faith. They must also allow access to religious items and texts that are required by an individual's faith. The prison chaplaincy is often seen as a valued and safe space in prison, providing crucial support for vulnerable prisoners, particularly those struggling to manage the demands of incarceration. Often the building(s) is one of the few quiet and calm spaces inside prison, whereby prisoners can escape the noise and commotion that is a common feature of prison life and take time to reflect and process their current situation. The Cardiff Centre for Chaplaincy Studies (2011) found in their report that all key individuals within a prison (chaplains, prisoners and prison officers) identified the primary role of the chaplain as being pastoral. Their role was to provide one-to-one support to prisoners in a non-judgemental way, irrespective of beliefs; this was particularly seen as crucial during times of personal crisis (for example, in times of bereavement) (Cardiff Centre for Chaplaincy Studies, 2011). This has moved beyond the preconceived notion that chaplains are there to convert prisoners to their religion/faith. They are often identified as those with time for prisoners, who prioritise availability and offer prisoners elements of friendship and/or humanity. Because of this, chaplains are often viewed, particularly by prison officers and governors, as having something of a 'neutral' or 'independent' status in prison; their role is seen as different from that of a prison officer, who is perceived to be more focused on security and control (Cardiff Centre for Chaplaincy Studies, 2011). Prison chaplaincy has become much more of a multi-faith activity with chaplains now working in teams of individuals drawn from a range of faiths. The multi-faith, multicultural model of prison chaplaincy appears to work in drawing together faiths, which outside prison walls can often see nothing in common with one another and can be the source of so much tension and in some cases violence. Prison chaplaincy has the responsibility alongside the broader prison to facilitate the marking and observing of various recognised religious festivals. For example, the annual observance of Ramadan, which is the month of fasting when Muslims abstain from food and drink from dawn until sunset, is a significant time in the Islamic faith but can provide a major challenge to prisons that run on a regime and strict timetable. Over the years, through consultation with Muslim prisoners and Islamic leaders, guidance has been created to help prisons support Muslim prisoners in the observation of this practice. Prisoners are entitled to one hour of worship per week, but they can be prevented from attending if they are held in a close supervision centre or in exceptional individual cases which have been authorised by the governor. PSI 05/2016 (HMPPS, 2016) states that exclusions may be granted on grounds of exceptional and specific concerns for the prisoner's mental or physical wellbeing; or in agreement with the chaplain leading worship if it has been judged that the prisoner has previously seriously misbehaved at a time of worship; or that the governor judges that their presence is likely to cause a disturbance or be a threat to security or control.

Extremism and radicalisation

One of the most concerning issues that has affected prisons and life inside them in recent years has been radicalisation and extremism. While many prisoners enter prison with a faith and others find one during their time in prison, a small number of these prisoners will be 'radicalised' while in custody. Radicalisation is understood in this context as a process by which an individual or a group comes to adopt increasingly extreme political, social and religious ideas and aspirations including the need to use violence to achieve political change (Rushchenko, 2019). Prisons have historically played an important role in many radical organisations and their growth, as they are, in an obvious way, clear locations for the potential recruitment of new followers. Radical political organisations such as the Irish Republicans, German Marxists and Neo-Nazi groups have all used prisons as recruiting grounds for new members and to spread their ideologies over the course of the 20th century. Significantly, the growth in the number of prisoners adopting an anti-state Islamist stance that condones or encourages violence against non-Muslim prisoners, prison officers and the public has caused major concern for prison managers and counter-terrorism officers over the last decade. The current terrorist threat in prisons in England and Wales is Islamist terrorism (Hall, 2022: 7). While gangs and hierarchies are seen as inevitable in prison life, Islamist group behaviour has come to be seen as part of the prison landscape and the harm it can potentially cause has not been appreciated by prison authorities until more recent times (Hall, 2022). For instance, Powis et al (2019) identified in their study how these groups, operating in an environment of high levels of fear among staff and prisoners, enabled 'heavy players' and 'extremist prisoners' to exercise significant power and influence at several high security prisons within the estate. There can be a tendency, due to the fear of discriminating against Muslim prisoners, to disregard disturbing gang-like behaviour; at the frontline level, there has been a predisposition to regard Islam as a 'no-go area' leading to a reluctance to focus on Islamist group behaviour (Hall, 2022: 10). Such an attitude can result in prisons becoming breeding grounds for extremist views, which can potentially result in violence and terrorist incidents occurring both inside and outside prison. This is particularly important because some prisoners, especially those who are vulnerable, can be very susceptible to extremist ideological messages which if not challenged can have drastic consequences. For instance, in 2020 at HMP Whitemoor, Brusthom Ziamani and Baz Hockton attempted to murder a prison officer by stabbing him. Ziamani, a convicted terrorist, is said to have radicalised Hockton by disseminating his extremist ideology (Hall, 2022: 22). The offence was ruled a terrorist incident as both individuals had written a martyrdom letter and made makeshift bladed weapons and fake suicide belts which they wore while carrying out the attack (BBC News, 2020b). Among the perennial problems that prisons face, overcrowding, lack of resources and understaffing exacerbate the risk of radicalisation and extremism:

> Badly run prisons also create the physical and ideological space in which extremist recruiters can operate at free will and monopolise the discourse about religion and politics. (International Centre for the Study of Radicalisation and Political Violence, 2010: 2)

In response to the Hall (2022) report, which was viewed as a landmark review of terrorist legislation, the UK government has stated it will invest £7.2 million in tackling extremism within prisons. Part of the plan involves the expansion of close supervision centres. These centres are essentially prisons within a prison; they hold the most dangerous men in the prison system, in small, highly supervised units contained within high security prisons. They hold a range of offenders, not just those convicted of terrorist offences. These units have the most restrictive regime in the prison system with extremely limited stimuli and human contact provided to prisoners within them. The expansion of these units is seen as key by the government as a way to prevent convicted terrorists from their potential recruitment for extremist causes (UK Government, 2022a). Alongside this, the government is establishing a team whose job it will be to quickly identify and target the most influential and charismatic terrorists so that they can be moved to one of the Prison Service's three 'separation centres' where they will reside completely apart from the main prison population (UK Government, 2022a).

The separation centre model was introduced in 2017 to manage extremism within the prison estate. These three centres were designed to be used solely for prisoners of any political or religious viewpoint who were thought to be at risk of radicalising other prisoners; so far they have only been used for Muslim men (HMCIP, 2022). These measures, alongside the removal of the right to automatic early release of terrorist offenders, tougher sentences for the most serious offences and further training to be provided to prison officers to help them to spot signs of terrorist activity are all designed to tackle the increased threat of prison-based extremism.

Summary

This chapter has explored several key elements that are features of everyday life in prison. While it is not exhaustive regarding covering all elements of prison life, it has provided an overview of the day-to-day regime of prison and then focused on a number of key areas such as education, work and training, which are considered vital if prison is to perform its function of rehabilitating individuals in its care. It has also discussed some of the more unheard-of areas of prison life such as association, as well as some of the more negative aspects such as radicalisation and extremism.

Questions to consider

1. What do you understand the notion of 'doing time' to mean?
2. Is a prisoner's time in prison spent productively?
3. What should prisons do to support prisoners with their health, both physically and mentally?

TAKING IT FURTHER

There are several texts that explore the issues presented in this chapter, which you might wish to consult for further detail:

- James, E. (2003). *A Life Inside: A Prisoner's Notebook*. London: Atlantic Books. James, now known under the name Monahan, is a *Guardian* columnist and convicted murderer. Since his release from prison, he has published several books detailing his experience of life in prison.

- Nichols, H. (2021). *Understanding the Educational Experiences of Imprisoned Men: (Re)education*. London: Routledge. This empirical study explores the benefits and challenges of the prison education system.

- Ugelvik, T. (2014). *Power and Resistance in Prison: Doing Time, Doing Freedom*. Hampshire: Palgrave Macmillan. While this book focuses on Norwegian prisons, it provides some very useful insights into what the notion of 'doing time' can mean to prisoners.

It is also worth consulting various websites of the organisations that actively campaign for improved prison conditions as they often have the most up-to-date sources for contextual information:

- Howard League for Penal Reform: https://howardleague.org

- Prison Reform Trust: http://www.prisonreformtrust.org.uk

- Prisoners' Education Trust: https://www.prisonerseducation.org.uk

6

Theorising punishment and the pains of imprisonment

Key learning outcomes

By the end of this chapter, you should be able to:

- Explain the differences between reductivist and retributivist principles of punishment

- Describe the pains of imprisonment

- Understand how prison can be considered as harmful

Introduction

This chapter introduces how the experience of being in prison can be seen when looking at broader philosophies of punishment. It explores the four main theories behind the use of prison as a punishment: incapacitation, deterrence, just deserts and rehabilitation. Examples of various legislation are introduced to show how governments have, over time, moved through all these different philosophies of punishment, often leaving the prison system in a state of constant reforms with very little time to embed them into practice. It is argued that political thinking shapes the policy designed to inform how we treat people in prison, with various reforms often being put forward to satisfy the media and public outcry rather than being evidence based. For instance, New Labour introduced the indeterminate sentence of imprisonment for public protection (IPP) as a mechanism to deal with 'dangerous offenders' using a risk-based approach to punishment yet it resulted in a big increase in the prison population and the subsequent overwhelming of the Parole Board and Probation Service. The chapter also focuses on the 'pains of imprisonment' and how violence, self-harm and self-inflicted deaths are sadly all features of prison life.

Philosophies of punishment

Exploring and understanding the different ways in which punishment can be handed out to individuals who have broken the law is the study of penal theory. Penal theory seeks to provide explanations as to on what grounds we are justified in punishing individuals who have broken the law and to what end different punishments can be used. When an individual breaks the law, it is assumed, if they are caught and found guilty, that they should be punished. This punishment, it is also thought, should involve some element of suffering for the guilty party, be it physical, mental or financial. Through handing out a punishment, the guilty party has been told that what they have done is wrong; it is a communicative act according to Duff (1998) whereby the offender is being informed that their behaviour is wrong. In Western societies, including England and Wales, punishments are handed out mostly by the criminal courts through judges and magistrates who interpret the law and sentencing guidelines to hand out the appropriate punishment. Other punishments are handed out through out-of-court disposals which are mainly police led, such as on-the-spot fines, penalty notices and so on. There are a range of punishments available through the courts ranging from fines, to community punishments and of course imprisonment, which is regarded as the most severe. This has been the case since the 19th century when capital punishment fell out of favour with the Victorians (see Chapter 2) although it is worth noting that capital punishment (the death penalty) was not fully abolished until 1969 in England and Wales; the last hanging took place in 1964. The use of sentencing guidelines by judges and magistrates when considering and delivering punishments is key to preventing the infliction of unnecessary harm. Punishment must have a stated aim or function, in part so that its effectiveness can be measured but also in that it needs to have a purpose to have legitimacy. What this aim or function is, is often the cause of controversy within the CJS. According to Duff and Garland (1994: 2) '[p]unishment requires justification because it is morally problematic. It is morally problematic because it involves doing things to people that (when not described as "punishment" [and thereby legitimised]) seem morally wrong.' The power to punish derives from the legal authority of the state to do things that would otherwise be '*prima facie,* morally wrongful' (Lacey, 1988: 14) but it raises important ethical dilemmas given that punishment causes pain, suffering and harm.

There are a number of competing explanations and justifications that are rooted in contrasting ideas over what the purpose of punishment should be. These fall into two typologies: reductivist and retributivist. Reductivists tend to be forward-looking, focusing on the aim of punishment being to prevent future crimes. In comparison, retributivists tend to be backward-looking, focusing on punishing individuals for past crimes and handing out punishments because the individual deserves it. It is important to remember that in practice the CJS does not subscribe to one justification of punishment at any one time. More often than not, the CJS fashions quite contradictory justifications so that they often coexist and operate together, despite this often causing greater problems due to the incompatibility of these approaches. This is particularly evident in the context of prisons as ever since their creation the purpose of them has been unclear, making it particularly difficult to manage them effectively and potentially is the root cause of many of the challenges prisons face today. The focus will now turn to exploring these different and competing justifications of punishment and their relevance to understanding imprisonment.

Reductivist principles

Reductivist justifications for punishment lie in the belief that punishment is justified on the grounds that it can prevent future offending and therefore future harm being caused. This is why reductivist justifications for punishment are considered to be forward-looking; they are about the prevention of further crime. The routes of reductivist approaches to punishment are found in a form of moral reasoning known as utilitarianism which was most famously advanced by Jeremy Bentham. Bentham (1998) argued that moral actions are those which produce 'the greatest happiness of the greatest number' of people. Cavadino and Dignan (2002: 34) interpret this to mean that for punishment to reduce future crimes the pain and unhappiness caused to the offender must be 'outweighed by the avoidance of unpleasantness to other people in the future – thus making punishment morally right from a utilitarian point of view'. The principles of reductivist justifications for punishment, therefore, focus on the end goal of punishment by focusing on the future or greater good principle. In practice, this is rationalised in that, through spending money on such forward-looking punishments, money is saved in the long term because of the future benefits they bring (Bennett, 2008). Such principles, however, rely on sentencing practices to work towards this end goal, yet the evidence regarding the successes of forward-looking justifications for doing this remains controversial and inconclusive at best (Bennett, 2008). Deterrence, incapacitation and rehabilitation are the three main forward-looking, reductivist justifications for punishment. It is argued, including by the great philosopher Bentham (1998), that through such approaches crime can be restricted as deterrence deters potential criminals, incapacitation keeps actual or potential offenders out of circulation and rehabilitation takes away their desire to offend. Each of these justifications will now be looked at in turn.

Deterrence

Deterrence as a justification for punishment is based on the notion that you can discourage crime being committed through making the public fearful of the punishment they would receive if they committed it. The two key criminological philosophers in this area are Cesare Beccaria and Jeremy Bentham, both of whom were writing about deterrence in the 18th century. Beccaria (1986 [1764]) argued that 'individuals make decisions based on what will garner them pleasure and avoid pain and unless deterred, they will pursue their own desires, even by committing crimes'. Yet, through using swift, proportionate punishments people could be deterred from committing crime, especially if what would happen to them was made clear to the public. Bentham (1998) drew up differences between individual and general deterrence. Individual deterrence occurs when someone experiences something so unpleasant that it deters them from repeating the experience in the future. In contrast, general deterrence is targeted at the public to discourage crime on a broader scale. For instance, take public service announcements such as the various advertisements on television and radio that we see and hear about not drinking and driving. Such advertisements are designed to deter people from the act and clearly emphasise the consequences of doing so, not just in terms of criminal prosecution but also regarding the harm that potentially can be caused by such an act. Both individual and general deterrence operate under the assumption that the severe and certain nature of punishment following an act of criminal transgression will reduce offending directly at the individual level but also indirectly through frightening society at large not to break the law.

Empirical evidence regarding the success of a deterrent-based punishment is modest at best (von Hirsch et al, 1999). There have been several attempts by different governments to introduce particularly harsh punishments on the grounds that they will create individual and general deterrent effects. For instance, in the 1980s the Conservative government as a mechanism to deal with young offenders introduced the 'short, sharp shock' approach to punishment whereby young people who broke the law were sentenced to short spells in custody and placed under an intensive regime with a view to shocking them out of committing further offences. Similarly, the US-style 'boot camps' of the 1990s that the Conservative government experimented with were based on aggressive army regimes and designed to shock and deter people from offending. However, the results from such approaches show success rates are no better than alternative punishments. There are also concerns raised regarding deterrent-based approaches on moral grounds as well as the lack of empirical evidence.

- Questions have been asked as to whether it is possible to quantify the individual human experiences of pain and harm and to devise a way to create equivalence. In that way, can we associate the pain of being a victim of crime to that of a punishment?
- Is it possible to assume that we will react to the deterrent in the same way? What may deter one person may not deter another.
- There is a lack of evidence regarding cause and effect; how do we know that harsher punishments have a deterrent effect?
- Is it possible that deterrent approaches will allow for punishment that is disproportionate to the offence committed?
- Deterrence is primarily concerned with offences that might be committed in the future rather than those that have been committed so we run the risk of assuming that people cannot change their behaviour and are destined to continue to offend. (Hudson, 2003)

Incapacitation

Incapacitation is the term given to the process of physically or geographically preventing an individual from being able to commit further offences either by restraining them (in other words, locking them behind bars) or through removing their ability to commit further offences (that is, by removing limbs, transporting them or killing them). In the context of England and Wales, this has been done through various ways over the course of history: originally through the removal of limbs, the application of the death penalty, and transporting individuals to foreign lands, and most recently by imprisoning people. There are other means of incapacitation in operation in England and Wales, through punishments such as curfews, exclusion zones and the removal of licences (for example, driving licences) as these restrict people's movements. Incapacitation, on a logical level, does not seek to change a person's behaviour nor try to understand it, it simply operates as a justification to restrict their capacity to commit offences. The rights of the offender are forgone in this justification with the focus being on the protection of potential victims. The justification of incapacitation dates as far back in history as that of rehabilitation, whereby under the traditional rehabilitation justification of punishment those offenders assessed as treatable were cured and those who were not were detained for purposes of incapacitation. Somewhat interestingly, the approach does not presume that incapacitating individuals will result in any transformative change despite the fact that rehabilitation is attempted within settings of incapacitation (that is, prisons).

There have been numerous policies created over the years with incapacitation used as a justification for them, largely to deal with 'dangerous offenders', those who are the most 'risky'. Individuals categorised as dangerous offenders can be sentenced to disproportionate lengths of imprisonment in comparison to 'normal' offenders who are sentenced proportionately under legislation provided by the Criminal Justice Act 2003. This is because certain offences have been categorised as dangerous and under this legislation, based on notions of public protection, individuals who commit serious sexual, violent and terrorist-related offences can be held for lengthy periods of time in custody and face significant challenges in being released once they have served their sentence. Other examples of policy approaches which have an incapacitation focus are the 'three strikes and you are out' law in the USA, whereby the three-strikes law significantly increases the prison sentence of an individual who is convicted of a third felony after having been previously convicted of two or more serious or violent felonies. Under this legislation, such individuals are referred to as 'persistent' offenders and if a person meets this criteria then the court has little option but to impose a mandatory life sentence. The use of incapacitation as justification for punishment has been attractive over time because it can lead to the removal of dangerous offenders from circulation in society. It also is viewed to have led to a reduction in crime rates and therefore reduced the need of governments to spend money on crime control. Furthermore, it is viewed as a politically popular justification as it is particularly difficult to argue against imprisoning dangerous individuals to prevent them from harming the public.

There are, however, criticisms about using incapacitation as a justification for punishment. These largely centre on the issue that for it to be justified as a punishment there needs to be a high level of assurance that those who are dangerous are accurately assessed as being so. It relies on assessments of risk being carried out by professionals such as probation officers and the use of actuarial risk assessment tools. Yet, it is known that humans are fallible and actuarial risk assessment tools have numerous problems (Haines and Case, 2009; Hudson, 2003). This is mainly due to the comparison that is made by such tools between an individual and the amassed knowledge of past events of a cohort of convicted offenders. The problem is statistical fallacy, in that it is assumed that information about one offender group can be easily generalised and applied to an individual placed under assessment (Haines and Case, 2009). The consequence can be false negatives, where an individual is assessed as low risk but is dangerous or a false positive, where an individual is assessed as dangerous but is not. Consequently, some individuals will therefore be incapacitated for disproportionate lengths of time without due justification. A policy example of this is the indeterminate sentence of IPP, which will be discussed as a case study later in this chapter.

Rehabilitation

Rehabilitation is arguably one of the main terms associated with imprisonment; it is seen as one of the main goals of prison to rehabilitate those who enter the prison gates. As a justification for punishment, rehabilitation seeks not to change the individual who is being punished but to try to restore them to the state they were in before the crime was committed. There are two approaches to rehabilitation. The first is the treatment model, which aims to 'treat' an individual who has broken the law and through such intervention it is assumed that an 'offender's personality, outlook, habits or opportunities can be changed to make them less inclined to commit crime' (von Hirsch, 1998). The treatment is centred on a psychological approach of trying to change an individual's mindset so they avoid reoffending. The treatment model was favoured as the approach to rehabilitation throughout the first half of the 20th century, and was at its height in the 1960s and 1970s. Trust and faith was placed in therapists, probation workers and social workers to rehabilitate individuals who broke the law. The approach to sentencing was centred on how best to treat an individual; the seriousness of the offence was not at the forefront of sentencing decision making. Offending was therefore treated as though it was a medical problem; if you could correctly diagnose the problem, it was thought you would be able to fix the person and prevent them from reoffending, because it was assumed that individuals who committed crimes did so because they were under some form of mental, physical or moral deprivation. The treatment model of rehabilitation lasted as the main justification for punishment in England and Wales until the early 1970s when research findings emerged which concluded that 'nothing worked' in the context of trying to 'treat' offenders. Martinson's (1974: 25) USA-based research had significant influence on government policy in the UK. His seminal paper argued that based on the analysis of 231 studies published in the USA between 1945 and 1967, with a few isolated exceptions, the rehabilitative efforts that had been reported thus far had had no appreciable effect on recidivism (Martinson, 1974). Such conclusions brought into question the appropriateness of rehabilitation under the treatment model as a justification for punishment. Subsequently, it started to fall out of favour as a basis for punishment and as the aim of imprisonment.

To survive as a justification for punishment, what is understood as the model for rehabilitation has had to change and evolve. Rehabilitation is now understood in a modern context, under the welfare model which aims to address the underlying causes of crime such as socioeconomic disadvantage: for example, the lack of education, training and employment. Prisons have continued to be seen as places where rehabilitation takes place although questions have consistently been raised as to whether this is possible given the context in which they operate; rehabilitation is also central to probation practices. It is now more commonly seen and understood as education rather than 'treatment', the goal being to educate individuals who have broken the law to recognise the situations which may lead them into reoffending and to provide them with the tools and mechanisms to avoid making the decision to reoffend. The shift in emphasis was recognised by Bean (1981) who argued that this approach to rehabilitation is a positive approach to punishment because it treats people who break the law as individuals and attempts to work with the individual and the context of the crime. It also holds the individual to account and moves the responsibility for the individual's behaviour back to them rather than to the CJS or the state. The rehabilitative approach to punishment, then, means that something positive is able to be achieved with the prisoner. They are not written off as unable to change. Through a focus on trying to understand an individual's reasons for offending in the first instance – their criminogenic needs (Clark, 2013) – it is possible that an individual can be 'reformed' or changed and that something good comes from the process of punishment.

Rehabilitation has been criticised, however, as a justification for punishment for potentially being too idealistic and not considering the rights and needs of victims nor the safety of the public. It is therefore hard to see it ever being considered as a justification for punishment on its own, but instead in tandem with incapacitation and deterrence, for example, as a trifecta of justifications for punishment. Given that crime is a social construct, it is hard to see that treating it as a medical problem whereby the individual can be cured does not circumvent that understanding. Indeed, not all medical illnesses can be cured, so why should crime be viewed as something that can be treated and resolved? It is also difficult to establish empirical evidence that a programme or approach to rehabilitation works because of the difficulty in establishing cause and effect. In recent years, this has led to a shift in the language and understanding about whether rehabilitation works to a focus on desistance from crime instead (see Chapter 8).

Case study: Indeterminate sentence of imprisonment for public protection (IPP)

The IPP was a product of the Criminal Justice Act 2003. It stated that it must be imposed on individuals who were convicted of a serious offence (that is, a specified sexual or violent offence carrying a maximum penalty of ten years' imprisonment or more – there were 153 offences for which this was applicable) or where 'the court is of the opinion that there is a significant risk to members of the public of serious harm'. In a similar manner to a life sentence, those sentenced to an IPP were given a 'tariff' that they must serve in custody before being considered for parole. The sentence was introduced in a context of increasing emphasis being placed on public protection as a goal of sentencing under the New Labour government. The increasing frequency of those sentenced to an IPP had a visible impact on the wider prison population, with the MoJ (2007) commenting at the time that the largest proportionate increases since April 2006 were for those sentenced to indeterminate sentences which increased by 31 per cent or from 1,000 prisoners in June 2006 to almost 3,000 the following year. It also had a significant impact on the workload of the Parole Board, something which was not initially factored in when the sentence was created. In response to these initial critiques, New Labour amended the sentence through the Criminal Justice and Immigration Act 2008 to try to limit the use of IPP sentences. It worked in that there was a reduction in the number of people sentenced to an IPP but problems remained with the lack of serving IPP prisoners being released. This was due to the huge increase in the workload of the Parole Board, which was caused by IPP. The other key problem for the indeterminately sentenced prisoner was not knowing the amount of time they would serve, making it very difficult to be productive in custody. Often offender behaviour programmes are allocated to individuals based on their time left in custody; for an IPP prisoner this is potentially endless, meaning they could struggle to access vital support as there would always be someone on a determinate sentence ahead of them on the waiting list. Under the coalition government and via the Legal Aid and Sentencing of Offenders Act 2012, the sentence was abolished. Ken Clarke (Hansard, 2011), Home Secretary at the time, said: 'IPPs were unclear, inconsistent and have been used far more than was ever intended. ... That is unjust to the people in question and completely inconsistent with the policy of punishment, reform and rehabilitation' (Hansard, 2011). There are individuals in prison today still serving this type of sentence; they have served beyond their tariff due to the delays in the parole system. Some have served five times the amount of time they should have been in custody. Because of the harms caused by imprisonment, this potentially could be irreversible and make it very difficult for IPP-sentenced prisoners to readapt to life outside.

The Justice Committee, at the time of writing, were holding an inquiry into the IPP sentence; it will be interesting to see the result of it. Visit their website at https://committees.parliament.uk/committee/102/justice-committee to find out more.

Retributivist principles

Retributivist justifications for punishment in their simplest form are justified on the basis that individuals who break the law deserve to be punished regardless of any future positive consequences of that punishment. This principle has its roots in ancient times dating as far back as the biblical notion of an 'eye for an eye', and is present in many religious doctrines. Kant, the German philosopher, argued that the duty to punish was absolute and unconditional to restore the moral equilibrium of society. Retributivist approaches to punishment are justified on the basis that if we harm someone, we deserve to be harmed because of our actions. However, retributivist justifications are not as unreasonable in their approach to punishment as the terminology might suggest. They do not aim to punish individuals who break the law more than for which they deserve to potentially deter, incapacitate or rehabilitate them; they argue the punishment should fit the crime. As Kant states:

> Punishment can never be inflicted merely as a means to promote some other good for the criminal himself or for civil society. It must always be inflicted upon him only because he has committed a crime. For a man can never be treated merely as a means to the purposes of another. (Kant, 1796, cited in Walker, 1991: 72)

Punishment, therefore, is justified under retributivist terms because it aims to restore justice, obtain redress for victims or express the 'justified outrage of reasonable people' (Bennett, 2008: 14). The increasing draw of reductivist justifications for punishment led to retributivist approaches falling from favour as they were considered outdated and embroiled with feelings of revenge, which did not sit well with more utilitarian thinkers. Yet, there has been something of a revival of retributivist ideas in the last few decades in England and Wales and other Western countries; this has been through the main penal approach of just deserts.

Just deserts

The premise of just deserts theory is a relatively simple one to absorb. It states that what happens to someone convicted of a crime should be determined by the seriousness of the offence and nothing else. In this sense, it is the task of the judge or magistrate responsible for the sentencing to find a punishment that fits the crime. Justice is central to this approach in that it insists that offenders should only be punished as severely as they deserve. This contrasts with justifications such as rehabilitation, which can be excessive, and incapacitation, which can be overzealous. However, it should not be assumed this means harsh punishments cannot be used, just that the punishment should be in line with the harm caused by the offence. Von Hirsch (1976) argued, as a key proponent of this approach, that at the centre of the CJS should lie greater consistency and certainty about what would happen if you committed an offence with the punishment fitting the crime, rather than the person being central to that provision. It is important that the individual who has committed the offence is punished but also that they understand they are being treated as someone who deserves punishment. In this sense, two further principles are key to understanding this approach: proportionality, whereby the offender should be sentenced in proportion to what the offence deserves; and denunciation, whereby through punishing the behaviour it is being denounced through social disapproval with a view to restoring the moral equilibrium. Proponents of just deserts argue that offenders are free willed and therefore are accountable for their actions, particularly those committed in the past as opposed to having any concerns about future offending (von Hirsch, 1976). Through doing this, it is viewed that punishment can be definite, consistent and just.

The challenge posed by just deserts is how to determine which offences are more serious than others. It is often left to judges and/or magistrates to determine this, although the introduction of sentencing guidelines has somewhat helped to alleviate this burden. There have been attempts through the creation of legislation over time to try to grade punishments with a view to determining seriousness. The Criminal Justice Act 1991 which was influenced by just deserts theory tried to grade punishments into three groups according to seriousness: fines or discharge; those that should result in a community punishment; and those that were so serious only a custodial sentence would be appropriate. One of the challenges of just deserts is whether the offender's motives for committing the offence or the consequences of their actions should be the focus of the assessment of seriousness. It is also important to consider issues of power about who gets to decide how serious an offence is. Given that the vast proportion of judges and magistrates are from privileged backgrounds, it is perhaps unlikely they would understand reasons to do with poverty and socioeconomic disadvantage as the causes of offending. Another challenge regarding the just deserts approach to punishment centres around whether it is justifiable to increase the severity of punishment for repeat or persistent offenders. Von Hirsh (1976) supports the notion of a 'discount' for first-time offenders but disagrees with the idea of increasing punishments for persistent offenders as this results in disproportionality. In this context, increased sentences for individuals labelled as persistent offenders are considered unjust (Roberts, 2007) as is the application of the 'three strikes and you are out' laws in the USA. The lack of a clear and just way to measure seriousness remains one of the key criticisms of just deserts theory. The justification for punishment assumes that all individuals' experience of punishment is the same; conversely, enacting the same punishment for the same offence could undermine a victim's experience of the harm caused by the offence because victims may not experience harm in the same way. Two people sentenced to custody may experience it differently because the impact of the environment on an individual is felt differently; therefore, the punishment would not be just because the punishments are unequal. Finally, even if these issues could be rectified, retributivists have never adequately explained why it is necessary to use punishment as a response to criminal behaviour as opposed to other sanctions such as naming and shaming (Bennett, 2008).

The impact of being in prison

The aims of imprisonment continue to change over time with different justifications used in different eras to rationalise the use of imprisonment as a punishment. While deterrence, retribution, rehabilitation and incapacitation (now seen through the lens of public protection) are still used as the main mechanisms to explain the use of imprisonment, the core purpose of imprisonment is to deprive an individual of their liberty. This is something it has always been used for and will continue to be used for. Historically, other purposes may also have been present such as subjecting prisoners to forced labour or penal servitude (see Chapter 2), yet the actual punishment of prison is to deprive an individual of their freedom and to remove them from society. Alexander Paterson, the Prison Commissioner in the 1920s, famously declared that people 'come to prison as punishment not for punishment' (Paterson cited in Ruck, 1951: 23). Yet, it is regularly documented in HMIP inspection reports, Independent Monitoring Board reports and through prisoners' autobiographical accounts that prison is often experienced in numerous painful ways. Prison is therefore always more than a restriction of liberty; perhaps Paterson (1925 as cited in Ruck, 1951) was only expressing an ambitious desire which was and still is yet to be achieved. Prison life is characterised by vulnerability, powerlessness, routine humiliations and the constant reminder that, as a prisoner, irrespective of whether you have been convicted or not, you have forfeited your rights (Moore, 2008). The inherent deprivations of prison life are often referred to as the 'pains of imprisonment'. One of the most well-known studies that has laid the foundation for theorising about how imprisonment is experienced is by Gresham Sykes (1958). His study, detailed in his book *The Society of Captives* (Sykes, 1958), identified the five pains of imprisonment and laid the foundations for many subsequent studies. Sykes (1958) undertook an ethnographic study in New Jersey's maximum security prison where he explored prison subcultures and the exercise of power. He concluded that prison inflicted psychological pains on the prisoners and that these pains were just as damaging, if not more so, than the physical pains endured by prisoners in the 18th and 19th centuries:

> Such attacks are less easily seen than a sadistic beating, a pair of shackles on the floor, or the caged man on a treadmill, but the destruction of the psyche is no less fearful than bodily affliction. (Sykes, 1958: 64)

Prisoners suffer, Sykes (1958) argued, five deprivations: the deprivation of liberty, deprivation of security, deprivation of autonomy, deprivation of goods and services and the deprivation of heterosexual relationships. These five core deprivations, Sykes (1958) argued, mark prison life. Studies have been undertaken which explore the psychological harm that imprisonment can cause alongside other impacts of being inside. Foucault (1977) in his now classic text, *Discipline and Punish*, made similar observations to Sykes (1958) in that the psychological harms caused by imprisonment were potentially more harmful than the physical methods that had been used in the past to punish individuals. The movement, Foucault (1977) argued, was from the punishment of the body through, for instance, the use of the stocks, whipping and hanging to one of the punishment of the soul through the use of imprisonment. Imprisonment therefore opened up new possibilities for punishment as there were only so many ways you could physically punish the body (before the individual died) but the punishment of the soul through imprisonment opened up new possibilities for endless suffering.

Since the work of Sykes (1958) and the many other studies which have contributed to the literature on the impact of imprisonment on individuals (see Cohen and Taylor, 1972; King and McDermott, 1995; Liebling, 2004; Liebling, 2011), a new pain of imprisonment can be added to the list: the pain of uncertainty and indeterminacy. For those individuals who are serving IPP sentences, whereby their sentence has no stated end date, they experience a further pain of a lack of certainty. The key consideration for the indeterminately sentenced prisoner is that the amount of time they will eventually serve in prison is unknown; this makes it impossible to plan for their future as their release date is undetermined. The notion of being on a Penrose staircase is a useful metaphor here, in that it is the sense of going round and round but not getting anywhere which individuals serving such sentences find so difficult (see Crewe, 2011). Moreover, Crewe (2011) has added to the pains of imprisonment literature and attempted to reconceptualise them to make them relevant to the modern day prison experience. He has argued that pains associated with 'tightness' should be added to the list, whereby:

> The term 'tightness' captures the feelings of tension and anxiety generated by uncertainty, and the sense of not knowing which way to move, for fear of getting things wrong. It conveys the way that power operates both closely and anonymously, working like an invisible harness on the self. It is all-encompassing and invasive, in that it promotes the self-regulation of all aspects of conduct, addressing both the psyche and the body. (Crewe, 2011: 522)

From Sykes' (1958) study to more recent accounts of experiences in prison (Crewe, 2009), the common theme that prison is more damaging than rehabilitative is quite profound. While it is open to debate and deliberation as to whether such effects and impacts are intended, they are nevertheless ever present within the prison estate. The consequences of the impact of that environment on individuals will be discussed now with a focus on violence, self-harm and self-inflicted deaths within the secure estate.

Violence within the secure estate

Prisons have long been thought of as violent places. Despite one of the primary goals of the secure estate to be rehabilitation, a significant amount of violence in various forms occurs in prisons on a day-to-day basis. There were 20,049 assault incidents in the 12 months up to September 2021, which is a reduction of 18 per cent when compared with the previous 12 months to September 2020 (MoJ, 2022d). It should be noted that these statistics cover the exceptional period of the COVID-19 pandemic and thus a period where prisons were running on a restricted regime whereby prisoners were locked down in their cells with their movements restricted. Therefore, it is important to look at the trend of assault incidents in the secure estate over time to get a true sense of the level of violence present within it. Figure 6.1 illustrates across a period of 20 years the levels of recorded assaults in the secure estate broken down into the two main ways it is documented: prisoner-on-prisoner assaults and assaults on staff. The drop-off in the number of assaults taking place during the COVID-19 pandemic is also illustrated in Figure 6.1, but violence is on the rise again as prisons return to normal regimes post-COVID-19; in the most recent quarter of July to September 2021, assaults increased by 9 per cent to 5,569 incidents (MoJ, 2022d).

Assaults within prison can range in seriousness with the MoJ specifically collecting statistics on what it terms to be 'serious assaults'. Serious assaults are those which fall into one or more of the following categories: a sexual assault; an assault requiring treatment in an outside hospital as an in-patient; an assault requiring medical treatment for concussion or internal injuries; an assault incurring any of the following injuries: a fracture, scald or burn, stabbing, crushing, extensive or multiple bruising, black eye, broken nose, lost or broken tooth, cuts requiring suturing, bites, temporary or permanent blindness (MoJ, 2022d). In the 12 months to September 2021, there were 2,042 serious assaults (a rate of 26 per 1,000 prisoners) (MoJ, 2022d). The levels of violence within the prison estate have long been of concern to governments, prison campaigners and the family and friends of those who reside in prison, as well as to those who work there. The volatility of prisons is well documented (see James, 2003), with many expecting them to be disordered and unruly places on account of the population they hold, but to carry out any of their stated aims prisons must be safe and orderly places. HMIP (2022) assesses prisons in regard to safety and considers it to be one of the four tests of a healthy prison. It is highlighted in various prison inspection reports that much of the violence in prisons is due to frustration caused by unpredictable and poorly communicated changes to regimes. Violence is also attributed to the systemic problem of drugs within the secure estate and individuals amassing drug debts while in custody. Physically poor conditions and highly controlling regimes, or by contrast, circumstances in which the rules are unevenly applied or not adhered to, or where prisoners do not experience staff decisions as fair or legitimate, can all heighten tensions and induce stresses, potentially giving rise to conflict and assaults (McGuire, 2018). Some aspects of prison life make the likelihood of violence occurring less likely; for instance, places where prisoners are engaged in purposeful activities they consider to be of value (workshops, education classes, rehabilitation programmes) are less likely to be sites of aggression than places with less focused objectives or less formal ground rules. Some of the most routine aspects of prison life such as movement from building to building

Figure 6.1: Annual rolling rate of prisoner-on-prisoner assaults and assaults on staff from 2000 onwards

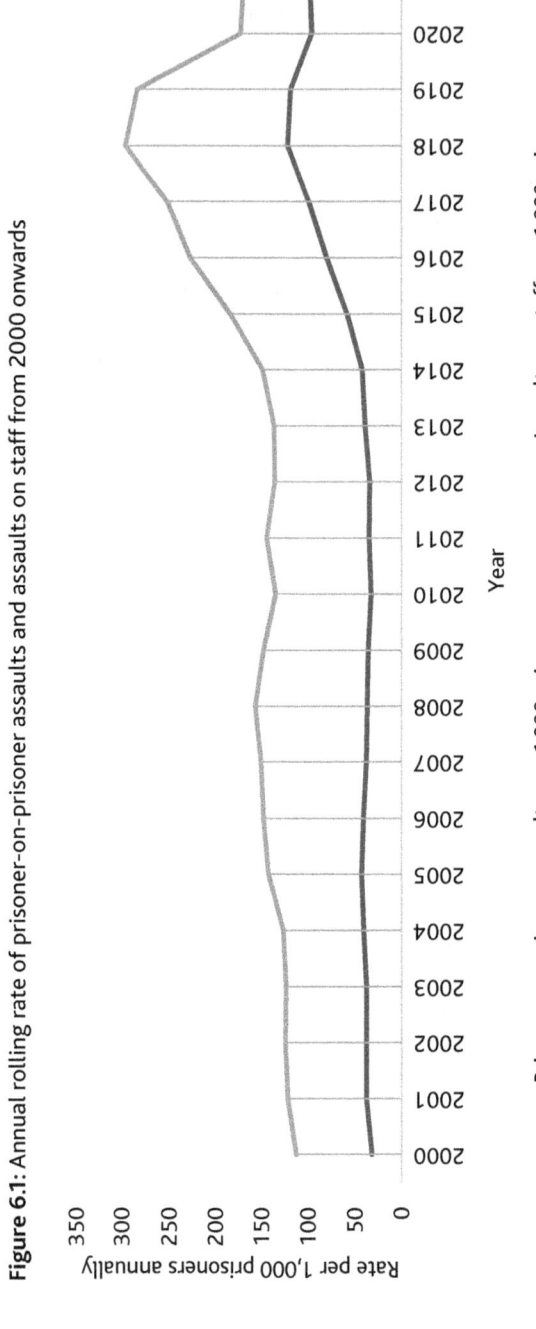

Source: MoJ, 2022d

are often the sites of violence because it is at these points where prisoners often outnumber the number of officers present to manage behaviour. A significant issue affecting prison violence is the rise of criminal gang activity inside prison walls. Just as such activity has increased outside prison, it has spilled into prisons with many individuals grouping together to continue their criminal activity inside. Wood (2006) found that prison gangs commit a disproportionate number of rule violations, assaults and violence in prison; despite this, there is no formal definition of a 'prison gang' provided by HMPPS (Maitra, 2020). Maitra (2020) found in his research that gangs are often formed in prison for protection from violence. Particularly in regard to the youth estate, gangs either exist in prison because they already exist on the outside or are formed once inside prison as young people from the same areas are placed together on wings. Interestingly, prison gangs can also be formed through racial and cultural solidarity. Maitra (2020) found that Pakistani and British Pakistani prisoners associated together in the prisons he researched; they collectively protected their reputation and engaged in retaliatory violence if an individual from the group was mocked or ridiculed. It is often the prison gangs that are the drivers of much of the illegal activity that goes on within prisons, such as bringing in and distributing illegal substances and using illegal mobile phones. There is very little clear policy and practice direction from HMPPS on the issue of prison gangs with individual prisons being left to deal with the problem themselves, often badly. More broadly, the management of violent behaviour has been as much of a concern as the violent behaviour itself within the prison estate. Research has shown that one way to potentially reduce the level of violence in prisons is to make them stricter and harsher environments on the assumption that this will make prisoners more compliant and less opposed to prison rules. Yet, contradictory evidence has shown that often the opposite occurs: the harsher and more restrictive regimes are often one of the causes of violence (Bierie, 2012; Listwan et al, 2013). In contrast, evidence such as that from McGuire (2018) shows that in order to reduce violence, establishing and communicating a system of rules that appears legitimate and justifiable to prisoners is key. This also requires them to be enacted fairly and consistently by staff, meaning good prisoner–staff relationships are needed (see Chapter 7).

Self-harm

One of the ways the impact of prison on an individual's mental health can be manifested physically is through self-harm. According to the leading mental health charity Mind (2020), self-harm is when a person hurts themself as a way of dealing with very difficult feelings, painful memories or overwhelming situations and experiences. Self-harm incidents, in the statistics collected prior to the COVID-19 pandemic, reached a record high of 63,328 incidents in the 12 months to December 2019 (MoJ, 2020f). Self-harm within the prison estate has always been of concern, particularly in women's prisons, but there are increased causes for concern as the rate of self-harm across the male prison estate has recently increased. The number of incidents in male establishments was recorded as 46,490 in the 12 months to September 2020; this had decreased to 40,934 in the 12 months to September 2021 (MoJ, 2022d). Given the population difference between men and women in the secure estate, women still account for a disproportionate number of self-harm incidents (Figure 6.2).

There have been many different reasons posed as to why this is but it is largely considered to be due to the acute nature of imprisonment that women experience and their sense of vulnerability while in custody (see Chapter 4). The nature of male and female self-harm in prison differs in nature as well as frequency. Women engage in a greater frequency of self-harm incidents, while the severity of self-harm in men tends to be much greater in both the severity of injuries and lethality of the method (MoJ, 2022d). Self-harm, in the prison context, is viewed as a mechanism that some individuals employ to cope with and manage their experience of prison. It can often be a consequence of emotional dysregulation (Pope, 2018), a way of coping with emotional distress and a way to achieve 'release' (Dixon-Gordon et al, 2012). Ramluggun (2013) found in his study that men often self-harmed because they wanted someone to talk to; they wanted some attention yet this was often perceived by some prison staff as 'manipulative' and not a 'genuine cry for help'. It has been a persistent concern that given the crisis in prison staffing (see Chapter 7) officers no longer have the time or training to appropriately deal with individuals in crisis (Howard League for Penal Reform, 2016b) with the consequence that individuals choose to self-harm as a way to manage their mental health crisis. Due to an overall lack of clarity regarding the increase in male self-harm in the custodial estate and the driving force behind it, HMPPS commissioned a small study to explore the experiences of male prisoners who had stopped self-harming to try to understand more about the act. Fitzalan Howard and Pope's (2019) research involved in-depth interviews with eight men about their experiences of self-harm and concluded that the following needs to be considered to prevent self-harm:

1. Men need to feel as though they matter and are cared for.
2. Trusting staff–prisoner relationships need to be developed.
3. Staff need to understand more accurately the complex reasons for individuals self-harming.

Self-inflicted deaths in custody

Prisons in England and Wales have seen a sharp decline in prison safety over recent years, largely driven by the increased availability of illegal drugs, poor living standards and the reduction in purposeful activities. The Prison Reform Trust (2021) maintains that people in prison – prisoners and staff – are less safe than they have been at any other time, with more self-inflicted deaths, self-harm and assaults than ever before. In the 12 months to March 2020, there were 286 deaths in prison custody; of these, 80 deaths were self-inflicted (MoJ, 2022d). People in prison are at an increased risk of suicide than the general population; this is

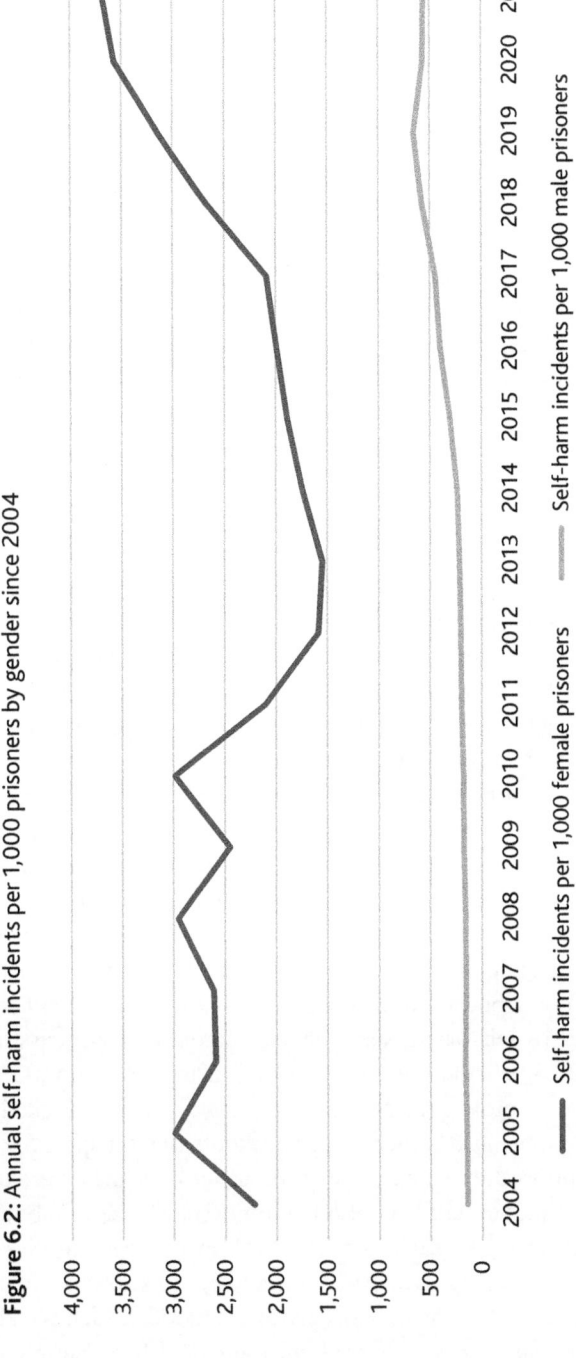

Figure 6.2: Annual self-harm incidents per 1,000 prisoners by gender since 2004

Source: MoJ, 2022d

true internationally, for both men and women (Tomaszewska et al, 2019). The reasons that people take their own life are complex, but the increased risk of suicide in prisons is suggested to be due to a unique combination of pre-existing vulnerabilities and features of prison life including the pains of imprisonment (Tomaszewka et al, 2019). A number of studies have been undertaken, trying to explore how to prevent self-inflicted deaths within custody. They often highlight that the initial arrival into custody is crucial in terms of trying to reduce the risk of suicide (Leese et al, 2006; Prisons and Probation Ombudsman, 2014; Ludlow et al, 2015). In 2018, almost a quarter (23 per cent) of all self-inflicted deaths occurred in the first 30 days in prison (PRT, 2021); it is crucial, therefore, that institutions are well staffed and that they have a clear arrival and induction programme to help settle new prisoners into prison life. Yet, HMCIP (2020) have repeatedly reported that first night accommodation centres do not have enough places for new prisoners due to overcrowding within the prison estate, despite the fact that new arrivals in prison should be 'allocated initially to dedicated first night accommodation, if available' or placed in another location which is suitable for them, according to PSI 52/2010. Van Ginneken et al (2017) conducted a study to explore whether overcrowding contributes to higher rates of suicide, concluding that on its own overcrowding could not be correlated with higher suicide rates; however, there are prison characteristics which could potentially contribute, including being a publicly managed prison, having a higher security category, having a larger population, having a male population and a higher turnover of population. Given that the highest suicide rates in prisons in England and Wales are found in male local establishments – those prisons which receive prisoners directly from courts, and house them during the early days of their sentence – it appears that some of these characteristics could be accurate. The Harris review published in 2015, was a government-commissioned review into the high rates of self-inflicted deaths among 18- to 24-year-olds in custody. Lord Harris in his review (2015) acknowledged that a range of different factors contributes to the risk of young adults taking their own lives while in custody and although the list was neither exhaustive nor conclusive, the review suggested that the harsh environment of the prison, a lack of purposeful activity, too little time out of cells, high rates of bullying and poor overall prison safety were key contributors to creating a high-risk environment for suicide. In a similar manner to self-harm, staff shortages are also a contributing factor to the increased risk of suicide. Due to a reduction in overall frontline operational staff (see Chapter 7), more prisoners are spending more time locked in their cells and subsequently missing healthcare appointments (see Chapter 5), which could have been the opportunity to raise concerns about how they were feeling with a professional. Shortages in staff have also led to potentially more subtle but arguably more concerning changes, such as the reduction in opportunities for frontline officers to build relationships with prisoners and get to know them. This is crucial for potentially noticing any changes in a prisoner's mood, which could sound alarm bells for potential risk factors associated with suicide. More training and guidance need to be provided to prison staff on how to prevent suicide but also staff should be encouraged to see relationship building as integral to their role, as well as part of good prison management and creating a safe and secure environment.

Summary

This chapter has explored the aims of imprisonment through the lens of philosophies of punishment. It has presented a framework, 'the pains of imprisonment', as a way to understand how prison can be considered harmful; this has been exemplified by an exploration of violence, self-harm and self-inflicted deaths in the custodial estate.

Questions to consider

1. What do you think the aims of imprisonment should be? How do you think these have changed over time?
2. In what ways do you consider prison to be harmful?
3. Can more be done to improve the conditions that prisoners live in? What do you think would reduce levels of violence in custody?

TAKING IT FURTHER

There are a number of texts that explore the issues presented in this chapter, which you might wish to consult for further detail:

- Crewe, B. and Bennet, J. (eds) (2012). *The Prisoner*. London: Routledge.

- Maruna, S. and Liebling, A. (eds) (2005). *The Effects of Imprisonment*. Cullompton: Willan.

- Matthews, R. (2009). *Doing Time: An Introduction to the Sociology of Imprisonment*. 2nd edn. Basingstoke: Macmillan.

To get the perspectives of current prisoners, it is worth exploring the website of the weekly (online) and monthly (printed) national newspaper for prisoners, *Inside Time*: https://insidetime.org

7

Doing prison work

Key learning outcomes

By the end of this chapter, you should be able to:

- Explain who works in a prison
- Describe the role of a prison officer
- Understand the challenges officers face through the nature of their work

Introduction

This chapter focuses on those who work within the prison environment. It presents relevant statistics and data to explore who works in prisons. The chapter also focuses on the role of the prison governor and issues about prison management before focusing on the prison officer. The role of the prison officer will be broken down to answer the following questions: what do they do; how do they do it; what training and education do they get; what is the impact of working in the environment on a prison officer; and what makes a good prison officer? The chapter discusses the notion of prison officer culture and the challenges officers face during their work. The focus of the chapter is deliberately on those with prisoner-facing roles but it provides an overview of who else works in a prison, the management structure and some key differences in working in public and/or private prisons.

Who works in a prison?

Prisons are staffed by a range of individuals who perform many different functions. It is often assumed that prison officers are the primary employees of the prison service but many different types of roles are available within the prison service to help with the management and running of a prison. A prison is run by a governing governor, often referred to within a prison environment as the 'No. 1 Governor'; this individual is responsible for the overall management of the prison and will have oversight of all areas of operation including security and prisoner wellbeing. They are also responsible for the prison budget and performance, and are often held accountable should a prison be viewed as failing after an inspection. The role of a prison governor can be difficult, particularly as those who perform well in the role can often be moved from high-performing prisons to prisons which are not doing so well to improve them, a role which is often a thankless task. Under the governing governor will be several other governors of various staffing pay grades who are all likely to hold a specialist responsibility, such as overseeing security, the residences, operations and rehabilitation services. Neither the governing governor nor the governors will wear a uniform but, at some point, they are likely to have been uniformed officers who rose through the prison ranks. Subordinate to the governors are the uniformed staff with whom most prisoners will interact every day: the prison officers and operational support staff. Prison officers all wear a distinctive uniform consisting of a white shirt and black tie, black trousers, black boots, black jumper and/or black softshell fleece jacket. Their rank can be distinguished by their epaulettes; a basic grade officer has one silver stripe, a supervising officer (previously known as a senior officer) will have two stripes and a custodial manager (previously known as a principal officer) has three stripes. Most prison officers, particularly if they are working on the wings of the prison residences, may carry additional items for protection or security purposes. All prison officers will carry keys on a long chain attached to a prison service-issued belt; the keys will open various doors and gates and are integral to movement around a prison. Some officers will carry a radio to communicate with colleagues and the control room at the centre of the prison. The control room has responsibility for the overall movement of prisoners around a prison. It is now increasingly common for officers who have direct contact with prisoners to wear a body camera attached to their chest. Body-worn video cameras were introduced by the MoJ to the prison environment in 2015 in response to rising levels of violence within prisons. International research suggests that the use of cameras can lower rates of assault in prison by increasing accountability and transparency, reducing staff reporting workloads, acting as evidence and potentially influencing a change in behaviour. Body cameras were introduced across several pilot sites before being rolled out more broadly across the prison estate in 2017. Some officers also wear a baton in a similar manner to police officers with the aim being to use it for self-defence should they need to; they may also carry handcuffs. One of the most controversial items that prison officers now carry is PAVA spray. PAVA spray is an incapacitating, synthetic pepper spray, which is used by police officers but also now prison officers as a mechanism to de-escalate and help control difficult situations. PAVA spray has been rolled out for use in all male category A–D prisons since April 2019. A thorough staff training programme has been created to ensure that all prison officers know how to use the spray, the legalities of using it, the effects it has and how to care for people exposed to it. Under the Assaults on Emergency Workers (Offences) Act 2018 the government also made it a clear illegal offence to assault (among others) a prison officer; it is punishable by up to 12 months in prison, as well as a fine should an individual be convicted. Moreover, the murder of a prison officer who was acting in the execution of their duty at the time can result in a whole-life order being imposed. Alongside the issuing of PAVA spray, handcuffs and body-worn cameras it is considered to be one of the key mechanisms that the government has employed to try to increase prison officer safety and deter violence in prisons.

The key operational grades in public sector prisons are the band 3 to 5 prison officers. They consist of band 3 prison officers, band 4 officer specialists, band 4 supervising officers, and band 5 custodial managers. As of December 2021, there were 22,156 full-time equivalent (FTE) band 3 to 5 officers, which is an increase of 592 FTE (2.7 per cent) compared with 31 December 2020 (HMPPS, 2022a). The vast proportion of prison officers are male (71 per cent) compared with only 28 per cent female officers (HMPPS, 2021c). They are also predominately under the age of 40 (51 per cent) compared with 47 per cent who are 40 and over (HMPPS, 2021c). Following the Lammy Review (2017), and the persistent criticism that the Prison Service was failing to attract and recruit talented individuals who were from an ethnically minoritised background, HMPPS made a public commitment that 14 per cent of all new recruits would come from a minority ethnic background by December 2020 (HMPPS, 2022b). This is because, according to workforce statistics, only 8.9 per cent of all public sector prison staff were from a minority ethnic background (HMPPS, 2022b). In the two years to December 2021, 13.9 per cent of successful prison officer applicants and 14.0 per cent of successful operational support grade applicants were from minority ethnic backgrounds, compared with 13.5 per cent of all successful HMPPS applicants (HMPPS, 2022b); this shows that HMPPS are attempting to address the lack of ethnic diversity among serving prison officers.

In regard to working in a private prison, there are different standards and expectations for staff. The pay is less compared with the public sector because the contractors of the private prison choose the pay grade. It is also likely that the job titles used for officers will be different; for instance, 'custody supervisor' is one name used for a prison officer within the private sector. There is evidence that staff within the private sector are generally less experienced and less well trained (House of Commons Justice Committee, 2009). The turnover of staff is higher in the private sector and there is less emphasis on sharing staff and good practice between sites due to the inevitable competition that privatisation has created among the companies who have the prison contracts (currently G4S, Serco and Sodexo). The staff also report having to work longer hours, and they have less annual leave and less generous pensions than their public sector counterparts.

While there have been numerous debates regarding the ethics of privatising prisons (see Schwartz and Nurge, 2004) and whether they perform better or not than their public counterparts (see Tanner, 2013; Crewe and Liebling, 2018), there have been significant incidents over the past ten years which have raised serious questions about the staff and management of private prisons. Substantial concerns were raised over HMP Northumberland, which is run by Sodexo, after a Panorama (2017) investigation found that drug use was widespread within the prison. The prison was chronically understaffed, which led to officers being left on their own to manage large groups of prisoners. Prisoners threatened staff daily and some staff said they did not feel able to confront prisoners because they were worried back-up support would take too long to arrive. There was a general decline in standards within the prison with other issues such as alarms not working and a hole in the perimeter fence also being found. The prison was privatised in 2014. This was done at a time when the government was aiming to cut £500 million from the prison budget; to win the contract, Sodexo pledged to save the taxpayer £130 million over 15 years. This meant that 200 jobs, including 96 prison officer posts, were cut. This led, therefore, to a chronic shortage of officers to manage prisoner behaviour and the prison has deteriorated since. In a similar manner, HMP Birmingham has also faced significant controversy during its period of privatisation; widespread and sustained periods of rioting in 2016 and again in 2017 alongside a spike in prisoner deaths at the prison caused the government to step in and take HMP Birmingham back into public control in 2018. It was said that staff had lost control of the prison and that ineffective frontline management and leadership were integral to the prison's problems. Perhaps the most controversial incident of note in recent times is that of Medway secure training centre, an institution that held 14- to 17-year-old children and was run by G4S until the government took it over in 2016 and it closed in 2020. Four G4S team leaders were arrested in January 2016, and four other staff members were placed on restricted duties, following an investigation by the BBC's Panorama TV programme (2016) into the centre. Allegations included foul language and use of unnecessary force – such as physical violence, overuse of restraint techniques (causing one teenager to have difficulties breathing) – on ten boys aged 14 to 17, as well as a cover-up involving members of staff avoiding surveillance cameras so as not to be recorded. Staff purposefully misreported incidents to avoid potential fines and punishment. The subsequent investigations into the conduct of officers at Medway led to the government taking back control of the centre and G4S putting up for sale its contract and that of another secure training centre.

There are a number of other job specifications for work in a prison environment, often collectively referred to as 'service providers'; individuals in these roles are not prison officers and therefore do not wear a uniform nor do they have access to keys to much of the establishment. They are often the providers of education, workshops, healthcare and catering. A range of administrative staff also work in a prison, carrying out key functions to assist with the smooth running of it.

Role of a prison governor

Despite their integral role in the shaping of prison life, prison governing as a topic of research has been neglected, particularly when compared with the volume of research on prisoners and prison officers. A number of prison governors have written memoirs about their working lives (see Anonymous, 2022; Frake, 2021) and there has been some detailed empirical work in the exploration of the working lives of prison governors/managers (see Bryans,

2007; Bennett, 2015) but it is still an under-researched area. The research that does exist shows that prison managers (governors) shape the social climate of the institutions they command (Bennett, 2016). Wilson (2000: 12) has described the distinctive role as:

> To work as a [prison manager], you had to understand prisoners, and be able to manipulate prison life to push it forward. This was not so much about management – or to further managerial ends – but to fashion and re-shape an essentially punitive structure into one that was positive and optimistic.

Wilson's description presents a role that seems difficult to achieve and one which is certainly likely to clash with others: namely, minsters of justice and prison officers. It also implies that prison governors can interpret their role in different ways depending on their own values and approaches, meaning that no two prison governors are alike. This may explain in some part why no two prisons are alike. The role of a prison governor is a challenging one that is shaped by external forces such as penal policy and the very population of the prison they are tasked with managing. It is also a role, which Bennett (2016) argues has been transformed fundamentally by the rise of managerialism. The development of performance management measures, the commercialisation of prison services, alongside the professionalisation of managers are all features which have been imposed on the prison system by the global shift towards managerialism (Bennett, 2016). This has resulted in prisons, according to Bryans (2007: 63), having to become managed in a more passionless and bureaucratic manner with efficiency and compliance as per the administratively defined goals of good prison management. What makes a good governor, then, in the eyes of the prison management system, has changed over time; it is now not necessarily someone who finds themself in a high-performing prison. Often the most skilled and successful prison governors are sent into the most difficult establishments to make improvements. This can make the role of a prison governor a tiresome one as success comes at the cost of being constantly moved from prison to prison to do repeated battle, often in the poorest conditions of the prison estate. For example, in October 2017, Peter Francis, No.1 Governor at HMP Liverpool, was dismissed from his role after an inspection by HMIP. HMP Liverpool had received one of the worst ever inspection reports reported, with the prison living conditions labelled as squalid and rat and cockroach infested with a lot of basic maintenance such as the repair of toilets and sinks lacking. Significant failures were found and claims were made that prisoners had been seriously injured and/or died through poor care (HMIP, 2018). Peter Clarke, the Chief Inspector of Prisons at the time, wrote in the report:

> I found a prisoner who had complex mental health needs being held in a cell that had no furniture other than a bed. The windows of both

the cell and the toilet recess were broken, the light fitting in his toilet was broken with wires exposed, the lavatory was filthy and appeared to be blocked, his sink was leaking and the cell was dark and damp. Extraordinarily, this man had apparently been held in this condition for some weeks. (HMIP, 2018: 5)

The conditions at the prison made newspaper headlines with the government prompted to take immediate action, starting with the removal of the governor alongside holding an unprecedented evidence session of the Parliamentary Justice Select Committee devoted to solely exploring the issues raised by the inspection. Peter Francis was replaced by Pia Sinha, the high-performing governor from HMP Thorn Cross, who, according to a recent reinspection report, has dramatically turned HMP Liverpool around with it now providing a culture of care that simply was not present previously (HMIP, 2020e). The outfall from HMP Liverpool also prompted HMIP to readdress its expectations and create some new measurements in terms of leadership. HMIP (2022) have strengthened their inspection criteria in regard to leadership in recognition that one of the most important factors in driving improvement and ensuring better outcomes for prisoners comes from quality leadership. This has all compounded the role of a prison governor, one that is difficult and shrouded in emotion. Crewe and Liebling (2015) found in their research that governors are emotional about their work; they also wished that their organisations were more emotional about them. Some of the governors in Crewe and Liebling's (2015) study reported on the personal and professional toll of being a prison governor with the role involving facing extraordinary levels of personal abuse and hostility from staff, particularly when they are tasked with making changes in the prison. It is argued that the failure of the Prison Service and the managerial culture that has been created among governors has led to a reluctance to acknowledge the emotional dimensions of prison work and the importance of being attentive to the emotional needs of its senior staff (Crewe and Liebling, 2015). However, in a similar manner to prisoners and prison officers, the showing of emotion among governors is viewed as weakness with many refusing to talk openly about the pressures of prison management. This leads to high rates of burn out with many governors leaving their roles. As Crewe and Liebling (2015) summarise:

> [T]he best governors seem to combine humanity with professionalism, and to like, and see the best in, prisoners and staff, whilst retaining a sharply well-developed sense of what can go wrong. This is highly skilled and demanding work. It is moral and emotional as well as bureaucratic work.

Such a role is an important one; it has the power to have significant influence over everything inside a prison but most importantly its culture and commitment to the purpose of prison. It is a unique role in a unique environment and one deserving of further exploration.

Role of a prison officer

Under the Prison Act 1952, prison officers working in public sector prisons have 'all the powers, authority, protection and privileges of a constable' while acting as such. It is a multi-faceted role which, contrary to popular opinion, requires a significant level of skill and knowledge to be able to perform it successfully. Historically, the work of prison officers has been under-researched within the context of criminology; they are often a neglected area of study, suffering to a certain extent from the broader notion of what it is to be in prison. Like prisoners themselves, they too have been ignored and disregarded as an important subject of research. The focus of much prison research has been on prisoners themselves or on the effects of imprisonment, yet through exploring the work of prison officers much can be learnt about the nature of imprisonment and the broader issues of power, punishment and inequality.

Many of the problems that were raised in Chapter 6 are exacerbated by inadequate staffing levels, with poor staffing levels often being held responsible for prisons failing to provide a decent, rehabilitative environment (HMCIP, 2020). As of December 2021, there were 22,156 full-time equivalent (FTE) band 3 to 5 officers, which is an increase of 592 FTE (2.7 per cent) compared with 31 December 2020 (HMPPS, 2022a). In part, this is due to a clear recruitment campaign by HMPPS to increase prison officer numbers; in 2016 the government promised under a new offender management model to recruit an additional 2,500 frontline officers (band 3–5) (MoJ, 2016). The government in its White Paper *Prison Safety and Reform* promised that 'each prison would have new dedicated officers, each responsible for supervising and supporting around six offenders, who will make sure prisoners get the help they need to quit drugs and get the skills they need to turn their lives around' (MoJ, 2016: 7). The recruitment was to take place nationally and be completed by 2018. This target was achieved, but there are still 12 per cent fewer staff than there were in 2010 (HMPPS, 2022a). It is impressive that the government achieved this target, which in part was largely due to the creation of a new scheme to recruit graduates to become prison officers, named Unlocked. The scheme was established in 2016 with the explicit aim of attracting high-calibre graduate talent to work in the UK prison service and inject new ideas, insights and energy into the rehabilitation of prisoners. Their stated goal is 'to lead change on the inside that delivers change on the outside' (Unlocked Grads, 2022). The programme has been running for over five years and has placed over 500 officers in prisons across London, the South East, the West Midlands and the North West of the UK. While this is a positive step to re-energise and invigorate the Prison Service, concerns have been raised regarding whether this and several other schemes the government has set up to increase recruitment will have a sustained impact on prison officer numbers. This is because the increase in numbers of officers also needs to be considered alongside the number of officers leaving HMPPS. There are, for example, over 700 fewer officers employed than there were in 2019 with overall retention of officers a particular problem as nearly half of the officers (48 per cent) who left the service in 2021 had been in the role for less than two years (HMPPS, 2022a). Concerns also remain in regard to the overall attractiveness of working in the Prison Service, with the job market now vast in the post-pandemic world. It remains a problem that there are a lot of competing roles out there that offer work in a safer and less-pressured environment for the same amount of money. This is a particular issue in southern England whereby the starting salary of £27,427–£30,927 is not seen as particularly competitive given the cost of living in the south. Another challenge that has become more acute over recent years is that the profile of staffing within HMPPS has become somewhat distorted through the recruitment of younger staff, meaning that there has been an overall decline in experienced staff within the service. Approximately four in ten officers have been in post for less than three years which is an increase from approximately one in eight in 2010 (HMPPS, 2022a). The nature of working in prison means that age and life experience is considered important and is something that cannot be learnt. The lack of experienced staff also means that new recruits are not benefiting from learning from established colleagues.

The nature of prison officer work is something that is beyond common sense; the prison officer is far from being merely a turnkey or warder (House of Commons Justice Committee, 2009) as was originally considered to be the function of the role. Yet, in a similar manner to prisons overall, the key role and functions of the prison officer, particularly in regard to rehabilitation, remain ill-defined and unclear. Since 1935, when formal training was introduced for prison officers, their primary function has been seen to be to maintain the order and security of the prison rather than having a role in reforming or rehabilitating those in prison. However, in more recent times, the role has become more professionalised; officers are recognised as having a leading role to play in an individual's rehabilitation through the key worker scheme. The key worker scheme was introduced in all closed prisons in the male estate with the role being gradually introduced across the female and open estate as well. It recognises that there is more to being a prison officer than locking and unlocking doors. The role of key worker is to develop constructive and motivational relationships with prisoners 'to counter the negative effects of imprisonment and to encourage people in prison to identify and resolve issues and concerns for themselves, in order to settle, feel safe and calm; and to engage in their rehabilitation and progress through their sentence' (HMPPS, 2017). Prison officers who undertake offender management in custody training are eligible to become key workers; all prisoners on entry to a prison are assigned a key worker to guide, support and coach them through their sentence. An average prison officer will have five or six prisoners to manage on a one-to-one basis. Importantly, key workers and prison-based offender managers (probation officers located within prisons) work together to try to provide effective rehabilitation during an individual's sentence. Prison officers are given time in their working week to meet the prisoners they have been assigned on an individual basis. The goal of these meetings is to help prisoners with their rehabilitation and to encourage them to take part in education, in drug recovery programmes and to keep in touch with family. The effective use of key workers has been reported as helpful in some prisons when prisoners can explore their concerns or get queries addressed in regular one-to-one sessions with their dedicated officer (HMCIP, 2020). There is no standardised model for how the key worker scheme works, meaning that there is variability between prisons. For example, in Warren Hill, HMCIP (2020) reported that the key worker scheme was the best that they had seen; all prisoners were quickly allocated a key worker who had regular, meaningful contact with them and who was involved in all aspects of their rehabilitation and progression. The key worker role exemplifies that prison officers have a range of roles to perform and essentially wear many hats when carrying out their duties; they act in many ways in loco parentis, acting as mentors, counsellors, teachers, social workers, comedians, psychologists and police officers (Crawley, 2004a). The key worker role is not something new; prisons have always had some form of personal officer scheme or prison officers have been encouraged to have these types of conversations with prisoners. Essentially, HMPPS has formalised them. Despite the role having reported initial success, the impact of the pandemic on prisons has meant that key working ceased at all prison sites in March 2020, but as prisons have been allowed to resume normal regimes it is hoped that the scheme will continue in its initial positive manner.

Prison officer work is still considered as low-visibility work despite the highly skilled nature of it (Liebling and Price, 1999); the approach an officer takes can set the tone on a wing, affecting the atmosphere and outcomes for prisoners. The skills of a prison officer, their 'prison [jail] craft', are vitally important to create a safe and positive environment – something which is largely developed over time and comes with life experience. The relationships that prison officers have with prisoners are a vital part of prison life and in some ways can make or break a 'healthy prison':

> As the prison staff unlock prisoners in the morning and lock them up last thing at night, in between these two key moments of each day, officers deal with prisoners when they are at their best and at their worst, at their strongest and at their weakest. There is a relationship of mutual dependency between prisoners and prison staff. ... On a day to day basis what makes prison life either tolerable or unbearable for prisoners is their relationship with staff. (Coyle, in House of Commons, 2009: 15)

Prison officers have responsibilities for the prisoners' welfare, meaning they have a caring role but this is often at odds with their role to maintain security and order. A high proportion of officers join the Prison Service because they want to make a difference to prisoners' lives. Yet, many officers have reported to the Howard League for Penal Reform (2017a) that they no longer felt that they could make a difference as the conditions in their prisons meant they could not form quality relationships with prisoners. Low staffing levels, high workloads and frequent rotations to different parts of the prison made many officers feel powerless to achieve what they saw as a central part of their role (Howard League for Penal Reform, 2017a). The detrimental aspects of prison life as raised in Chapters 5 and 6 are also experienced as much by prison officers as by the prisoners themselves. Prison officers are regularly exposed to violence, drug use, people in mental health crisis and the consequences of self-harm and suicide. In 2019–20, there were 9,995 recorded assaults on staff, of which 952 were serious; this number has tripled in only six years (MoJ, 2020f). The Prison Officer Association has made repeated calls on the government to address the issue of safety within prisons; part of this has been done, debatably, by introducing PAVA spray and body-worn cameras, the argument being that if overall conditions improved there potentially would be a reduction in violence.

In order to cope with their environment and working conditions, prison officers perform emotional labour (Hochschild, 1983) to manage the overwhelming and constant demands that they face. Prisons are highly pressurised and emotionally charged environments; prison officers must develop ways to manage and cope, not only where they work but with whom they work. Prisoners have often 'suffered a variety of personal traumas, difficulties and disappointments during their sentence', (Crawley, 2004b: 414) and it is prison officers whom prisoners often see first following potentially bad news. It is therefore key that prison officers learn how to cope emotionally with what can often be potentially volatile relationships. Crawley (2004b: 414) explains that staff–prisoner relationships are also emotionally charged because the degree of intimacy involved in working with prisoners is great; unlike, for example, police officers, whose relationships with offenders are relatively fleeting, prison officers often spend sustained periods of time with the same prisoners. They must therefore develop mechanisms to cope; this can be as simple but as important as going to the prison gym at lunchtime or spending time outdoors. It is also one of the reasons why prisoners are locked back in their cells at lunchtime, to allow officers to have an uninterrupted break.

Prison officer staff culture

In a similar manner to other occupations, prison officers have their own occupational culture. According to Crawley (2004a), 'occupational culture' is the term given to 'the commonly shared beliefs, values and characteristic patterns of behaviour that exist within an organisation'. Extensive research has been undertaken on police occupational culture (see Skolnick, 1966; Bowling et al, 2019; Loftus, 2009); less so on prison officer occupational culture and even less on probation officer occupational culture. It remains, however, an important element that to understand the attitudes and behaviours of prison officers, the conditions under which they work need to be appreciated. The culture of an organisation is key to understanding how and if that organisation can deliver on its stated aims and objectives. Crawley and Crawley (2008), two leading researchers in this field, have identified four elements of prison officer culture:

1. Solidarity: in a similar manner to police officers, prison officers are expected to show solidarity with and to their fellow officers. They are meant to be able to rely on colleagues when they are in danger, an obligation expected of any uniformed officer. Solidarity also ensures that prison officers have people to turn to when criticism is received from people 'outside' who do not understand the pressures of the job.
2. Cynicism and suspicion: being suspicious and cynical of behaviour that may seem out of the ordinary are elements of everyday prison officer life. Again, in a similar manner to the police, not trusting an individual's behaviour is part of the nature of prison work given that prison officers are there to watch over prisoners, all of whom by the nature of being in custody can be described as non-trustworthy individuals.
3. Humour: integral to prison life and particularly for maintaining staff morale. 'Banter' is important as it helps to break the ice, ease difficult situations, increase solidarity and make individuals feel part of a collective.
4. Machismo: it was initially conceived that the male traits of dominance, authoritativeness and aggressiveness were key to being a successful prison officer and therefore those who lacked these qualities would struggle to fit into the occupational culture. However, arguably the need for such qualities is fading as more women take up the role and as the role of a prison officer becomes more professionalised.

Elements of these characteristics may be present in some prison settings. These behaviours may also be more nuanced than described. Alongside is the reputation of the prison in that it may be viewed as harsh or brutal or, alternatively, as innovative or supportive. Together these elements can define the nature of a prison; the staff culture can have a significant impact on a prisoner's rehabilitation prospects (House of Commons, 2009). A negative staff culture can have a detrimental impact on officers, especially new recruits who join the Prison Service with the desire to help prisoners:

'It is really hard for a prison officer who really cares and wants to do his work to do it because he lives in a small community, a prison community with other prison officers. That showed at Feltham [in the Mubarek inquiry] with the POA that if you did not fit in with the clique who were the heavy boys then you had a hard time, you were seen to be too caring for prisoners and seen as the "welfare screw", which was a stigma, and that made it very hard.' (Cummins, 2015 as cited in House of Commons, 2009: 44)

It can also have an impact on prison officers themselves with many becoming hardened by the job through the nature of the work they are asked to do. Being changed by prison work is a common perception among prison officers (Crawley and Crawley, 2008); most feel that they have become desensitised to the distress and suffering of others due to what they see on a day-to-day basis. This can 'spill over' into family life, with evidence having been found of prison officers struggling not to be overly suspicious of their spouses and children, for instance (Crawley, 2004a).

The management of the self is an acute process and one that both prisoners and prison officers must do to cope with the stresses and strains of prison life. Potentially, in contrast with policing, prison work is arguably unseen work, work that goes on daily to keep people safe but work that the public does not want to hear about. It could be considered as 'dirty work', a phrase coined by Hughes (1958: 50) to describe occupational activities that are physically disgusting, that symbolise degradation, that wound the individual's dignity, or that run counter to the more heroic of our moral conceptions. In this context, prison officers are carrying out work where they have to mix with individuals who have transgressed the moral order of society and so therefore are 'dirty' (Cresswell, 1996). This was, for instance, a reason why the work of prison officers was not highlighted during the pandemic despite the fact that they were arguably as much at risk of contracting COVID-19 as care workers because of the environment in which they work (Youle, 2020).

Summary

This chapter has presented an analysis of who works in the prison environment with the focus on governors and prison officers. It has explored the nature of being a prison officer, what the role entails and who prison officers are in terms of an analysis of demographics. The chapter has also discussed prison officer occupational culture and how the impact of the job forces officers to develop ways to cope with it.

Questions to consider

1. What qualities do you think it is important that prison officers must have to be successful in their role?
2. Should the government aim to increase the diversity of prison officer staff?
3. Do you think public and private prisons should have the same expectations of their prison officer staff and pay them equally?

TAKING IT FURTHER

There are several texts that explore the issues presented in this chapter, which you might wish to consult for further detail:

- Crawley, E. (2013). *Doing Prison Work: The Public and Private Lives of Prison Officers*. Cullompton: Willan.

- Liebling, A., Price, D. and Shefer, G. (2011). *The Prison Officer*. 2nd edn. Cullompton: Willan.

- Samworth, N. (2019). *Strangeways: A Prison Officer's Story*. Hampshire: Pan Macmillan. Written by a former prison officer about his time working at HMP Manchester. There are several books like this that are worth reading for contextual purposes but be wary about using them as a source of evidence in academic work.

It is well worth exploring the following websites to explore job descriptions and blogs written by current officers about being a prison officer:

- HM Prisons and Probation Service. Become a prison officer: https://prisonand probationjobs.gov.uk/prison-officer

- Unlocked Prison Officer Graduate Scheme: https://unlockedgrads.org.uk

On the website there is a test you can do to see if you have what it takes to be a prison officer. Well worth a go!

8

Leaving prison, resettling and returning

Key learning outcomes

By the end of this chapter, you should be able to:

- Explain the theories behind what makes people stop offending
- Describe key elements of the desistance process
- Understand the challenges to assessing whether prison works

Introduction

This chapter focuses on the theory behind what makes people stop offending, the concept of 'desistance'. The key elements of desistance theory and how prison can either help or hinder that process will be discussed. The processes of release, resettlement and recall will be explored with a focus on the legislative framework that enables them to take place accompanied by a discussion of some of the practical challenges faced in their undertaking. This will include a brief discussion of the Parole Board, a much underexplored area of the CJS. The chapter also introduces the challenging notion of assessing whether prison works and how we might go about evaluating this. It explores different ways of assessing whether prison works or not, including a discussion of reoffending rates and recidivism.

Desistance from crime

Since the birth of the prison, academics, practitioners and penal policy makers have been captivated by the notion that prisons can be used to instil a change of behaviour in the individuals they hold. The idea that prisons can influence individuals to change their behaviour and likelihood of reoffending is common across many jurisdictions, particularly in the West. The emergence of a body of work that aims to contribute to this thinking falls under the concept of desistance. Desistance refers to the end of a criminal career or the cessation of offending behaviour. It is viewed as difficult to know when an individual stops offending for as Maruna (2001) states, 'desistance takes place all the time – a person can steal a purse on a Tuesday morning, then terminate criminal participation for the rest of the day. Is that desistance? Is it desistance if the person does not steal another purse for a week? A month? A year?' Due to it being difficult to know when exactly cessation from offending permanently occurs (indeed scholars have argued that we can only truly know that one has desisted from crime when that person has died), desistance is now conceptualised as a process (Farrall, 2002; Laub and Sampson, 2003). The movement from criminal behaviour to the maintenance of a crime-free lifestyle is a process which can be problematic both for the individual who has offended and for professionals to initiate and understand how best to support. Primary desistance is the name given to the period when individuals decide to stop offending while secondary desistance is the name given to the time when individuals have stopped offending permanently because they have achieved a shift in their identity (Maruna and Farrall, 2004). It is arguably the shift in identity from one of an 'offender' to one of an 'ex-offender' which is most crucial regarding successful desistance from crime yet perhaps the hardest movement to achieve because of the stigma associated with being an offender and in particular being someone who has spent time in prison. McNeill and Schinkel (2016) suggest that desistance is a social and political process as much as a personal one, in that securing long-term change depends not just on how one sees oneself but also on how one is seen by others and on how one sees one's place in society. Questions remain about the prisons' role in this; prisons clearly cannot achieve this in isolation.

Desistance research focuses on the role of maturation and age, social bonds and ties, subjective changes in identity, and social environments and activities. One of the few near certainties in criminal justice is that for the overwhelming majority of people who engage in offending it peaks in their teenage years and then starts to decline (Farrington, 1986). This is the pattern depicted in what is known as the 'age–crime curve'. Maturity is one of the key elements in regard to understanding how and why people give up offending; for some, they simply grow out of it (Rutherford, 2002). For others, research indicates a range of factors can start the process of abandoning crime. There is a significant evidence base on the causes of crime but desistance research suggests that the factors behind the start of offending behaviour are often different from those behind its abandonment. The actual decision to give up crime is considered to be as important as the process, in that the decision to desist and actually desisting are two very different things (Maruna, 2001: 23). Moreover, the decision is not one an individual makes in isolation but involves social structural factors. Across the breadth of desistance research, most of which involves qualitative longitudinal research whereby cohorts of individuals are tracked over time by researchers who engage with them at various points of their lives to see how they are getting on, several key factors are cited repeatedly as reasons why individuals stop offending:

- securing employment
- giving up illegal substances
- marriage
- having children
- gaining an alternative identity (for example, father, mother, student, employee)

The CJS can have little to no impact on the factors listed, therefore its role in desistance from crime is a somewhat questionable one. It is often viewed in a policy context that the process of giving up crime is one that is straight, indeed it is colloquially known as 'going straight' yet arguably the process is not straight at all. The CJS works on the basis of a conveyer belt in stages: a crime is committed; it is detected; the individual is arrested, prosecuted, convicted, sentenced, does their sentence and comes out at the end of it not wanting to commit crime again. This is a somewhat flawed understanding of the complexities involved in offending; Leibrich (1993) suggests that it is more beneficial to understand the process of giving up crime as not linear but curved. In her study on desistance, she argued that the people she interviewed who were identified as trying to give up crime did not fall into neat categories of 'straight' or 'crooked' but more that 'going straight' needed to be viewed as a zig-zag or curved process because people may change the type, rate or frequency of their offending on their way to desistance and that this should not be viewed as not 'going straight'.

Prison, it is viewed by most desistance researchers, presents a fundamentally problematic context in which to support desistance. According to McNeill and Schinkel (2016: 612), there are four key ways in which prison is problematic for desistance:

1. The experience of imprisonment often deprives people of their responsibility and may delay maturation.
2. Imprisonment often damages positive social ties and weakens bonds between prisoners and society.
3. Imprisonment tends to cement spoiled identities rather than nurturing positive ones.
4. The routine activities of life in prison, even if rendered 'purposeful' are detached from the desistance-supporting routines that need to be established in the community.

There is evidence that being in prison can be criminogenic (Joliffe and Hedderman, 2012) and that community sanctions are better at reducing reoffending; yet, the preference among the judiciary, policy makers and in part the general public is for the use of imprisonment, arguably for reasons of penal populism (Pratt, 2007). Despite the aforenoted problems, there is some evidence that imprisonment can have a reforming effect on individuals. For instance, Schinkel (2015) found in her study that some prisoners credited their imprisonment with transforming them and making their desistance from crime more likely. This was due in part to the very nature of 'doing time', in that for some individuals prison provided them with the space and time to think and reflect on their lives (Schinkel, 2015), ironically something for which prisons are often criticised (too much time spent in the cell; see HMCIP, 2020). Similarly, Aresti et al (2010) found that, for some, 'defining moments' happened while in prison whereby they re-evaluated their lives by reflecting on the amount of time they had to serve and the impact of the environment on their sense of self. In contrast, however, Comfort (2008) has argued that some ex-prisoners may be trying to cast their imprisonment in a positive light to make the experience mean something, 'time well served', rather than having found the experience truly rehabilitative. What prison does, however, is to sequester individuals from negative influences that might have been leading them to offend; for instance, troubled peers, involvement in gangs, the influence of illegal substances and so on. On the other hand, prison can result in important protective factors such as family ties, employment and secure housing being severed. Sampson and Laub (2005) refer to this as 'knifing off' with imprisonment often giving, as others have found (mentioned previously), the time and space for individuals to form new hopes and goals for release. What is important when considering the influence of desistance research on policy making and practice is that most of it shows that a one-size-fits-all approach to interventions does not work (Weaver and McNeill, 2010). Desistance processes are different for different types of individuals depending on the crime they have committed, whether it is their first offence or not and how long their sentence is. In regard to imprisonment, perhaps it is better to view it, despite the grand promises the government makes about its reforming and rehabilitative effects, as less of a 'hook for change and more like a shaky peg' (Schinkel, 2015).

Exploring release, resettlement and recall

Release from prison

The majority of the 75,000 individuals who are held within prison at any one time will be released at some point back into the community. It is only those who are serving a whole-life tariff who will never be released. It is the prison's job to prepare prisoners for release and it is the role of the Probation Service to support prisoners on their return to the community. For most individuals, release will be an automatic process once they reach the halfway point of their sentence. For those who are designated as 'dangerous', the Parole Board will determine release. For release to be successful and an individual not to end up back in custody, those who are serving a long sentence should move through the prison system from closed conditions to a resettlement prison and then eventually to open prison conditions. This is important preparation for long-serving prisoners because release from prison can be a significant challenge. That is not to say it is not problematic for short-sentenced prisoners but the challenges they face are somewhat different, as they are released without the preparation that long-term prisoners receive. The loss of accommodation, employment and family support that can result from even the shortest spell in custody make readjusting to life after prison unfailingly difficult.

The release from prison into the community is referred to as parole; the original meaning of the word parole is 'word of honour' (Justice, 2017). It is said that to be granted early release prisoners had to promise to abide by certain conditions, what is now more commonly understood as licence conditions. The point at which someone can leave prison is determined by three key factors:

- the length of their sentence
- their behaviour in custody
- any time spent on remand awaiting their trial

Most prisoners will be on determinate sentences (see Chapter 3), whereby once they reach the halfway point of their sentence they will be automatically released. All individuals released from custody regardless of whether they have spent one week or ten years in prison will be required to be supervised by the Probation Service for the remainder of their sentence. Post-sentence supervision was introduced by the Offender Rehabilitation Act 2015; originally, those who were deemed low to medium risk would have been supervised by community rehabilitation companies, the privatised part of the Probation Service. High-risk offenders would have been supervised by the publicly owned Probation Service. Following the failure of the privatisation of the Probation Service (see Tidmarsh, 2020; National Audit Office, 2019), community rehabilitation companies ceased to exist. Henceforth, the supervision of low- and medium-risk offenders and the delivery of unpaid work and behavioural change programmes would be carried out by the public sector Probation Service, alongside the supervision of high-risk offenders which was already the responsibility of the public sector.

If an individual is serving an extended sentence or a determinate sentence of either four years or more or for a serious violent or sexual crime committed before 4 April 2005, they must apply for parole to be released. If a prisoner is serving an indeterminate sentence or life sentence, then the government applies for parole on the prisoner's behalf (see the following information for clarification). There are further considerations regarding the release of individuals from prison, in that poor behaviour and compliance with prison regimes can result in the punishment of additional days being added to a person's time in custody. Very little is known about this area but the Howard League for Penal Reform (2018) have sought to illuminate this potentially unjust practice. According to their research, a total of 359,081 days of additional imprisonment were imposed as punishment in 2017 across prisons in England and Wales – the equivalent of 983 additional years of imprisonment (Howard League for Penal Reform, 2018). The vast proportion of these additional days are imposed for non-violent infractions of rules; days can be added for something as simple as disobeying an order to go back to one's cell (Howard League for Penal Reform, 2018). The use of additional days as a punishment has been heavily criticised for being unfair and unjust because the process is varied and unpredictable (Howard League for Penal Reform, 2018). If a prisoner is very poorly behaved it could result in them spending the entire length of their sentence in custody. Conversely, prisoners can have time taken off their sentence in recognition of any time spent on remand or on bail (section 240, Criminal Justice Act 2003).

When will prisoners be released?

Life or indeterminate sentences

They will be contacted either:
- three years before the earliest release date ('tariff') runs out if they are serving a sentence of four years or more
- at least six months before the tariff runs out if they are serving a shorter sentence

Extended or fixed-term sentences

They will be contacted up to six months before their earliest release date if they have either:
- an extended sentence
- a fixed-term sentence of four years or more, given before 3 December 2012 for a serious violent or sexual crime committed before 4 April 2005

UK Government (2022b)

All prisoners who are released will be supervised by the Probation Service while in the community on licence. Licence conditions are the set of rules prisoners must follow if they are released but still have a part of their sentence to serve in the community. The aim of a period on licence is to protect the public, to prevent reoffending and to secure the successful reintegration of the individual back into the community. They are not a form of punishment and must be proportionate, reasonable and necessary (Parole Board, 2019a). If the Parole Board has granted the release of a prisoner, then the licence conditions will be proposed by the community offender manager (also known as a probation officer) but it is the Parole Board who will have to agree to them before the individual can be released; the Secretary of State for Justice can also have a final say in some extreme cases. There are a set of standard licence conditions which are included in every prisoner's licence; these are as taken from the Parole Board (2019a):

> An offender must:
> (a) be of good behaviour and not behave in a way which undermines the purpose of the licence period;
> (b) not commit any offence;
> (c) keep in touch with the supervising officer in accordance with instructions given by the supervising officer;

(d) receive visits from the supervising officer in accordance with instructions given by the supervising officer;

(e) reside permanently at an address approved by the supervising officer and obtain the prior permission of the supervising officer for any stay of one or more nights at a different address;

(f) not undertake work, or a particular type of work, unless it is approved by the supervising officer and notify the supervising officer in advance of any proposal to undertake work or a particular type of work;

(g) not travel outside the UK, the Channel Islands or the Isle of Man except with the prior permission of the supervising officer or for the purposes of immigration deportation or removal.

Additional conditions can be added to an individual's licence should they be viewed as necessary to keep victims or members of the public safe. The conditions, which fall under the following categories, need to be specifically asked for by the community offender manager:

- residence at a specified place;
- restriction of residency;
- making or maintaining contact with a person;
- participation in, or cooperation with, a programme or set of activities;
- possession, ownership, control or inspection of specified items or documents;
- disclosure of information;
- curfew arrangement;
- freedom of movement;
- supervision in the community by the supervising officer, or other responsible officer, or organisation.

While the community offender manager can request the conditions, usually after consultation with prison-based offender managers, the local police and other such interested parties which can include the victim(s) and their families, it is for the Parole Board to decide whether the conditions are necessary and proportionate in light of the prisoner's behaviour in prison and original offence.

Parole Board

The Parole Board is an independent body that was established in 1967 to advise the Home Secretary who originally had responsibility for the release of prisoners on licence. The Parole Board is now a judicial body which has significant power over determining the length of time that many prisoners will spend in custody; it also determines when some of the most dangerous and 'risky' individuals will be released. The weight of that responsibility falls to approximately 246 Parole Board members who are mostly part time and hold other positions such as judges, psychiatrists and independent lay members. As a non-departmental executive public body, the Parole Board receives its funding from the MoJ but its operations are independent from it. Somewhat crucially, however, it is the Secretary of State for Justice who appoints members of the Parole Board and issues guidance about how decisions should be made, something which over recent years has led to questions being raised about the extent of its independence. The Parole Board is required to determine whether it is 'satisfied that it is no longer necessary for the protection of the public' for a prisoner to be detained; this test is contained in section 2767B Legal Aid, Sentencing and Punishment of Offenders Act 2012.

Most of the Parole Board's work is done through the process of paper hearings. When a prisoner is eligible for parole they will be notified by letter and asked to complete an application form. The Parole Board will also be notified via a referral letter received from the Secretary of State; following this a single board member will be appointed to the case. The prisoner and the prison will prepare a dossier of parole papers which will contain the following information:

- pre-trial and sentence reports;
- offender management assessments which include current risk factors for further offending and information about behaviour in custody;
- sentence plan compliance and courses completed in prison;
- prison-based offender managers', key worker prison officers' and other relevant professionals' views on suitability for release;
- risk management plans for management in the community;
- letters of support from relevant professionals.

Parole papers can also include information such as a victim impact statement from the victim or victim's family. The single board member can decide as to whether the prisoner is suitable for release or not; they can also decide if the case requires an oral hearing. If the single member decides, based on a paper hearing, that the prisoner is not suitable for release, then the prisoner has the right to ask for an oral hearing to determine their case (Parole Board, 2019b: rule 15). There were 21,063 paper hearings in 2019/20; after the assessments it was decided that 8,140 would be rejected and remain in custody, 6,795 were to have an oral hearing and 478 were directed to be released (Parole Board, 2020). According to the annual report, a paper hearing costs £315 in comparison to an oral hearing which costs £1,443 (Parole Board, 2020).

If they are to be used, oral hearings must take place within 26 weeks of the original referral from the Secretary of State for Justice. Most oral hearings now take place via video link or via telephone conferencing rather than in person, although they can still take place in person in some instances. An oral hearing consists of up to three members of the Parole Board listening to the prisoner and any witnesses they may wish to speak on their behalf; the victim may also be present. It is up to the prisoner to decide whether to attend or not; they can also bring a legal representative. The decision as to the outcome of the panel is decided after the hearing and must be communicated to the prisoner within 14 days. The oral hearing panel can make several recommendations including:

- direct release
- direct release at a future date
- recommend a transfer to open conditions
- make no direction to release
- adjourn the case for further information
- defer the case for a set period (Parole Board, 2019b)

The Parole Board has been subject to a number of issues over recent years; first, in relation to the significant number of delays in the system, and second, regarding its independence from the state. Delays in the system to get prisoners to even have a parole hearing have been a concern for several years. The increase in lengths of sentences alongside a burgeoning prison population has meant the Parole Board has had a significant increase in its workload but not necessarily in its staffing. Due to the austerity measures put in place by the government following the economic downturn in 2010, the Parole Board has been restricted in its ability to recruit new members (Hardwick and Jones, 2017). Increased delays in the system have resulted in prisoners suing because their cases have not been heard, with the Parole Board paying over £1 million in compensation between 2016 and 2019 (Parole Board, 2020). Paying compensation has meant that any cost savings made under the austerity measures have been nullified. A significant contributing factor to the delay is the failure of HMPPS staff, largely prison-based offender managers, to deliver reports on time. As the information they provide is critical to the Parole Board's decision making, such failures inevitability result in hearings being cancelled or flawed decisions being made due to incomplete paperwork.

The other important issue is the Parole Board's independence. Given that the Secretary of State for Justice has influence over appointing new members, decides the rules of procedure, issues directions and allocates funding, questions have been raised over whether the Parole Board is independent of the state or not. This debate has been added to in recent years as significantly controversial cases have hit the headlines, such as the case of John Worboys. In 2009, John Worboys was convicted of a range of offences including rape, five sexual assaults and 12 drugging charges and sentenced to an IPP with a minimum custodial term of eight years. In 2018, it was reported that Worboys was to be released under strict licence conditions after a parole hearing in November 2017. The High Court overturned the parole release decision following a judicial review case brought by two of his victims. The court ruled that due to a lack of risk information, the Parole Board had not fully explored the evidence of his wider offending. Moreover, the court decreed that rule 25, which prohibited information about hearings being made public, was unlawful. The case also raised concerns about the Parole Board's communication with victims and whether they were doing so sufficiently as several of his victims had reported they were unaware of his impending release. The government subsequently amended rule 25 to instruct the Parole Board to provide a summary of its reasons for release to victims. The chair of the Parole Board at the time, Nick Hardwick, resigned after a successful legal challenge quashed the Parole Board's decision to release Worboys. It was met with widespread condemnation from policy makers, practitioners and academics who argued the government had attempted to deflect responsibility from the MoJ and had instead blamed the chair of the Parole Board. In his resignation letter, Nick Hardwick (2018) raised questions about the independence of the Parole Board and how its independence could be safeguarded. The government at the same time commissioned a comprehensive review of all Parole Board rules.

Resettlement

For an individual to not reoffend or break their licence conditions, successful resettlement back into the community is key. Success depends on practical things like accommodation being sourced but also the more personal and social elements of desistance such as identity change. According to the MoJ (2022e), all prisoners get help to prepare for life outside prison; specifically, in the last 12 weeks of their sentence they are given advice and support on getting a job, finding somewhere to live and money management. Individuals who have abused substances, are sex workers or are the victims of domestic violence (MoJ, 2022e) can get additional support due to their perceived vulnerability. The vast proportion of prisoners who have spent considerable time in prison (that is, years) will spend the last few months of their sentence ideally in a prison close to where they plan to live. This is usually a prison which is classed as 'open conditions', whereby through the ROTL process prisoners are gradually allowed to leave the prison, usually for the purposes of visiting family, volunteering, education or work. They are allowed out during the day and must return at night. The scheme was designed to gradually acclimatise long-sentenced individuals to community life. It is thought to be a better process than release directly into the community without preparation, at which point the risk of reoffending would likely be high because of the 'shock' of being back in the real world. This relates in part to some of the pains of imprisonment and the challenges of life inside. While in custody their lives are on hold, but in the meantime, the lives of relatives and loved ones move on. Mathiesen (1990) referred to this as entering prison in a pseudo-static state, a state of 'abeyance', in comparison with one's family and friends whose lives continue. Part of the key to successful resettlement is to reintegrate a prisoner back into the lives of their family and loved ones; for instance, children moving from infant school to high school or one's spouse changing jobs all come with new routines and systems that the individual in prison will be unaware of. They must, therefore, be integrated to feel a part of the family once more rather than a voyeur or someone who is on the outside looking in. This can be one of the most challenging aspects of release from prison.

Moreover, the 'responsibilisation' agenda whereby the CJS holds individuals to account for their actions is contradictory when it comes to releasing prisoners. Prisoners are put in a position in which they must take responsibility for their actions and their rehabilitation but have little means of doing so. For instance, they cannot source accommodation or find a job. Nor are they encouraged to assume responsibility for themselves; prison is infantilising and strips the notion of 'adult' from the prisoner (Haney, 2001). Ironically, the prisoner is then punished for being 'irresponsible' and not doing what was 'expected' of them, despite it not being possible for them to do it in the first place. For instance, to source a job most people look on the internet but prisoners are not allowed access to the internet so they do not possess this skill; when they leave prison they are disadvantaged because they may not know how to use the internet to find a job. This is a particularly acute problem for 'lifers'; they are in a Catch-22 situation whereby they need to prepare for release but the outside world may have changed dramatically during the many years they have spent in custody (Warr, 2016). Thus, through having no substantive interaction with the world at large when in closed conditions, 'planning' can be problematic and result in unrealistic plans being devised which are unachievable (Warr, 2016). Often prisoners are set up to fail by the very fact they need to change a significant number of things in their lives all in one go, which for the average individual is impossible to achieve.

Resettlement also brings with it the practical challenges of accommodation and employment. Moving into secure accommodation on release is vital from the outset. Having a conviction can cause considerable problems for individuals released from prison; it is often a significant barrier to getting onto waiting lists for accommodation. The importance of having an address has only recently come to light regarding the interconnected relationship between having an address and getting a bank account. You cannot open a bank account without an address; you cannot claim for Universal Credit (the main benefit in the UK that supports people with living costs). This places individuals in a Catch-22 situation: they are stuck. A high proportion of prisoners each year are released to no fixed abode – they are homeless, in other words – because it is impossible for them to have the right identification documentation needed to open a bank account. This has recently been recognised by several banks, with the government and charities for homeless people working together to establish a scheme to set up bank accounts for ex-prisoners, people experiencing homelessness, those living in insecure housing and others who have previously fallen under the radar. The high-street bank Halifax has reportedly helped more than 2,000 vulnerable people to open a bank account, with the bank working closely with the MoJ to give ex-offenders access to an account when they leave prison as part of efforts to help them readjust to life in the community. Since the COVID-19 lockdown, Halifax has reported supporting more than 450 former prisoners in this way (*The Guardian*, 2020).

The other challenge that comes from the lack of having a bank account is that individuals can pay hundreds of pounds extra each year for bills and basic services because they often miss out on preferential deals and discounts on utilities, mobile phone contracts, broadband and personal loans, all of which creates another barrier to resettlement for individuals leaving prison (*The Guardian*, 2019). In some prisons there are good arrangements in place to help people source accommodation prior to release. One example is the monthly sessions attended by local housing providers where prisoners learn about and apply for accommodation. The Probation Service must refer a prisoner to a council's homeless team if they are already homeless, likely to be homeless in the next eight weeks and/or are staying in probation or bail accommodation with no suitable move-on option. Prisoners can also make a homeless application themselves before they leave prison if they are legally threatened with homelessness. Legally, they are threatened with homelessness if their release date is in the next eight weeks and they do not have anywhere suitable to stay on release.

Some licence conditions will dictate that prisoners cannot live in certain areas or they must stay in 'approved premises' (APs); an individual's offender manager must therefore inform them of the conditions and help them to source alternative accommodation if, for example, the family home is in the exclusion area. Formerly known as probation or bail hostels, APs are premises approved under section 13 of the Offender Management Act 2007; they provide intensive supervision for those who present a high or very high risk of serious harm. There are significant challenges in regard to APs as they can be sporadically located, meaning that individuals can be placed further away from home if their local AP is full at the time of their release. There is also a particularly acute problem regarding APs for women. As with women's prisons there are very few of them, meaning that a woman can end up being placed even further away from home yet again if directed to stay in one on release. APs have faced several criticisms and challenges over the years. They are interesting as an idea of providing further 'through the gate' support to individuals who may be struggling with release and obviously provide reassurance for the public about extra management of risky individuals. Yet, for the people placed in them, they provide further control and restrictions on their lives, further extending the reach of the prison and by extension some of the pains of imprisonment. There is a significant amount of research (see O'Leary, 2013) showing that former prisoners who are in stable accommodation are significantly less likely to reoffend within a year than those who are homeless or in temporary accommodation; therefore, it is vital that as much assistance as possible is provided by the state to source suitable accommodation.

Secure employment is the other practical factor that is important to have in place before someone is released. Having a job is a well-documented protective factor against offending in the first place and subsequent reoffending. As a job provides a legitimate source of income, so it is vital that when individuals leave prison they ideally have employment already set up to prevent possible reoffending. However, it is not just the fact that employment provides income; it also provides other aspects that people's lives are based around. Employment can provide routine, socialisation, time being occupied and an identity. Those individuals who have a job up to four weeks before they are released are more likely to stay employed post-release than those who leave prison without a job (Smith and Hopkins, 2014). It is critical therefore that prisons work with organisations to provide opportunities for individuals to secure roles prior to their release. It is also important that appropriate training and accreditation are provided before release; courses should be relevant and useful. Research has further shown the factors that reduce the likelihood of employment after release include the lack of accommodation, needing help with job-related skills and being engaged in treatment for addiction (Smith and Hopkins, 2014). As evidenced, prisoners must be provided with appropriate opportunities before they are released to maximise their chances of successful rehabilitation.

It is an 'imagined' penal reality (Carlen, 2008) to believe that prison aids the prisoner to prepare for release. Prisons can and should aim to be capacity-building places if they want to meet the goal of being contributors to public safety and ex-prisoner reintegration (McNeill and Schinkel, 2016). Yet they are, by their very nature, incapacitating places where individuals adapt within them not to prepare for life after the experience but to survive the experience itself (McNeill and Schinkel, 2016).

Recall to prison

Should things go wrong and an individual released from prison commits a further offence, breaks the conditions of their licence or their offender manager is concerned their behaviour might lead to further offending, they can be recalled to custody. The offender manager (probation officer) has the power to recall an individual in such circumstances. The police may get involved should the person not comply with the recall. There are two different types of recall:

1. Fixed-term recalls: these apply to individuals serving sentences of either less than 12 months or more than 12 months but who are assessed as not high risk. Individuals will be sent back to prison for:
   a. 14 days – if the original sentence was less than 12 months
   b. 28 days – if the original sentence was 12 months or more
   When released they will be back on probation and licence until the end of their sentence.
2. Standard recalls: in this case, the person will go back to prison until the end of their sentence unless the Parole Board or the Secretary of State for Justice decides to release them. Their case will be sent to a parole hearing automatically after 28 days; the decision will be either to release them straight away or set a date (within one year) when they can be released on licence. An individual has the right to challenge their recall; if they do so, the Parole Board will hear their case. The individual can make representations against their recall with the Parole Board being able to make one of four decisions:

- order immediate release back onto licence
- refuse immediate release but order release at a future date
- make no recommendation at all
- send the case to an oral hearing

Significant numbers of individuals are subject to recalls every year; from January to September 2021, 16,278 individuals were recalled to prison for breach of their licence. In June 1995, the average number of recalled prisoners was approximately 150; by June 2016 this had increased to 6,600, an increase of 4,300 per cent (Howard League for Penal Reform, 2017b). Most people are recalled to custody not because they have committed a further offence but for more technical reasons largely relating to not complying with licence conditions. MoJ (2022c) figures show that most recalls to prison are for technical licence breaches, such as failing to keep in touch with probation officers, failing to reside at a specified address and taking drugs or alcohol. It is interesting that if the person were not on licence, these behaviours would not be serious enough to warrant attention from police or probation, let alone a custodial sentence. The Howard League for Penal Reform (2017b) reported the following cases where young people had been recalled to custody for breach of their licence conditions:

- A 20-year-old man was recalled to prison for spending one night away from his approved premises after he received some difficult news about his late sister. He had returned of his own accord. He was re-released after a further seven months in custody.
- A 21-year-old man was recalled to custody for getting into a taxi without the prior approval of his probation worker and having a second SIM card without prior approval. He was recalled to custody for seven months.
- A 19-year-old man missed two appointments with his probation worker – on the first occasion he rang ahead after his motorbike broke down; on the second occasion, he was ten minutes late. He spent one night away from his mother's house after she asked him to leave during tensions over his missing sister. He was recalled to custody for 11 months.

Most people who are recalled serve only 14 or 28 days in prison before being released on licence again. The disruption to the life they have established on the outside by the recall process for technical breaches can be considerable with homes and jobs put at risk as well as disruption to their relationships with families. The process of recall can be understood as the most bureaucratic form of imprisonment. In her research with individuals who had been recalled to prison, Padfield (2012) found that of the 46 recalled, 33 had been recalled on suspicion of committing a further offence and ten for licence condition breaches. Of those in the first group, several were not charged with the further suspected offence, had the charges dropped or were found not guilty in court – yet they remained in custody (Padfield, 2012). Many of the individuals reported that their licence conditions were 'unreasonable' and that their conditions had been 'inadequately discussed with them' (Padfield, 2012: 20).

Does prison work?

The usual assessment of whether imprisonment works or not is through rates of recidivism. Reoffending is notoriously difficult to measure because only a proportion of crime is detected and it is not recorded on one central system. Proven reoffences are measured over a one-year follow-up period with a further six-month waiting period to allow for offences to be proven in court. The figures presented in MoJ (2022f) show the proven reoffending statistics for the January to March 2020 offender cohort. The overall proven reoffending rate, over time, has fluctuated between 24 per cent and 30 per cent (MoJ, 2022f). The statistics also show that juveniles reoffend at a higher rate than adult offenders (MoJ, 2022f). The other interesting statistical fact is that the proven reoffending rate for adult offenders was 40.3 per cent. However, adults who served sentences of 12 months or more reoffended at a substantially lower rate (22.8 per cent) compared with those who served sentences of less than 12 months (57.5 per cent). Those released from sentences of less than or equal to six months had a proven reoffending rate of 59.3 per cent (MoJ, 2022f). While caution should be exercised when comparing the effectiveness of different sentences because the presented statistics do not control for offender characteristics, it is telling that short-term sentences are less effective than longer-term sentences at reducing reoffending. The MoJ (2019) has estimated the annual total economic and social cost of reoffending to be £18.1 billion. It is a problem that has plagued ministers for decades – ever since prison became the focus for punishment.

Nevertheless, the question remains: how effective is imprisonment at preventing reoffending? Does it work? The questions are tricky to answer and dependent on several interconnected issues which can be difficult to untangle. Three of the most important are presented here:

1. Prisons are not rehabilitative; they can largely be viewed as de-habilitative primarily because they are dehumanising in the manner and way in which they treat individuals. There is a wealth of evidence showing that prisoners are poorly treated, much of which has been presented in earlier chapters. This poor treatment cultivates an environment in which prisoners come to accept that they are not wanted in society, so it encourages them not to strive to reform. The very act of being a prisoner is stigmatising; this coupled with the successive failures of prison to reduce the propensity of individuals to reoffend results in an overall crisis of legitimacy for the institution.
2. The use of draconian sentencing approaches further fuels de-habilitation rather than enabling rehabilitation. This largely relates to the overuse of short-term sentences which do not allow adequate time for prisons to work with individuals to create opportunities for reform. While this may seem a

contradiction – and longer prison sentences present their own challenges for rehabilitation – it is clear that a policy approach to overall penal sentencing is needed whereby plans for rehabilitation are timely, focused and underpinned by joint working between prisons, probation and broader community services.

3. Prisons also do not adequately prepare prisoners for the return to the outside world. They are isolating environments built on creating a place where little to no functions of normal life exist. This is contradictory in terms of the evidence that works towards desistance. Evidence from a global exploration of imprisonment (see Chapter 9) shows that prisons which are premised on a normalisation approach, in which they reflect 'normal' life, are much more successful in reducing reoffending than those that are not.

Given the extraordinary cost of imprisonment, the negligible deterrent effect it has and its lack of success at preventing reoffending, an alternative approach is needed. There is arguably a stronger case now, more than ever, for a significant policy change towards penal policy; justice reinvestment might hold the solution to the ongoing perpetual prison crisis. Reinvesting the money that is currently spent on incarceration and diverting it towards rehabilitation and prevention programmes would arguably result in more success than prison currently does. Investing in local education, mental health, drug and alcohol services and community programmes in socioeconomically deprived areas – which is where most crime occurs – is likely to result in a reduction in offending/reoffending. This would subsequently reduce the capacity in prisons to allow for staff to deal more effectively with the smaller group of serious persistent offenders for whom there is little alternative other than custody. Moreover, a justice reinvestment approach recognises and puts at its heart the fact that prisons are not the solution to social problems even though they have become them. As Garside (2018, emphasis in original) argues:

> [T]he prisons crisis is not, fundamentally, a crisis *in* prisons: one that can be resolved if the right reforms, the right action, is taken. It is a crisis *of* prisons: of our unbending attempts to treat a complex set of social problems – violence, drug, alcohol and mental health problems, poverty and disadvantage, social antagonisms – as if they are a simple set of crime problems, [to] be resolved through punishment.

A fundamental recognition of this may result in more successes in the prison system – more than the few successes there are at present.

Summary

This chapter has explored the concept of desistance and how it affects our understanding of what people need to not return to prison. The processes of release have been described, including a discussion of the Parole Board and the current challenges it faces. Recall, the process of returning people to prison if they have not complied with their licence conditions was also discussed. Finally, the chapter ended with a discussion of whether prison works and how this can be assessed.

Questions to consider

1. What support do you think prisoners need on leaving prison?
2. Who should have more of a say in the process of parole? The victim, the state or the prisoner?
3. How should we measure whether prison works? Are proven re-offences the best way?

TAKING IT FURTHER

There are several texts that explore the issues presented in this chapter, which you might wish to consult for further detail:

- Appleton, C. (2010). *Life after Life Imprisonment*. Oxford: Clarendon Studies in Criminology.

- Maruna, S. (2001). *Making Good: How Ex-Convicts Reform and Rebuild Their Lives*. London: American Psychological Association.

- Soothill, K., Fitzpatrick, C. and Francis, B. (2009). *Understanding Criminal Careers*. Cullompton: Willan.

It is well worth exploring the following sources for further information about the topics discussed in this chapter:

- Bilal's First Day Out: https://wearestraightline.com/video/bilals-first-day-out. Featured on the website Wearestraightline, a subpart of the National Prison Radio, is the story of Bilal and his first day out from prison. Well worth a listen.

- The Parole Board: https://www.gov.uk/government/organisations/parole-board

- The Road from Crime: https://www.iriss.org.uk/resources/videos/road-crime. This is an excellent film produced as part of a project to understand why people desist from offending.

9

Prison on an international scale

Key learning outcomes

By the end of this chapter, you should be able to:

- Explain the current trends of prison populations on a global scale

- Describe a series of different countries' approaches to imprisonment

- Understand the challenges prisons face on a global scale

Introduction

This chapter will take you on a tour of prisons around the world. It will introduce you to a global look at imprisonment, starting with an overview of the current prison population internationally before moving on to discuss key reasons why it is important to compare penal policies. The tour of prisons focuses on six different countries with contrasting approaches to imprisonment: Australia, Brazil, India, Japan, Norway and the USA. A factfile will be presented for each country documenting a breakdown of the current prison population, the size of the prison estate, the capacity of the prison estate, an overview of prison conditions and key notable points about the country's approach to imprisonment. The chapter concludes with a discussion as to which country arguably has the 'right' approach to prison.

A global look at imprisonment

The treatment of prisoners says a huge amount about a country's approach to its people, as described by Nelson Mandela (UNODC, nd), 'A nation should not be judged by how it treats its highest citizens, but its lowest ones.' It can also be said that one of the best ways to understand a nation is to understand whom it decides to put in prison and why. There are over 10 million people in some form of custodial detention across the world at any one time. Prisons and penal systems vary depending on their geographical location but also according to the social and cultural values of a country. It is important to note that prison populations vary between different regions of the world and between different parts of the same continent.

Tables 9.1 and 9.2 respectively show the top ten countries in the world with the highest prison population totals and the highest rates of imprisonment. Rates

Table 9.1: Prison population total: global top ten

Rank	Country	Prison population total
1	USA	2,068,800
2	China	1,690,000
3	Brazil	811,707
4	India	478,600
5	Russian Federation	471,490
6	Thailand	309,282
7	Turkey	291,198
8	Indonesia	266,259
9	Mexico	220,866
10	Iran	189,000
23	England and Wales	78,789

Source: World Prison Brief, 2022a

Table 9.2: Prison population rate: global top ten

Rank	Country	Prison population rate
1	USA	629
2	Rwanda	580
3	Turkmenistan	576
4	El Salvador	564
5	Cuba	510
6	Palau	478
7	Virgin Islands	477
8	Panama	452
9	St Kitts and Nevis	423
10	Grenada	413
115	England and Wales	132

Source: World Prison Brief, 2022b

of imprisonment are different from prison population totals; the countries on each of the top ten lists are different. When looking at the lists, some of the countries are not particularly comparable in geographic size or economic status, but they are in terms of prison population totals and rates of imprisonment. The USA has the highest total prison population in the world; it alone houses one fifth of the world's prison population. The USA also has the highest rate of imprisonment in the world, which means they lock up more people per 100,000 than any other country.

England and Wales rank 23rd on the list of the world prison population, the highest in Western Europe and third overall in the whole of Europe. Yet, England and Wales are only 115th in terms of the global ranking for the prison population rate. Whether you are likely to end up in prison if you commit a crime varies across the globe, and no matter what country you are in it is still determined in part by your social characteristics: age, gender and ethnicity. For example, Roma people make up around 40 per cent of Hungary's prison population, despite representing only 6 per cent of the national population; and Indigenous people in Australia represent 27 per cent of adult prisoners while making up around 2 per cent of all adult Australians. Across the board, poor and marginalised communities are overrepresented in prisons (Jacobson et al, 2017). What is key is that an exploration of crime rates cannot on its own explain prison rates; there is something much more nuanced going on that warrants further investigation. Therefore, it is important to compare and contrast prisons across the globe for several reasons:

1. It allows us to understand the similarities, differences and broad trends in the ways imprisonment has been deployed historically around the globe.
2. It helps us to understand why changes occur in our country, both through examining the policies of similar countries and analysing the influences that other penal initiatives have had on our country.
3. The complex relationship between 'crime' and punishment can be examined. (Cavadino and Dignan, 2012)

It is also important to be cautious when comparing statistical information from different countries. This is because not all countries collect statistics in the same manner; for example, statistical information from Eastern Europe is known to be lacking. It is also important to consider that not all forms of detention are included in countries' official records so in many countries the figures that are often used are estimates which are usually on the low side. There are also differences in the way statistics are gathered and in how individuals are categorised, and significant legal differences between criminal justice systems; for example, there are no data on the numbers detained pre-trial or prior to sentencing in China, making it too difficult to compare remand statistics. Moreover, as data are collected in different countries at different times of the year, there can be nuances in the data missed. Similarly, as the data that are often used for comparisons look at daily population totals, the significant annual totals and throughputs of prisoners in a system can be missed. That said, it is important to compare for many reasons; it should just be done with caution.

There is a considerable weight of international evidence against the use of imprisonment; yet, imprisonment continues to be the main form of punishment in most Western countries. Some of the most chronic problems that plague the prison system in England and Wales are problems that face prisons on a global scale: overcrowding, inhumane conditions, high levels of violence and lack of staff are all features that can be found in prison systems from Australia and France to the USA. Several non-governmental organisations scrutinise the conditions within prisons and the treatment of prisoners around the world. Organisations such as Amnesty International, Human Rights Watch and Penal Reform International regularly visit prisons and report on the conditions they find inside, usually to pressure governments to do something about what are often appalling environments. Despite the differences in economies, geographic size and political economy, the consequences of rapid prison population growth as experienced by a significant number of countries on a global scale are clear. An increase in punitive penal policy whereby prison is overused as the sentence for criminal offences results in overcrowded, inhumane and degrading conditions in prisons. It also results in limited rehabilitation being done by the prison as the staff and available resources struggle to cope with the swell of the demand. It also imposes a considerable cost to the public in terms of the actual financial cost of imprisonment being extortionate and the little good it is doing because the cost is not being offset by a reduction in (re)offending. Statistics show that global prison populations have risen steadily in recent decades but when looking at continental trends, a mixed picture is presented. From 2000 to 2015, the total prison population of Oceania increased by 59 per cent, while that of the Americas increased by 41 per cent, that of Asia by 29 per cent, and that of Africa by 15 per cent. Europe, in contrast, saw a 21 per cent fall in total prisoner numbers (Jacobson et al, 2017: vii). Furthermore, continental trends mask disparities at the country level; for example, the rate of increase in prisoner numbers in the USA has slowed and then reversed over the past 15 years, whereas some European countries have seen periods of growth in prisoner numbers followed by periods of decline (such as the Netherlands), and others vice versa (such as Hungary) (Jacobson et al, 2017: vii). This is interesting when compared with other countries throughout the world (such as India) in which levels of imprisonment have always been relatively low, and in which this continues to be the case (Jacobson et al, 2017: vii). What this shows is that prison population growth fluctuates as multiple factors can influence an increase in the use of imprisonment as well as decrease it. Political pressures, economic challenges and broader social conditions can all have a key bearing on the use of imprisonment. Weiss and South (1998: 2) suggest that there have been five important developments shaping imprisonment in recent times:

1. The rise of neoconservative governance and neoliberal political economy in the West, alongside economic decline, class polarisation and fiscal crisis.
2. The introduction of the market economy in China.
3. The collapse of the Soviet Union and associated communist regimes.
4. The return to civilian rule in most of Latin America, as well as a renewed push towards privatisation and other neoliberal economic prescriptions.
5. The fall of apartheid in South Africa.

Scott and Flynn (2014: 81) suggest the following two major developments can be added to the list:

6. The consequences of the USA-led war on terrorism and the subsequent increase in global insecurities.
7. The re-emergence of (the visibility of) slavery and human trafficking.

What these seven events show is the interconnected relationship between macro socioeconomic and political events and new patterns of crime, protest and repression. When these connect, imprisonment rates appear to increase or decrease depending on the nature of the event.

A tour of prisons around the world

The focus of the chapter now turns to take you on a tour of six different countries around the globe with contrasting approaches to imprisonment. These countries are, as presented in alphabetical order: Australia, Brazil, India, Japan, Norway and the USA. While many countries could have been chosen as case studies to highlight different elements of imprisonment around the globe, these have been chosen to compare and contrast a variety of different issues to the prison system described in this book as a whole, namely that of England and Wales.

Australia

Australia has an interesting relationship with England and Wales considering it is a former British colony and in part was originally a place of imprisonment and exile. As the country was colonised by British explorer James Cook, it was decided to use it as a place to send individuals from Britain's most overcrowded prisons via the means of penal transportation. It is reported that more than 160,000 convicts were transported to Australia between 1787 and 1868 when transportation ended. Despite popular belief, most individuals who were transported to Australia did not end up in Australian prisons but were put to work and subjected to various degrees and methods of control during their sentences. Australia became an independent nation in 1901; at that point, the country's prisons held approximately 5,000 prisoners with a prison population rate of 126. From that point onwards the prison population remained at around 5,000 despite the increase in the country's overall population. In 1950, Australia's prison population numbered around 4,000, and the prison population rate was 53, but since then the country has seen sustained and accelerating growth in prisoner numbers. By 2016 the total prison population rate of 162 was three times the 1950 figure (Jacobson et al, 2017: 31). The Federation of Australia constitutionally consists of six federated states (New South Wales, Queensland, South Australia, Tasmania, Victoria and Western Australia) and ten federal territories, out of which three are internal territories (the Australian Capital Territory, the Northern

Table 9.3: Factfile: Australia's prison system

Country	Australia
Ministry responsible	Ministry of Justice and Customs
Prison administration	Corrective departments of the individual states
Prison population total (including pre-trial detainees/remand prisoners)	42,403 (September 2021)
Prison population rate (per 100,000 of national population)	165
Female prisoners (percentage of prison population)	7.5% (September 2021)
Number of establishments/institutions	111 (2015: 85 government-operated prisons, 9 privately operated prisons, 4 transition centres, 12 court cell centres, 1 periodic detention centre)
Official capacity of prison system	36,730 (2017)
Occupancy level (based on official capacity)	112.2% (2017)

Source: Adapted from World Prison Brief, 2022c

Territory and Jervis Bay Territory) contiguous to the Australian mainland. These states and territories assume major responsibilities and powers for social issues, including legislative powers for the administration of criminal justice. Australia, therefore, has no single CJS; states and territories have separate and independent systems of police, courts, prisons and juvenile institutions. There is wide variation in prison population rates between states and territories with the Northern Territory having the highest rate of imprisonment at 971 prisoners per 100,000 adult population contrasting with that of the Australian Capital Territory of 113 prisoners per 100,000 adult population (Australian Bureau of Statistics, 2022). Explanations for the overall rise in the prison population in Australia centre on a general movement to an increasingly punitive approach to criminal justice policy and practice. The introduction of mandatory sentencing and stricter sentencing guidelines has led to people spending longer in custody. When this is considered alongside the reduction in the use of bail so more people are remanded into custody alongside a reduction in the granting of individuals' parole, it is the perfect storm for an increase in the prison population. The result of this is an overcrowded prison estate in a significant number of states and territories. Cunneen et al's (2013: 195) examination of imprisonment across Australia found that the growth of risk management and a punitive turn had affected the prison population but the 'penal/colonial complex' was also an explanatory factor. One of the most concerning features regarding imprisonment in Australia is the significant overrepresentation of Indigenous people in the prison population. According to the Australian Bureau of Statistics (2022), in 1990, 14 per cent of prisoners identified themselves as being Indigenous; this had increased to 27 per cent by 2016, yet only 2 per cent of the overall Australian population identify themselves as Indigenous. The statistics show a significant disproportionality within the Australian CJS and has been characterised as 'hyperincarceration' of Indigenous Australians (Cunneen et al, 2013). The cause of such huge disparities is said to lie in the ongoing issues of dispossession, exploitation and disempowerment of Indigenous people across Australia. The prison system of Australia also essentially suffers a similar fate to that of England and Wales in that it does not work; almost one in two adults released from prison in Australia are back in custody within two years (Australian Productivity Commission, 2020).

Brazil

Brazil was the first Latin American nation to build a prison, borrowing the idea from the southern states of the USA. The country is the fifth most populated country in the world, and it has the third highest prison population in the world; a total of 811,707 people are in prison at a rate of 381 per 100,000 people (World Prison Brief, 2022b). Brazil has some of the worst prison conditions in the world with the majority of the country's prisons reported as dilapidated, overcrowded and disease-ridden places. The vast proportion of the prison estate is run by Brazilian gangs with extreme levels of violence being a feature of everyday prison life; survival in a Brazilian prison depends on gang protection. Brazil as a country is a federal republic with 26 states; around 25 per cent of the population lives below the poverty line and many survive on less than £35 a month. It is a country that suffers from significant political instability; despite its return to democracy the impact of its previous brutal and repressive military dictatorship in the mid-1900s has left a legacy of poor respect for human rights and the rule of law

Table 9.4: Factfile: Brazil's prison system

Country	Brazil
Ministry responsible	Ministry of Justice
Prison administration	Department Penitenciário Nacional (DEPEN)
Prison population total (including pre-trial detainees/remand prisoners)	811,707 (December 2020)
Prison population rate (per 100,000 of national population)	381
Female prisoners (percentage of prison population)	5.1% (December 2020)
Number of establishments/institutions	2,608 (2019: according to the National Council of Justice)
Official capacity of prison system	455,283 (December 2020: places in *sistema prisional* [prison system])
Occupancy level (based on official capacity)	146.8% (December 2020: prisoners in *sistema prisional*)

Source: Adapted from World Prison Brief, 2022d

alongside a general mistrust of the CJS. The vast proportion of the individuals who make up the prison population are largely unemployed men who are sentenced for robbery, theft or drug trafficking offences. Brazil's largest criminal organisation, Primeiro Comando da Capital, was formed behind prison walls, in response to the massacre in 1992 of 111 prisoners at São Paulo's Carandiru prison. This organisation and similar organised crime groups control 90 per cent of Brazil's prisons, from where they organise drug trafficking, extortion and prostitution operations across large swathes of the country (Miraglia, 2015). Overall, law enforcement and the CJS are marked by corruption and inefficiency in a Brazilian context as is the vast proportion of most public sector services. Drugs are an epidemic in Brazil with the majority of those in custody there for drugs-related offences, usually in connection with gang activity. Additionally, a high proportion of the prison population is also due to large numbers of people on remand as over 40 per cent of the total prison population is waiting to be sentenced. Overcrowding, coupled with extreme staff shortages, often leads to rioting and violence within the prison estate. In the first two weeks of January 2017 over 125 prisoners were killed in five separate riots. In the state of São Paulo, a single guard oversees 300 to 400 prisoners in some prisons. Resources are also scarce with prisoners often being forced to compete for basics such as mattresses and food (BBC News, 2017). In recent times, José Eduardo Cardozo, the then Minister of Justice, stated, 'we have a medieval prison system, which not only violates human rights, it does not allow for the most important element of a penal sanction which is social reintegration. From the bottom of my heart, if I were given many years in some of our prisons, I would rather die' (Amnesty International, 2013).

India

India consists of 29 states and seven union territories, each of which has responsibility for its prisons, rules and regulations as per the Government of India Act 1935. India is something of a contradiction regarding its prison population; the total prison population has grown continually since 2000, and currently stands at between 478,000 and 490,000 making it the fifth-largest prison population in the world. The contradiction lies in the fact that as the world's second most populated country, India has one of the lowest prison population rates (35 per 100,000) ranking at 210 out of 223 countries (World Prison Brief, 2022b). Despite having a low rate of imprisonment, India's prison system is still overcrowded as can be seen in Table 9.5. There is, however, variation across India in terms of overcrowding as occupancy levels vary between states and union territories: Uttar Pradesh has reported the highest number of prisoners (107,395) in its jails contributing 22.0 per cent, followed by Bihar (51,934), Madhya Pradesh (45,484), Maharashtra (31,825), West Bengal (25,863) and Jharkhand (22,190). Together, these states contribute around 58.3 per cent of total prisoners in the country (NCRB, 2022). A particular issue affecting Indian prisons specifically

Table 9.5: Factfile: India's prison system

Country	India
Ministry responsible	Ministry of Home Affairs
Prison administration	Governments of States and Union Territories
Prison population total (including pre-trial detainees/remand prisoners)	488,511 (December 2020)
Prison population rate (per 100,000 of national population)	35
Female prisoners (percentage of prison population)	4.1% (December 2020)
Number of establishments/institutions	1,306 (December 2020: comprising 145 central jails, 413 district jails, 565 sub jails, 29 women's jails, 88 open jails, 19 borstal schools, 44 special jails, 3 other jails)
Official capacity of prison system	414,033 (December 2020)
Occupancy level (based on official capacity)	118.0% (December 2020)

Source: Adapted from World Prison Brief, 2022e

is the significant number of prisoners who are being held on remand (that is, awaiting trial), currently 76 per cent of the total prison population (World Prison Brief, 2022e). There is a considerable delay in the Indian CJS in processing people, which is largely driven by a shortfall of judges in the high courts and a lack of modern technology to improve case management. This adds considerably to the overcrowded nature of Indian prisons, resulting in poor conditions. Prisons in India have been described as lacking in food, medical care and sanitation and having inadequate environmental conditions (US Department of State, 2020). There are also significant reports of severe staff shortages alongside high levels of corruption. Prisoners being severely mistreated is a regularity in Indian prisons with some reported as having died from the beatings received from prison guards. Overall, Indian prison conditions are described as 'frequently life threatening' (US Department of State, 2020) and despite some attempts to improve the conditions little has been achieved in recent years.

Japan

Japan is viewed as one of the world's most technologically advanced nations; it has a very low imprisonment rate compared with other developed countries. Japan had a prison population of 55,000 prisoners in 1950 which had risen to 61,000 in 2000 and hit a peak of 81,000 in 2006. Since then the numbers in custody have gradually fallen to a population now of 47,064 (World Prison Brief, 2022f). The Japanese prison system is one of the small number in the world which has never been classed as overcrowded. Japanese culture is unique and centred on being a group–oriented society whereby citizenship is closely tied to the collective

Table 9.6: Factfile: Japan's prison system

Country	Japan
Ministry responsible	Ministry of Justice
Prison administration	Correction Bureau
Prison population total (including pre-trial detainees/remand prisoners)	47,064 at mid-2020 (via Asian & Pacific Conference of Correctional Administrators)
Prison population rate (per 100,000 of national population)	37
Female prisoners (percentage of prison population)	8.5% (mid-2020)
Number of establishments/institutions	184 (2018: comprising 62 adult prisons, 8 branch prisons, 6 juvenile prisons, 8 detention houses and 100 branch detention houses. The prison administration also has responsibility for juvenile classification homes and juvenile training schools, whose occupants are not included in the prison population)
Official capacity of prison system	89,310 (December 2020)
Occupancy level (based on official capacity)	56.6% (December 2020)

Source: Adapted from World Prison Brief, 2022f

identity of the nation. Family is considerably important in Japanese culture as are the values and bonds that education and the workplace bring to people's lives. Due to this, those who break the law in Japan are treated harshly under the authoritarian rules that the country has. Yet, those who show remorse and shame for their behaviour and apologise for it are much more likely to receive a more lenient sentence than those who do not. This is because the Japanese culturally favour more informal mechanisms of social control than penal harshness. For those who break the law the experience of prison is harsh as everything within the environment is highly regimented and orderly. All movement around the prison is heavily controlled with limited free time available to prisoners. Prisoners are banned from talking except during periods of association and engagement with work is compulsory, similar to the 'separate system' once used in Victorian prisons in England and Wales (see Chapter 2). For nearly a century, Japan's prisons were run under the Prison Law which provided the basic rules and regulations for penal institutions. However, in 2006, this Act was revised to define the rights and duties of prisoners more clearly. It was reported that when the new law came into force many of the current prison officers objected to the changes, arguing that the numerous provisions protecting the rights of prisoners made their jobs more difficult. The new law also increased access to visits, letters and the receipt of care packages that had been strictly regulated and almost banned under the previous legislation. The new law aimed to create a more consistent practice across the penal estate in Japan, as previously prisoners could experience significantly different treatment depending on the prison they were located in. Overall, regimes in Japanese prisons now are characterised as being more tightly regulated; this is in part due to the relatively small number of officers who manage a large prisoner population. Japan has been repeatedly criticised for violating human rights due to its adherence to strict rules of conduct and the widespread use of solitary confinement as its main punishment for rule breaking. Its reliance on solitary confinement as a punishment for contravening prison rules has been widely condemned because officials are ignoring the considerable evidence base on the detrimental impact the practice has on the mental health of prisoners.

Norway

The Norwegian approach to imprisonment is one where the system aims to get prisoners out and back into society. The country, while small in population when compared with other European countries, also has a considerably small prison population averaging around 3,000 prisoners at any one time (World Prison Brief, 2022g). Among all the countries in the world, Norway is considered to have the most compassionate approach to imprisonment; Halden Prison, Norway's flagship institution, is classed as the world's most humane prison. Norwegian institutions are small; Halden, its top institution, holds just 259 male prisoners. Prisons are centred on a regime that is built on the principle of normality, whereby the goal is to build a society behind walls that is as close as possible to the normal world outside the prison. This reflects the key principle that those inside will at some point return to society and the aim is to make that transition back as effortless as possible. Norwegian prisons boast some of the best facilities in the world; prisoners are provided with kitchens to cook in, fully purpose-built workshops for learning new skills and single occupancy rooms resembling university student accommodation, fitted with private en suites and bar-less open windows. Most prisons are in vast

Table 9.7: Factfile: Norway's prison system

Country	Norway
Ministry responsible	Ministry of Justice and Public Security
Prison administration	Department of Corrections
Prison population total (including pre-trial detainees/remand prisoners)	3,088 (March 2022) national prison administration
Prison population rate (per 100,000 of national population)	57
Female prisoners (percentage of prison population)	5.6% (March 2022)
Number of establishments/institutions	33 (2021: 33 units consisting of 58 prisons)
Official capacity of prison system	3,638 (August 2021)
Occupancy level (based on official capacity)	83.4% (August 2021)

Source: Adapted from World Prison Brief, 2022g

green, open spaces and have artwork on the walls designed to inspire and motivate prisoners to improve their lives. 'Better out than in' is the unofficial motto of the Norwegian Correctional Service, which makes a reintegration guarantee to all released prisoners (Benko, 2015). The Correctional Service works with other government agencies to secure accommodation, a job and access to a support network for each prisoner prior to release. As might be expected, all of this comes at a cost. Norway spends considerable money on imprisonment; more than £71,000 is spent per prisoner per year compared to just £35,000 spent by the MoJ in England and Wales and £23,000 spent in the USA on each prisoner. The outcome of this is that Norway has one of the lowest prison reoffending rates in the world; only 20 per cent of those in prison come out and subsequently reoffend (Deady, 2014). This is in part attributed to the work that the prison system does to train prisoners for employment after prison; 'the Norwegian prison system is successful in increasing participation in job training programmes, encouraging employment and discouraging crime, largely due to changes in the behaviour of individuals who were not working prior to incarceration' (Kristofferson, 2013). It appears that the Norwegian approach to imprisonment has recognised that the actual punishment of imprisonment is to take away an individual's freedom; the subsequent purpose of the prison is then to work to reintegrate them back into society.

USA

As a total and complete opposite to Norway, alongside being the richest and most advanced capitalist society in the world, the USA also boasts the largest prison population. The prison population has remained relatively stable over the last 20 years with the USA having on average two million people in prison at any one time (World Prison Brief, 2022h). The continual growth of the prison population is attributed to a very clear, tough law and order stance started in the late 1960s by President Nixon. This led to a dramatic rise in the rate of imprisonment alongside the increase in the prison population in every decade since. Before this tough penal stance, imprisonment levels had been fairly stable; yet, the 1970s–2000s produced a 500 per cent increase in prisoner numbers. President Reagan's 'war on drugs' in the 1980s fuelled this dramatic rise; it is estimated that one third of all admissions to state and federal prisons over the period 1993–2009 were for drug offences (Rothwell, 2005). Zimring (2010: 1230) states that the 35 years from 1972 'produced a growth in rates of imprisonment that has never been recorded in the history of developed nations'. The prison population reached its peak of 2.3 million in 2008; there were 755 people in US prisons or jails for every 100,000 of the national population (World Prison Brief, 2022h).

The USA also has the highest rate of imprisonment in the world. No other country has a rate over 600, with Rwanda and Turkmenistan behind it at 580 and 576 respectively (World Prison Brief, 2022b). There is considerable variation between states in the USA as to the rate of imprisonment; Louisiana, Oklahoma and Mississippi have the highest rates of imprisonment per 100,000 people at 684,

Table 9.8: Factfile: USA's prison system

Country	USA
Ministry responsible	Department of Justice
Prison administration	Federal Bureau of Prisons, state and local correctional authorities
Prison population total (including pre-trial detainees/remand prisoners)	2,068,800 (2019 US Bureau of Justice statistics: 734,500 in local jails (June 2019), 1,159,900 in state prisons, 174,400 federal prisoners. In addition there are prisoners in the 84 Indian Country Jails that operate on reservation land (2,870 at mid-year 2018))
Prison population rate (per 100,000 of national population)	629
Female prisoners (percentage of prison population)	c.10.3% (2019)
Number of establishments/institutions	4,455 (2014: 3,163 local jails; 2005: 1,190 state confinement facilities and 102 federal confinement facilities)
Official capacity of prison system	c.2,163,235 (2019: 907,700 local jails; c.1,121,402 operational capacity in state prisons, 134,133 rated capacity in federal prisons)
Occupancy level (based on official capacity)	c.95.6% (2019: 80.9% in local jails, 130.0% in federal prisons, c.103.4% in state prisons)

Source: Adapted from World Prison Brief, 2022h

639 and 632 respectively (World Population Review, 2022). The USA penal system is broken down into 'jails', which hold individuals pre-trial and those sentenced to under a year's custody; they are mostly run by city or county authorities. They also have 'prisons', which are operated by state authorities or the Federal Bureau of Prisons and house those convicted of federal crimes and who are likely to be serving lengthy sentences. The USA has clear sentencing legislation about some offences carrying mandatory minimum prison sentences; judges have very little discretion to use and must follow the set guidelines. One of the most controversial sentencing practices is the 'three strikes' law, which usually requires a sentence of at least 25 years to be imposed for specific third felony convictions. Until recently, California had the toughest three strikes law, which resulted in sentences of 25 years to life for 'third strike' offences of drug possession or theft. This has since been amended to follow what most of the other states do, which is to use it to punish persistent, serious offenders. Alongside the tough sentencing policies, which have kept the overall numbers of people incarcerated high, is the reduced use of parole – or the elimination of the possibility of parole altogether – for certain categories of prisoners. Both issues are responsible for the bulging prison population. The USA has been heavily criticised for the conditions in which it keeps prisoners, particularly regarding its overuse of solitary confinement and the creation of 'supermax' (super-maximum security) prisons. Many international

rules and regulations specify solitary confinement should only be used in the most exceptional of circumstances and for minimal periods (Nelson Mandela Rules 43–5, UNODC, 2015) due to the significant amount of evidence that exists of the harm it does to a person's mental health. Yet, the USA has one of the most widespread uses of this punishment, so much so it is almost a standard tool used to control and punish incarcerated people. It is estimated that 80,000–100,000 individuals are being held in some form of isolation at any one time in the USA (Penal Reform, 2022). To facilitate this widespread practice, supermax prisons were designed and built specifically to hold prisoners in strict isolation. Shalev (2009) outlines the typical features of a supermax prison:

- Cells measure 70–80 square feet.
- Prisoners are kept alone in their cells for 22.5 to 24 hours a day.
- Prisoners exercise alone in a cage or concrete exercise block.
- No congregating areas and no group activities.
- No work opportunities and few, if any, in-cell educational programmes.
- Family visits are limited and held through a thick glass barrier.
- High-tech measures of control, surveillance and inspection.

Under the presidency of Barack Obama, there had been attempts to reduce the use of solitary confinement at federal and local levels, largely due to sustained international and national pressure, particularly regarding its use on juveniles and those with existing mental illnesses. One of the other most salient issues about the USA's use of imprisonment is that it demonstrates significant racial disparities. As the prison population increased in the 1970s, the existing racial inequalities in the overuse of imprisonment for ethnically minoritised individuals became starker. One in three African Americans is sent to prison during their lifetime, although they only constitute 13 per cent of the wider population. In the USA, racial disparities, in a similar manner to England and Wales, plague the CJS, with discriminatory practices embedded at every stage of the process. The USA spends on average the equivalent of £62 billion a year on imprisonment. It does not work, and it has one of the highest rates of recidivism with almost 44 per cent of individuals released returning to prison within a year (World Population Review, 2022). Policies brought in by Barack Obama slowed the prison population rate and for the first time reduced some of the racial disparities experienced by ethnically minoritised individuals. They were reversed under the presidency of Donald Trump.

Who does prison best?

The tour of countries demonstrates a range of different approaches to imprisonment. There are significant themes when a global look is taken at imprisonment:

- overcrowding
- poor prison conditions

- disproportionality
- poor provisions for social reintegration
- penal populism

Overcrowding is a global issue when it comes to prisons; it plagues a high proportion of prisons across the world. Overcrowding often exacerbates many of the other problems that prisons face; it makes poor conditions worse, fuels disproportionality and restricts the opportunities for rehabilitation. Prisons in over 124 countries exceed their maximum occupancy rate, which results in violence, higher rates of death in custody, a lack of healthcare provision and low rehabilitative opportunities. Many countries have, despite attempts, failed to build their way out of the overcrowding problem. Overcrowding is not a new problem, however; since prisons have been created, there has been overcrowding. This is largely due to the way they are seen: as places to send people that society does not know what to do with. It is easier to put them somewhere and forget about them than to deal with them. It is also due to a chronic lack of investment. The solution to prison overcrowding lies in a broader look at sentencing policy and alternatives to prison, as well as providing prisoners with clear financial stability. Poor conditions are another ingrained problem in prisons across the world. Some of the most economically rich countries have some of the worst prison conditions; the wealth of a country is not an indicator of good prison conditions. Countries have an obligation towards people in prison; they are in the care of the state from the moment they are deprived of their liberty. Those in prison should expect to be treated humanely; states have a responsibility to provide adequate accommodation, food and water, healthcare, sanitation, access to light, fresh air and exercise. There are also clear international standards relating to contact with the outside world, access to legal representation, provision for religious practice and even standards relating to clothes and bedding. Rules regulating the prison regime cover how prisoners can be disciplined and punished, as well as providing guidance on instruments of restraint to ensure fair and equal treatment and safeguard against abuse. Yet, despite all the international standards to which most (Western) countries are signatories there are still consistent breaches and reports of human rights violations.

Disproportionality is also something that crosses borders. In many prison systems around the world, individuals who are ethnically minoritised are overrepresented, from the USA and Australia to England and Wales. Those who are underrepresented in the population are often disproportionally overrepresented in the CJS, largely driven by discriminatory practices at every stage from arrest and prosecution to sentencing. Prison is often the consequence of these discriminatory practices and proceeds to accentuate them in a wholly negative way. Roberts and McMahon (2008) utilise the term 'ethnic penalty' to explain that a penalty or inequality in certain aspects of life exists even if a person of minority ethnicity has the same background as a White person. This disadvantage or 'penalty' is experienced because of a person's ethnic background.

Roberts and McMahon (2008) argue that underlying racism and discrimination is embedded in our institutions; the prison system is no exception to this. Those who enter the prison system face a significant further hurdle in that the stigma of prison increases discrimination; hence, the label of being a prisoner further compounds inequality.

What is also universally problematic is that most prisons poorly prepare individuals for social reintegration. It is evidenced across many countries that prison does not work, in the sense that prisons have high reoffending rates with considerably high numbers of individuals returning to prisons worldwide each year. In part, reoffending is driven by the lack of preparation by prisons to prepare individuals to reintegrate into society. The label of being an 'offender' and having a criminal record is stigmatising but having been to prison accentuates that and makes it worse. In a number of countries across the world but particularly in the West, little is done to aid rehabilitation in the prison environment. This is in part due to the aforementioned conditions that prisoners live in and the nature of overcrowding; it impedes any possible work to reduce reoffending as there is neither the space nor the staff capacity to do it. Prisons have become places of containment, for the most part. Prisoners often return to the circumstances they found themselves in before going to prison; sometimes they are even worse off, whereupon reoffending is almost inevitable. A lack of investment of money and resources to support prisoners, not only while in custody but also post-release, along with an overzealous focus on public protection (particularly in countries like England and Wales and the USA) has resulted in high rates of recall to prison. Often this is due to individuals failing to follow licence conditions as opposed to further offending. Despite the significant supporting research, there are often gaps in provision in key areas of broader social policy that need to be filled for reoffending to be reduced. More also needs to be done to integrate prisons with their local communities so the public can be made aware of the work being done to help prisoners. Moves to reduce stigmatisation to enable successful reintegration should also be made.

Finally, there exists a trend across the world, particularly in the West, towards penal populism (Pratt, 2007). As crime has been politicised by politicians so too has the response to it. An increase in public anxiety and insecurity, fuelled by battles for political supremacy, has led to punitive rhetoric being created towards people who transgress the law. The result is a perceived increased desire by the public for harsher and stricter punishment with prison being the primary tool to achieve this. With the media and politicians continually highlighting rises in serious violence the response has been a lengthening of prison sentences, the justification for this being that the public wants people in prison for longer. In the USA, Australia, England and Wales and other countries, this populist punitiveness, or penal populism, has fuelled new sentencing provisions, such as mandatory sentencing with fixed minimum terms, 'three strikes' systems and, in some cases, indeterminate sentences being used. These provisions contradict the evidence base that exists regarding incarceration and are largely designed to show toughness as a response to serious forms of offending. It is unclear how such policies contribute to the goal of rehabilitation, which is assigned to most prison systems. Instead, they make a significant impact on prisoner numbers, which subsequently contribute to the other previously mentioned issues, such as levels of violence, self-harm and risk of suicide.

When thinking about who does prison best, what a comparative analysis does show is that it can lead to a greater understanding of the use of imprisonment and how different countries justify and deliver the punishment. This in turn can potentially enable penal policy transfer, whereby ideas and approaches are shared between countries to improve practice. While this can be positive by allowing countries to learn from one another, it is not straightforward. It would be naive to assume that taking a successful policy or practice from one country and simply transferring it to another would result in equivalent success; it would not. For instance, for England and Wales to build a prison based on the design of Norway's Halden prison would not work. The reason why Norway's approach to imprisonment works is that the country has a less punitive and more pro-social reintegration approach to criminality, so the culture allows for a prison like Halden to work. That is simply not the case for England and Wales, which has a much more populist punitive approach to law and order, fuelled by the constant shift and uncertainty in penal policy created by the government. This is why cultural, social and economic contexts are important to consider before exploring whether different approaches to imprisonment would work in different countries. It is also important to recognise political, geo-political and economic contexts, both nationally and internationally, and the bearing that these have on shaping a country's approach to punishment. All these factors must be considered because they define or affect the structure and content of criminal justice policy and how it is interpreted and applied at all stages of the criminal justice process. These forces shape which kinds of conduct are perceived and treated as criminal and therefore ultimately determine who ends up in prison. The size and nature of a country's prison population are intricately bound up with many of its most important features, including its political culture, economy, structural inequalities and the real and perceived internal and external threats it faces. To determine who does prison best the question must be considered in all these contexts, not just the reoffending rates.

Summary

This chapter has taken a tour of a range of different prison systems around the world, providing a global sense of where England and Wales sit on the spectrum of prisons. It has provided an overview of global prison population trends and justified why it is important to internationally compare countries. While acknowledging this can be tricky because countries differ so much in geographic size, economic stability, political management and cultures, it is worth attempting to do, so that the true sense of the challenge the English and Welsh penal system faces can be seen in a global light. Sadly, in some ways the chapter illustrates that

England and Wales are not alone in the current problems their penal system faces. The chapter has concluded with a discussion of the difficult question of who does prison best and whether lessons can be learnt from who does and who does not with a view to improving the English and Welsh prison system.

Questions to consider

1. What is the solution to the global prison crisis?
2. What policies/practices could England and Wales adopt from other countries to improve the prison system here?
3. Would a prison like Halden ever work in England? Why do you think this?

TAKING IT FURTHER

There are several texts that explore the issues presented in this chapter, which you might wish to consult for further detail:

- Allen, R. (2012). *Reducing the Use of Imprisonment: What Can We Learn from Europe?* London: Criminal Justice Alliance.

- Jewkes, Y., Bennett, J. and Crewe, B. (eds) (2016). *Handbook on Prisons*. 2nd edn. London: Routledge. Several chapters look at different prison systems across the world.

- Wooldredge, J. and Smith, P. (eds) (2018). *The Oxford Handbook of Prisons and Imprisonment*. Oxford: Oxford University Press. Several chapters look at different prison systems across the world.

It is well worth exploring the following sources for further information about the topics discussed in this chapter:

- Penal Reform International – https://www.penalreform.org

- United Nations Office on Drugs and Crime, prison reform information – https://www.unodc.org/unodc/en/urban-safety/prison-reform.html

- World Prison Brief – https://www.prisonstudies.org

10

What next for prisons?

Key learning outcomes

By the end of this chapter, you should be able to:

- Explain the current state of the penal system in England and Wales

- Describe how power, legitimacy and rehabilitation can help us understand the penal policy in relation to prisons

- Understand what the future challenges for prisons are

Introduction

This concluding chapter provides an overarching summary of the state of the prison system in England and Wales. The key points from each chapter are presented to show how the three concepts of power, legitimacy and rehabilitation can help us understand all aspects of prisons and imprisonment. The chapter provides an overview of the future challenges for prisons. It argues that by looking at imprisonment we can understand the broader trajectories of punishments and the philosophies and policies that surround them.

Current state of the prison system in England and Wales

The prison system in England and Wales can be described as in crisis, a phrase which has been used for more than a decade now to describe the persistent problems and challenges it faces. Since the population boom in the mid-2000s, the prison system has struggled to cope with swelling numbers in an estate that was not designed with either the infrastructure or the policy directives for it to cope with such a high volume of people. The drivers of this increase in numbers were caused by a series of interconnecting issues:

1. More individuals sentenced to immediate custody
2. Increase in the average time served in prison
3. Decline in the parole rate
4. Increasing numbers of ROTL prisoners being recalled

These issues have combined to create a system whereby the conditions found within prisons are some of the worst that have been documented since the turn of the 20th century. High levels of violence, self-harm and self-inflicted deaths are all key indicators of a prison system struggling to cope with the constant and perpetual state of crisis it finds itself in, despite in most cases the best efforts of staff. Cavadino et al (2013) have described the problems that plague the English and Welsh prison system as a set of interlocking crises:

- increasing numbers and overcrowding
- poor organisation and management
- dysfunctional security, conditions and regimes
- difficulty maintaining order and control
- the lack of effective accountability mechanisms or grievance procedures

Many of these crises are related to the general crisis of chronic underfunding, which has intensified as the prison population has continued to grow. In the past decade, there has been an air of almost permanent crisis management throughout the penal system but specifically in prisons. This is compounded by policy makers of both governments (Conservative–Liberal Democrat coalition, 2010–15, and the Conservative Party, since 2015 and at the time of publication) lacking the vision and courage to take effective action to tackle the underlying causes of the crisis. This has resulted in there being a deep-seated crisis of legitimacy within prisons. Imprisonment must be considered within the wider framework of approaches to punishment and who is being punished. To understand prisons without considering the social context in which they operate is to not understand them at all. Prisons are representations of the broader social divisions and inequalities within society. We do not lock up the rich or the powerful but instead those who are poor, vulnerable and powerless. Prisons, therefore, lack not only moral legitimacy but also political legitimacy. Fitzgerald and Sim (1982: 4) state:

> Imprisonment is invoked consistently against marginal, lower class offenders. In so doing, imprisonment serves a class-based legal system, which first, defines the social harms which are singled out for punishment and second, invokes different types of sanctions for different categories of social harm.

Through the crisis of legitimacy, Fitzgerald and Sim, and others, have called for the abolition of imprisonment. Penal abolitionism is a sociological, philosophical, criminological and political position that developed in the late 1960s, although it has its roots much further back in time, in connection with the abolition of slavery and the slave trade. The present social movement emerged to challenge the very existence of the prison system through the development of a series of policies, practices and philosophies which try to move the debate away from traditional ideas about imprisonment. Abolitionists have argued that new philosophies for dealing with those who break the law are needed. Penal abolitionists such as Joe Sim (2009) talk about restoration and reparation, as opposed to punishment, as being better overall philosophies to adopt. They also advocate for decarceration and removing different groups from the prison system such as women and children. Yet, despite the best attempts of penal abolitionists, prison reform campaigners, researchers and advocates to highlight the ongoing inhumane and dehabilitating treatment of prisoners, prisons persist as our main form of punishment. Why is this?

Social functions of imprisonment

Foucault (1977) described the birth of the prison as part of a much broader movement known as the 'great confinement', in which a range of institutions was created as the solution to a range of social problems. Removing people who do not fit or comply with the rules of mainstream society has driven the creation of prisons, secure mental health units and immigration removal centres. It all began with prisons and the movement from the punishment of the body (corporal punishment) to the punishment of the soul, 'the great transformation' (Foucault, 1977) triggered by the impact of industrialisation at the start of the 19th century. The continued use of imprisonment as the dominant form of punishment, however, is driven in part by a number of the issues discussed in Chapter 6 but also by potentially the broader social functions it performs. Mathiesen (1974) argues that prison performs five key social functions in advanced capitalist societies, which is why it continues to be the main method of punishment despite all its faults:

1. Expurgatory function: those who are both unproductive and disruptive of the normal processes of production are liable to find themselves siphoned off and contained in prison where they can do the least damage. The demographic profile of the prison population reflects this. As Carlen (2008) has put it, 'today the prison still fulfils its age-old function of catering for the homeless, the mentally ill, the stranger, the non-compliant poor, the abused and the excluded'.
2. Power-draining function: prisons drain people of their autonomy and decision-making powers; they are unable to interfere with the modes of production that are so vital to the success of a capitalist society.
3. Symbolic function: prison is stigmatising; through applying the label of 'prisoner' individuals on the outside can avoid those whom they might not wish to morally interact with.
4. Diverting function: as prison continues to focus on punishing poor and vulnerable people it has a diverting function whereby those who actually cause more harm are able to continue because society refuses to address the crimes of the powerful. Mathiesen (1974) highlights that more harm is caused by those who pollute the environment, flout health and safety requirements to prioritise profits and damage ecosystems through ignoring international law, yet few are held to account for such behaviour.

5. Action function: imprisonment continues to have a high value within political rhetoric as it reassures the public that something is being done about crime and disorder within society.

Drawing attention to the more understated symbolic functions of the modern prison can help us to understand why the use of imprisonment persists despite its clear and well-evidenced failings. As Cavadino et al (2013) state, 'there is a heavy price to be paid, not only in terms of resources and human suffering but also in managing the increasing tensions that are associated with the enduring penal crisis'. The heavy price that is paid appears to be the inhumane treatment of those in prison and the little to no prospect of rehabilitation they face on release.

What next for prisons?

There have been the beginnings of change in recent years with moves to improve prisons initiated by the Conservative government. The White Paper *Prison Safety and Reform* (MoJ, 2016) demonstrated that changes were needed to improve safety and increase rehabilitation. This was to be done against a backdrop of providing prison governors with greater autonomy to do what was right for their specific prison populations and contexts (MoJ, 2016). To trial this new approach and new ways of operating, six reform prisons were established whereby greater freedom was given to the governors in relation to staffing, budgets and regime design; effectively, they had overall control of their prisons. The recommendations in the White Paper were enacted in the Prison and Courts Bill 2017. The Bill was a significant moment in the history of imprisonment because for the first time it was to enshrine in legislation that one of the key purposes of prison is to reform and rehabilitate prisoners. The proposed legislation stated:

> In giving effect to sentences or orders of imprisonment or detention imposed by courts, prisons must aim to −
> (a) protect the public,
> (b) reform and rehabilitate offenders,
> (c) prepare prisoners for life outside prison, and
> (d) maintain an environment that is safe and secure. (Prison and Courts Bill 2017: c.1)

This would have been a watershed moment for prisons. The work they do in rehabilitating prisoners would have been legally recognised and mandated. Yet, sadly, the Bill was cancelled when then-Prime Minister Theresa May called the snap 2017 general election to secure a bigger majority and shore up her position as she went into negotiations for the deal for the UK to leave the European Union (Brexit). The Bill never resurfaced after the election and the White Paper, along with many others, which had promised significant and potentially positive changes for the prison system, faded into the ether. The demise of the Prison and

Courts Bill 2017 shows just how vulnerable penal policy is to political changes. As O'Brien and Robson (2016: 44) state:

> Prison policy often gets buffeted in the winds of media, scandal and fear; with little short-term political capital to be gained by improving prison policy, an unsympathetic client group and a largely invisible and undervalued workforce.

The question remains: what next for prisons? As the UK and the world emerge from the COVID-19 pandemic, the challenges that prisons face continue to be ever present. The strategy adopted by the government to lock down prisons during the pandemic for longer periods than the general population has had an interesting impact on the various measures traditionally taken to assess the health of a prison. Early statistics (MoJ, 2022d) show that levels of violence have reduced, largely explained by the fact prisoners were locked in their cells for sustained periods. Moreover, levels of self-harm and self-inflicted deaths may have stabilised, all of which is potentially good news. Yet, what is perhaps concerning is the impact that lockdowns have had on the prospects of those currently in prison being successfully rehabilitated. All programmes to reduce the risk of reoffending ceased during the pandemic along with education and training. Cohorts of prisoners lost out on vital opportunities to gain new skills and qualifications as well as an understanding of their triggers for offending, all of which will make the prospect of successful resettlement and desistance from crime more challenging on release. Additionally, many experienced an isolated prison sentence as all visits and contact with family and friends stopped; these fragmented connections now add to the pressures of release. The pandemic also had a significant impact on the work of the Parole Board, which continued to function at the time but faced significant challenges. Now there are even more delays in the system.

The Conservative government has been focusing attention elsewhere in recent years with Brexit and the COVID-19 pandemic creating significant policy challenges for them. Consequently, criminal justice policy and, specifically, penal policy have seen little movement aside from the revival of some of the 'tough on crime' rhetoric seen in the mid-2000s. The Conservatives have launched the building of several new prisons and started to close some of the not-fit-for-purpose Victorian institutions. The solution to fixing the problem with prisons does not lie in building our way out of it – it is a very costly and ultimately flawed way to solve the crisis. The solutions to the problems lie in a broader exploration and addressing of the complex social problems that lead people into prison in the first place. Violence, substance abuse, poverty, discrimination and mental health problems are all social problems that are attempted to be resolved through the CJS and subsequently the use of imprisonment; they cannot be. Until those in positions to do so recognise this and invest in improving the broader systems of social policy then prisons will continue to be used for people society does not know what to do with. Prisons need a clearly articulated purpose if they are to be successful in their aims; without this, they will continue to exist as institutions that remain in a continual state of crisis.

Before you go ...

What are your views of the prison system now?
Have they changed from what you wrote at the start?
What do you think the solution to the prison crisis is?

This book has attempted to provide you with an overview of prisons and penal policy in England and Wales. It has given you a historical outline of the birth of imprisonment as well as the modern context. The fact that some groups within society experience prison differently and that this results in discrimination has also been discussed. What 'doing time' entails as well as the overall experience of what prison is like and the conditions prisoners face have been established. The role of the prison officer provided insights into the nature of working in a prison as well as what the role in enabling rehabilitation requires. The processes of release have been presented alongside the consequences of not complying with release conditions. Finally, the book took you on a tour of prisons around the world and explored why it is good to compare approaches. A global outlook allowed us to see not only where England and Wales are positioned but also what the global strains and stresses are regarding imprisonment. The book has attempted to provide various insights to challenge your thinking. It is hoped that it has inspired you to think broadly about penal policy and to have a deeper appreciation of the challenges that prisons and those inside them face.

References

Amnesty International. (2013). Carandiru and the scandal of Brazil's medieval prison system. [Online]. https://www.amnesty.org/en/latest/news/2013/04/carandiru-and-scandal-brazil-s-medieval-prison-system [accessed 25/03/22].

Anonymous. (2022). *The Secret Prison Governor*. London: Welbeck Publishing Group.

Aresti, A., Eatough, V. and Brooks-Gordon, B. (2010). Doing time after time: an interpretative phenomenological analysis of reformed ex-prisoners' experiences of self-change, identity and career opportunities. *Psychology, Crime and Law*, 16(3), 169–190.

Ashforth, B. and Kreiner, G. (1999). 'How can you do it?' Dirty work and the challenge of constructing a positive identity. *The Academy of Management Review*, 24(3), pp 413–434.

Australian Bureau of Statistics. (2022). Prisoners in Australia [Online]. https://www.abs.gov.au/statistics/people/crime-and-justice/prisoners-australia/2021#state-territory [accessed 25/03/22].

Australian Productivity Commission. (2020). Report on Government Services 2020: Corrective services [Online]. https://www.pc.gov.au/research/ongoing/report-on-government-services/2020/justice/corrective-services [accessed 25/03/22].

BBC News. (2017). Brazil prison riots: what's the cause? [Online] 7 January. www.bbc.co.uk/news/world-latin-america-38534769, [accessed 25/03/22].

BBC News. (2020a). George Floyd: what happened in the final moments of his life [Online] 16 July. https://www.bbc.co.uk/news/world-us-canada-52861726, [accessed 20/02/22].

BBC News. (2020b). Whitemoor prison terror attack inmates handed life terms [Online] 8 October. https://www.bbc.co.uk/news/uk-england-cambridgeshire-54462241, [accessed 25/08/22].

BBC News. (2021). Probation services return to public control in England and Wales [Online] 28 June. https://www.bbc.co.uk/news/uk-57632663, [accessed 25/08/22].

Bean, P. (1981). *Punishment: A Philosophical and Criminological Inquiry*. Oxford: Martin Robertson.

Beard, J. (2021). *The Prison Estate*. London: House of Commons Library.

Beccaria, C. (1986 [1764]). *An Essay on Crimes and Punishments*. Indianapolis, IN: Hackett Publishing Company.

Benko, J. (2015). The radical humaneness of Norway's Halden Prison [Online] *New York Times*. https://www.nytimes.com/2015/03/29/magazine/the-radical-humaneness-of-norways-halden-prison.html [accessed 25/03/22].

Bennett, C. (2008). *The Apology Ritual: A Philosophical Theory of Punishment*. Cambridge: Cambridge University Press.

Bennett, J. (2015). Managing prisons in an age of austerity. *The Prison Service Journal*, 222(November), 15–25.

Bennett, J. (2016). Prison managerialism: global change and local cultures in the working lives of prison managers. In Jewkes, Y., Bennett, J. and Crewe, B. (eds) *Handbook on Prisons*. 2nd edn. London: Routledge, pp 131–147.

Bentham, J. (1998). Deterrence and punishment. In von Hirsch, A. Bennett, J. and Ashworth, A. (eds) *Principled Sentencing Readings on Theory and Policy*. Oxford: Oxford University Press, pp 53–57.

Bierie, D. M. (2012). Is tougher better? The impact of physical prison conditions on inmate violence. *International Journal of Offender Therapy and Comparative Criminology*, 56, 338–355.

Bottoms, A. (1990). The aims of imprisonment. In Garland, D. (ed.) *Justice, Guilt and Forgiveness in the Penal System*. Edinburgh: University of Edinburgh.

Bowling, B., Reiner, R and Sheptycki, J. (2019). *The Politics of the Police*. 5th edn. Oxford: Oxford University Press.

Bryans, S. (2007). *Prison Governors: Managing Prisons in a Time of Change*. Cullompton: Willan.

Cabinet Office Social Exclusion Unit. (2009). *Short Study on Women Offenders*. London: Cabinet Office.

Cardiff Centre for Chaplaincy Studies. (2011). *The Role and Contribution of a Multi-Faith Prison Chaplaincy to the Contemporary Prison Service*. Cardiff: Cardiff Centre for Chaplaincy Studies.

Carlen, P. (1983). *Women's Imprisonment: A Study in Social Control*. London: Routledge.

Carlen, P. (ed.) (2008). *Imaginary Penalties*. Cullompton: Willan.

Carlen, P. and Tombs, J. (2006). Reconfigurations of penality: the ongoing case of the women's imprisonment and reintegration industries. *Theoretical Criminology*, 10(3), 337–360.

Cavadino, M. and Dignan, J. (2002). *The Penal System: An Introduction*. 3rd edn. London: Sage.

Cavadino, M. and Dignan, J. (2012). *Penal Systems: A Comparative Approach*, London: Sage.

Cavadino, M., Dignan, J. and Mair, G. (2013). *The Penal System: An Introduction*. 5th edn. London: Sage.

Clark, A. (2013). Criminogenic needs. In Canton, R. and Hancock, D. (eds) *Dictionary of Probation and Offender Management*. Cullompton: Willan Publishing, pp 666–672.

Coates, S. (2016). *Unlocking Potential: A Review of Education in Prison*. London: MoJ.

Cohen, S. (1985). *Visions of Social Control*. London: Polity.

Cohen, S. and Taylor, L. (1972). *Psychological Survival: The Experience of Long-Term Imprisonment*. Harmondsworth: Penguin.

Comfort, M. (2008). The best seven years I could'a done: the reconstruction of imprisonment as rehabilitation. In Carlen, P. (ed.) *Imaginary Penalties*. Cullompton: Willan, pp 252–274.

Commission for Racial Equality (CRE). (2003a). *A Formal Investigation by the Commission for Racial Equality into HM Prison Service of England and Wales – Part 1: The Murder of Zahid Mubarek*. London: CRE.

Commission for Racial Equality (CRE). (2003b). *A Formal Investigation by the Commission for Racial Equality into HM Prison Service of England and Wales – Part 2: Racial Equality in Prisons*. London: CRE.

Corston, J. (2007). *The Corston Report: A Report by Baroness Jean Corston of a Review of Women with Particular Vulnerabilities in the Criminal Justice System*. London: Home Office.

Crawley, E. (2004a). *Doing Prison Work: The Public and Private Lives of Prison Officers*. Cullompton: Willan.

Crawley, E. (2004b). Emotion and performance: prison officers and the presentation of self in prisons. *Punishment and Society*, 6(4), 411–427.

Crawley, E. and Crawley, P. (2008). *Understanding Prison Officers: Culture, Cohesion and Conflict*. Cullompton: Willan.

Cresswell, T. (1996). *In Place, out of Place: Geography, Ideology and Transgression*. Minneapolis, MN: University of Minnesota Press.

Crewe, B. (2009). *The Prisoner Society: Power, Adaptation and Social Life in an English Prison*. Oxford: OUP, Clarendon Press.

Crewe, B. (2011). Depth, weight, tightness: revisiting the pains of imprisonment. *Punishment and Society*, 13(5), 509–529.

Crewe, B. (2016). The sociology of imprisonment. In Jewkes, Y., Bennett, J. and Crewe, B. (eds) *Handbook on Prisons*. 2nd edn. London: Routledge, pp 77–101.

Crewe, B. and Liebling, A. (2015). Governing governors, *The Prison Service Journal*. 222(November), 3–11.

Crewe, B. and Liebling, A. (2018). Quality, professionalism and the distribution of power in public and private sector prisons. In Hucklesby, A. and Lister, S. (eds) *The Private Sector and Criminal Justice*, Oxford: Blackwell, pp 161–194.

Cunneen, C., Baldry, E., Brown, D., Brown, M., Schwartz, M. and Steel, A. (2013). *Penal Culture and Hyperincarceration: The Revival of the Prison*. Aldershot: Ashgate.

Deady, C. (2014). *Incarceration and Recidivism: Lessons from Abroad*, Newport: Pell Centre for International Relations and Public Policy. https://www.salve.edu/sites/default/files/filesfield/documents/Incarceration_and_Recidivism.pdf

De Graaf, K. and Kilty, J.M. (2016). You are what you eat: exploring the relationship between women, food, and incarceration. *Punishment and Society*, 18(1), 132–145.

Dixon-Gordon, K., Harrison, N. and Roesch, R. (2012). Non-suicidal self-injury within offender populations: a systematic review. *International Journal of Forensic Mental Health*, 11(1), 33–50.

Dolan, R., Hann, M., Edge, D. and Shaw, J. (2019). Pregnancy in prison, mental health and admission to prison mother and baby units. *Journal of Forensic Psychiatry and Psychology*, 30(4), 551–569.

Duff, R. (1998). Desert and penance. In von Hirsch, A. and Ashworth, A. (eds) *Principled Sentencing Readings on Theory and Policy*. Oxford: Oxford University Press, pp 161–167.

Duff, R. and Garland, D. (1994). Introduction. Thinking about punishment. In Duff, R. and Garland, D. (eds) *A Reader on Punishment*. Oxford: Oxford University Press.

Earle, R. (2016). Race, ethnicity, multiculture and prison life. In Jewkes, Y., Bennett, J. and Crewe, B. (eds) *Handbook on Prisons*. 2nd edn. London: Routledge, pp 568–585.

Eves, A. and Gesch, B. (2003). Food provision and the nutritional implications of food choices made by young adult males, in a young offender's institution. *Journal of Human Nutrition and Diet*, 16(3), 167–179.

Farmer, L. (2019). *The Importance of Strengthening Female Offenders' Family and other Relationships to Prevent Reoffending and Reduce Intergenerational Crime*. London: MoJ.

Farrall, S. (2002). *Rethinking what Works with Offenders*. Cullompton: Willan.

Farrington, D. (1986). Age and crime. *Crime and Justice*, 7, 189–250.

Farrington, D., Loeber, R. and Ttofi, M. (2012). Risk and protective factors in offending. In Farrington, D. and Welsh, B. (eds) *The Oxford Handbook of Crime Prevention*. Oxford: Oxford University Press, pp 46–70.

Fitzalan Howard, F. and Pope, L. (2019). *Learning to Cope: An Exploratory Qualitative Study of the Experience of Men Who Have Desisted from Self-Harm in Prison*. London: MoJ Analytical Series.

Fitzgerald, M. and Sim, J. (1982). *British Prisons*. 2nd edn. Oxford: Blackwell.

Foucault, M. (1977). *Discipline and Punish: The Birth of the Prison*. Harmondsworth: Penguin.

Frake, V. (2021). *The Governor: My Life inside Britain's most Notorious Prisons*. London: HarperNonFiction.

Garland, D. (1985). *Punishment and Welfare*. Aldershot: Gower.

Garside, R. (2018). The prison crisis: alternatives to incarceration [Online]. Centre for Crime and Justice Studies. https://www.crimeandjustice.org.uk/resources/prisons-crisis-alternatives-incarceration.

Gelsthorpe, L. and Morris, A. (2002). Women's imprisonment in England and Wales: a penal paradox. *Criminology and Criminal Justice*, 2(3), 277–301.

Gladstone, H. (1895). *Report from the Departmental Committee on Prisons* (1895). C.7702. London: Parliamentary Papers.

Godderis, R. (2006). Dining in: the symbolic power of food in prison. *The Howard Journal*, 45(3), 255–267.

Gunaratnam, Y. (2003*). Researching 'Race' and Ethnicity: Methods, Knowledge and Power*. London: Sage.

Haines, K. and Case, S. (2009). *Understanding Youth Offending: Risk Factor Research, Policy and Practice*. London: Routledge.

Hall, J. (2022). *Terrorism in Prisons*, London: The Stationery Office.

Haney, C. (2001). The psychological impact of incarceration: implications for post-prison adjustment [Online]. US Department of Health and Human Services. https://aspe.hhs.gov/sites/default/files/migrated_legacy_files//42351/Haney.pdf [accessed 27/02/22].

Hansard House of Commons Deb. Vol. 534 cols 785, 1 November 2011. [Online] [Accessed 25/03/2022]. Available from: https://hansard.parliament.uk/comm ons/2011-11-01/debates/11110173000002/LegalAidSentencingAndPunish mentOfOffendersBill

Harding, C. (1988). The inevitable end of a discredited system? The origins of the Gladstone Committee Report on Prisons 1895. *The Historical Journal*, 31(3), 591–608.

Hardwick, N. (2013). Foreword. In Champion, N. and Edgar, K. (2013). *Through the Gateway: How Computers Can Transform Rehabilitation*. London: Prison Reform Trust.

Hardwick, N. (2018). Letter of resignation from Nick Hardwick to the Secretary of State for Justice. 28 March. Press release. [Online]. https://www.gov.uk/ government/news/letter-of-resignation-from-nick-hardwick-to-the-secretary- of-state-for-justice [accessed 10/02/2023]

Hardwick, N. and Jones, M. (2017). Evidence given by Nick Hardwick and Martin Jones to the Justice Committee [Interview, 18 October]. London: Justice Select Committee.

Harris, T. (2015). *Changing Prisons, Saving Lives: Report of the Independent Review into Self-Inflicted Deaths in Custody of 18–24 Year Olds*. London: The Stationery Office.

Harrison, K. (2020). *Penology: Theory, Policy and Practice*, London: Red Globe Press.

Hay, D. (1975). Property, authority and the criminal law. In Hay, D., Linebaugh, P., Rule, J.G., Thompson, E.P. and Winslow, C. (eds) *Albion's Fatal Tree*, Harmondsworth: Penguin.

Henriques, U. (1972). The rise and decline of the separate system of prison discipline. *Past and Present*, 54(1), 61–93.

HM Chief Inspector of Prisons. (2020). *Annual Report 2019–20*, London: The Stationery Office.

HM Chief Inspector of Prisons. (2022). *Report on an Inspection of Separation Centres*, London: The Stationery Office.

HM Government. (2018). *Victims Strategy*. London: HM Government.

HM Government and NHS England. (2019). *National Prison Healthcare Board Principle of Equivalence of Care for Prison Healthcare in England*. London: HM Government.

HMIP (HM Inspectorate of Prisons). (2010). *Women in Prison*. London: HMIP.

HMIP. (2014). *A Review by HMIP. Release on Temporary Licence (ROTL) Failures*. London: HMIP.

HMIP. (2016). *Life in Prison: Food*. London: HMIP.

HMIP. (2017). *Report on an Announced Inspection of HMP Wormwood Scrubs*. London: HMIP.

HMIP. (2018). *Report on an Unannounced Inspection of HMP Liverpool*. London: HMIP.

HMIP. (2019a). *Report on an Unannounced Inspection of HMP Buckley Hall*. London: HMIP.

HMIP. (2019b). *Report on an Announced Inspection of HMP Wormwood Scrubs*. London: HMIP.

HMIP. (2019c). *Report on an Unannounced Inspection of HMP and YOI New Hall*. London: HMIP.

HMIP. (2019d). *Report on an Announced Inspection of HMYOI Feltham A*. London: HMIP.

HMIP. (2020a). *Report on an Unannounced Inspection of HMP Full Sutton*. London: HMIP.

HMIP. (2020b). *Report on an Announced Inspection of HMP Leeds*. London: HMIP.

HMIP. (2020c). *Minority Ethnic Prisoners' Experiences of Rehabilitation and Release Planning*. London: HMIP.

HMIP. (2020d). *Report on an Unannounced Inspection of HMP Warren Hill*, London: HMIP.

HMIP. (2020e). *Report on an Announced Inspection of HMP Liverpool*, London: HMIP.

HMIP. (2021a). *Report on an Unannounced Inspection of HMP Wormwood Scrubs*, London: HMIP.

HMIP. (2021b). *Report on a Scrutiny Visit to HMP/YOI Thorn Cross, 12–13 and 20–21 April 2021*. London: HMIP.

HMIP. (2021c). *Report on a Scrutiny Visit to HMYOI Feltham A*, 9th–17th February, London: HMIP.

HMIP. (2022). Our expectations [Online]. https://www.justiceinspectorates.gov.uk/hmiprisons/our-expectations/ [accessed 07/02/22].

HMPPS (Her Majesty's Prison and Probation Service). (2016). *PSI 05/2016 Faith and Pastoral Care for Prisoners*. London: HMPPS and MoJ.

HMPPS. (2017). *Offender Management in Custody Model*, London: HMPPS.

HMPPS. (2020a). *PSI 75/2011 Residential Services*. London: HMPPS and MoJ.

HMPPS. (2020b). *Incentives Policy Framework*. London: HMPPS and MoJ.

HMPPS. (2021a). About us [Online]. UK Government. https://www.gov.uk/government/organisations/her-majestys-prison-and-probation-service/about [accessed 05/12/2021].

HMPPS. (2021b). Breakdown of the prison estate [Online]. UK Government. https://www.gov.uk/government/publications/prisons-and-their-resettlement-providers [accessed 05/12/21].

HMPPS. (2021c). *Her Majesty's Prison and Probation Service Staff Equalities Report: 2020 to 2021*. London: HMPPS.

HMPPS. (2022a). *Her Majesty's Prison and Probation Service Workforce Quarterly: December 2021*. London: HMPPS/MoJ.

HMPPS. (2022b). *Recruitment Diversity Statistics December 21*. London: HMPPS.

HM Treasury. (2021). *Public Expenditure Statistical Analyses 2021*. London: HM Treasury.

Hochschild, A. (1983). *The Managed Heart*. Berkeley, CA: University of California Press.

House of Commons Justice Committee. (2009). *Role of the Prison Officer. Twelfth Report of Session 2008–09*. London: House of Commons.

House of Commons Justice Committee. (2020). *Ageing Prison Population. Fifth Report of Session 2019–21*. London: House of Commons.

Howard League for Penal Reform. (2016a). Prisoners' diaries reveal what it's really like to be inside as the crisis deepens [Online]. BuzzFeed. https://www.buzzf eed.com/patricksmith/prison-diaries?utm_term=.ukWMaYLB9#.mw2bKX 9LG [accessed 07/09/21].

Howard League for Penal Reform. (2016b). *Preventing Prison Suicide.* London: Howard League for Penal Reform.

Howard League for Penal Reform. (2017a). *The Role of the Prison Officer: Research Briefing.* London: Howard League for Penal Reform.

Howard League for Penal Reform. (2017b). Howard League calls on new government to act as recalls to prison spiral out of control [Online]. https:// howardleague.org/news/recallsspiraloutofcontrol/ [accessed 10/02/2023].

Howard League for Penal Reform. (2018). *The Rising Tide: Additional Days for Rule-Breaking in Prison.* London: Howard League for Penal Reform.

Howard League for Penal Reform. (2021). John Howard: the life and work of John Howard [Online]. https://howardleague.org/john-howard/ [accessed 19/08/21].

Howard League for Penal Reform (2022) Prisons [Online]. https://howardleague. org/prisons-information/ [accessed 20/08/22].

Hudson, B. (2003). *Understanding Justice.* 2nd edn. London: Sage.

Hughes, E. (1958). *Men & Their Work.* Glencoe, IL: The Free Press.

Hutton, M.A. (2017). Prison visits and desistance: a human rights perspective. In Hart, E.L. and van Ginnekin, E. (eds). *New Perspectives on Desistance: Theoretical and Empirical Developments.* London: Macmillan, pp 1–8.

Ignatieff, M. (1978). *A Just Measure of Pain: The Penitentiary in the Industrial Revolution.* London: Macmillan.

International Centre for the Study of Radicalisation and Political Violence. (2010). *Prisons and Terrorism: Radicalisation and De-Radicalisation in 15 Countries,* London: International Centre for the Study of Radicalisation and Political Violence.

Jacobson, J., Heard, C. and Fair, H. (2017). *Prison: Evidence of Its Use and Over-Use from around the World.* London: ICPR.

James, E. (2003). *A Life Inside: A Prisoner's Notebook.* London: Atlantic.

Jewkes, Y. (2008). Local prisons. In Jewkes, Y. and Bennett, J. (eds) *Dictionary of Prisons and Punishment.* Cullompton: Willan, pp 156–157.

Johnston, H. (2016). Prison histories, 1770s–1950s. Continuities and contradictions. In Jewkes, Y., Bennett, J. and Crewe, B. (eds) *Handbook on Prisons.* 2nd edn. London: Routledge, pp 24–38.

Joliffe, D. and Hedderman, C. (2012). Investigating the impact of custody on reoffending using propensity score matching. *Crime and Delinquency,* 61(8), 1051–1077.

Justice. (2017). The parole system of England and Wales [Online]. https://just ice.org.uk/parole-system-england-wales/ [accessed 25/02/22].

Keith, B. (2006). *Report of the Zahid Mubarek Inquiry,* HC 1082-I, London: HMSO.

Khan, Z. (2020). A typology of prisoner compliance with the Incentives and Earned Privileges scheme: theorising the neoliberal self and staff–prisoner relationships. *Criminology and Criminal Justice,* 22(1), 97–114.

King, R. and McDermott, K. (1995). *The State of Our Prisons*. Oxford: Clarendon Press.

Kneen, H. (2017). *An Exploratory Estimate of the Economic Cost of Black, Asian and Minority Ethnic Net Overrepresentation in the Criminal Justice System*. London: MoJ.

Kristoffersen, R. (2013). Relapse study in the correctional services of the Nordic countries: key results and perspectives, *Kriminalomsorgens høgskole og utdanningssenter KRUS*, https://krus.brage.unit.no/krus-xmlui/handle/11250/160435.

Lacey, N. (1988). *State Punishment: Political Principles and Community Values*. London: Routledge.

Lacey, N. (2008). *The Prisoners' Dilemma: Political Economy and Punishment in Contemporary Democracies*. Cambridge: Cambridge University Press.

Lammy, D. (2017). *The Lammy Review: An Independent Review into the Treatment of, and Outcomes for, Black, Asian and Minority Ethnic Individuals in the Criminal Justice System*. London: UK Government. https://www.gov.uk/government/publications/lammy-review-final-report.

Laub, J.H. and Sampson, R.J. (2003). *Shared Beginnings, Divergent Lives: Delinquent Boys to Age 70*. Cambridge, MA: Harvard University Press.

Leese, M., Thomas, S. and Snow, L. (2006). An ecological study of factors associated with rates of self-inflicted death in prisons in England and Wales. *International Journal of Law and Psychiatry*, 29(5), 355–60.

Leibrich, J. (1993). *Straight to the Point: Angles on Giving Up Crime*. Dunedin: University of Otago Press.

Liebling, A. (2004). *Prisons and Their Moral Performance: A Study of Values, Quality and Prison Life*. Oxford: Clarendon Press.

Liebling, A. (2008). Incentives and earned privileges revisited: fairness, discretion, and the quality of prison life. *Journal of Scandinavian Studies in Criminology and Crime Prevention*, 9(1), 25–41.

Liebling, A. (2011). Moral performance, inhuman and degrading treatment and prison pain. *Punishment and Society*, 13(5), 530–550.

Liebling, A. and Price, D. (1999). *An Exploration of Staff–Prisoner Relationships at HMP Whitemoor*. Prison Service Research Report No. 6. Available as Research Findings No. 87. London: Home Office.

Listwan, S.J., Sullivan, C.J., Agnew, R., Cullen, F.T. and Colvin, M. (2013). The pains of imprisonment revisited: impact of strain on inmate recidivism. *Justice Quarterly*, 30, 144–168.

Loftus, B. (2009). *Police Culture in a Changing World*. Oxford: Oxford University Press.

Ludlow, A., Schmidt, B., Akoensi, T., Liebling, A., Giacomantonio, C. and Sutherland, A. (2015). Self-inflicted deaths in NOMS' custody amongst 18–24 year olds: staff experience, knowledge and views. Santa Monica, CA: RAND Corporation. [Online]. https://pdfs.semanticscholar.org/210a/8831a3276ac45a64458985334ac72827040f.pdf

Lyon, J. (2012). Most prisons are overcrowded. [Online]. Prison Reform Trust. http://www.prisonreformtrust.org.uk/PressPolicy/News/vw/1/ItemID/159 [accessed 08/01/2022].

MacPherson, W. (1999). *The Stephen Lawrence Inquiry. Report of an Inquiry.* [Online]. London: The Stationery Office. http://webarchive.nationalarchives. gov.uk/20130814142233/http://www.archive.official-documents.co.uk/docum ent/cm42/4262/4262.htm [accessed 25/08/22].

Maitra, D.R. (2020). 'If you're down with a gang inside, you can lead a nice life': prison gangs in the age of austerity. *Youth Justice*, 20(1), 128–145.

Martinson, R. (1974). 'What works?' Questions and answers about penal reform. *The Public Interest*, 35, 22–54.

Maruna, S. (2001). *Making Good: How Ex-Convicts Reform and Rebuild Their Lives*, USA: American Psychological Association.

Maruna S. and Farrall S. (2004). Desistance from crime: a theoretical reformulation. *Kolner Zeitschrift fur Soziologie und Sozialpsychologie*, 43: 171–194.

Mathiesen, T. (1974). *The Politics of Abolition*. London: Martin Robertson.

Mathiesen, T. (1990). *Prison on Trial*. Winchester: Waterside Press.

McEwan, A. (1986). A typology of dispersal prisoners. *Personality and Individual Differences*, 7(1), 73–80.

McGuire, J. (2018). *Understanding Prison Violence: A Rapid Evidence Assessment*, London: HMPPS.

McNeill, F. and Schinkel, M. (2016). Prisons and desistance. In Jewkes, Y., Bennett, J. and Crewe, B. (eds) *Handbook on Prisons*. Cullompton: Willan Publishing.

Medlicott, D. (2007). Women in prison. In Jewkes, Y. (ed.) *Handbook on Prisons*. Cullompton: Willan, pp 240–248.

Milner, A. and Jumbe, S. (2020). Using the right words to address racial disparities in COVID-19. *The Lancet*, 5(8), 419–420.

Mind. (2020). What is self-harm? [Online]. https://www.mind.org.uk/ information-support/types-of-mental-health-problems/self-harm/about-self-harm [accessed 22/02/22].

Miraglia, P. (2015). *Drugs and Drug Trafficking in Brazil: Trends and Policies.* Washington DC: Brookings Latin America Initiative.

MoJ (Ministry of Justice). (2002). *PSO-4460 Prisoners' Pay*. London: MoJ.

MoJ. (2007). *Offending Management Caseload Annual Statistics*. London: MoJ.

MoJ. (2012). *PSI-17 2012 Certified Prisoner Accommodation*. London: MoJ.

MoJ. (2014). *Prisoners' Childhood and Family Background*. London: MoJ.

MoJ. (2016). *Prison Safety and Reform*. London: MoJ.

MoJ. (2017). *Freedom of Information Act Request 113134*. London: MoJ.

MoJ. (2018). *Female Offender Strategy*. London: MoJ.

MoJ. (2019). *The Economic and Social Costs of Reoffending*. London: MoJ.

MoJ. (2020a). *Annual HM Prison and Probation Service Digest: 2019 to 2020.* London: MoJ.

MoJ. (2020b). Answer to written question 121212, 7 December [Online]. House of Commons. https://questions-statements.parliament.uk/written-questions/ detail/2020-11-26/121212 [accessed 18/01/22].

MoJ. (2020c). *Security Categorisation Policy Framework*. London: MoJ.

MoJ. (2020d). *Offender Management Statistics Quarterly: April to June 2020*. London: MoJ.

MoJ. (2020e). *Incentives Policy Framework*. London: MoJ.

MoJ. (2020f). *Safety in Custody Statistics, England and Wales: Deaths in Prison Custody to March 2020 Assaults and Self-Harm to September 2019*. London: MoJ.

MoJ. (2020g). Four new prisons boost rehabilitation and support economy [Online]. https://www.gov.uk/government/news/four-new-prisons-boost-rehabilitation-and-support-economy [accessed 15/2/22].

MoJ. (2021a). New prison strategy to rehabilitate offenders and cut crime [Online]. https://www.gov.uk/government/news/new-prison-strategy-to-rehabilitate-offenders-and-cut-crime [accessed 8/1/22].

MoJ. (2021b). *Criminal Justice Statistics Quarterly June 2021*. London: MoJ.

MoJ. (2021c). *Progression Regime Policy Framework*, London: MoJ.

MoJ. (2021d). *Prison Education Statistics 2019–2020*, London: MoJ.

MoJ. (2022a). Prisons in England and Wales [Online]. https://www.gov.uk/government/collections/prisons-in-england-and-wales [accessed 08/01/2022].

MoJ. (2022b). Prison population figures: 2022 [Online]. UK Government. https://www.gov.uk/government/statistics/prison-population-figures-2022 [accessed 08/01/2022].

MoJ. (2022c). *Offender Management Statistics Quarterly: July to September 2021*. London: MoJ.

MoJ. (2022d). *Safety in Custody Statistics, England and Wales: Deaths in Prison Custody to December 2021 Assaults and Self-harm to September 2021*. London: MoJ.

MoJ. (2022e). Leaving prison [Online]. UK Government. https://www.gov.uk/leaving-prison/before-someone-leaves-prison [accessed 25/02/22].

MoJ. (2022f). *Proven Reoffending Statistics: January to March 2020*, London: MOJ.

MoJ/DfE (Ministry of Justice / Department for Education). (2017). *Exploring the Outcomes of Prisoner Learners: Analysis of Linked Offender Records from the Police National Computer and Individualised Learner Records*. London: MoJ.

Moore. J. (2008). Prison – more than detention? *Criminal Justice Matters*, 71 (Spring) https://www.crimeandjustice.org.uk/publications/cjm/article/prison-more-detention [accessed 17/03/22].

Nathan, S. (2003). Prison privatisation in the United Kingdom. In Coyle, A., Campbell, A. and Neufeld, R. (eds) *Capitalist Punishment: Prison Privatization and Human Rights*. London: Clarity Press, pp 113–129.

National Audit Office. (2019). *Transforming Rehabilitation: Progress Review*, London: NAO.

National Crime Records Bureau. (2022). Prison statistics India – 2020 [Online]. https://ncrb.gov.in/sites/default/files/Executive_ncrb_Summary-2020.pdf [accessed 25/03/22].

National Justice Museum. (2019). The 'Bloody Code'? [Online]. https://www.nationaljusticemuseum.org.uk/museum/news/what-was-the-bloody-code [accessed 18/08/21].

Nichols, H. (2021). *Understanding the Educational Experiences of Imprisoned Men: (Re) education.* London: Routledge.

O'Brien, R. and Robson, J. (2016). *A Matter of Conviction: A Blueprint for Community-Based Rehabilitative Prisons.* London: RSA Action and Research Centre.

O'Leary, C. (2013). The role of stable accommodation in reducing recidivism: what does the evidence tell us? *Safer Communities,* 12(1), 5–12.

Omolade, S. (2014). *The Needs and Characteristics of Older Prisoners: Results from the Surveying Prisoner Crime Reduction (SPCR) Survey.* London: MoJ.

Oxford Dictionaries. (2022). 'Punishment' [Online]. https://www.oed.com/view/Entry/154677?redirectedFrom=punishment#eid [accessed 29/03/22].

Padfield, N. (2012). Reflection on 'About Parole'. *Prison Service Journal,* 200, 379–380.

Panorama. (2016). *Teenage Prison Abuse Exposed.* BBC1, 11 January.

Panorama. (2017). *Panorama Behind Bars: Prison Undercover.* BBC1, 13 February.

Parole Board. (2019a). Licence conditions and how the Parole Board use them [Online]. UK Government. https://www.gov.uk/government/news/licence-conditions-and-how-the-parole-board-use-them [accessed 25/02/22.]

Parole Board. (2019b). *The Parole Board Rules.* London: Parole Board.

Parole Board. (2020). *Parole Board Annual Report and Accounts 2019–20.* London: Parole Board.

Penal Reform. (2022). Solitary confinement [Online]. https://www.penalreform.org/issues/prison-conditions/key-facts/solitary-confinement/ [accessed 25/03/2022].

Pennington, S. and Crewe, B. (2015). Open prisons: a governor's perspective. *Prison Service Journal,* 217(January), 12–13.

Pope, L. (2018). *Self-Harm by Adult Men in Prison: A Rapid Evidence Assessment (REA).* London: HM Prison and Probation Service.

Powis, B., Dixon, L. and Woodhams, J. (2019). *Exploring the Nature of Muslim Groups and Related Gang Activity in Three High Security Prisons: Findings from Qualitative Research.* London: MoJ Analytical Series.

Pratt, J. (2007). *Penal Populism.* London: Routledge.

Prison and Courts Bill 2017. (c.1). London: HMSO. https://www.publications.parliament.uk/pa/bills/cbill/2016-2017/0145/cbill_2016-20170145_en_2.htm#pt1-pb1-l1g1.

Prison Officers Association. (2021). Prison Officers Association submission to Justice Committee Inquiry on Mental Health in Prison [Online]. *House of Commons Justice Committee.* https://committees.parliament.uk/writtenevidence/36348/html/ [accessed 23/03/22].

Prison Reform Trust. (1991). *The Woolf Report: A Summary of the Main Findings and Recommendations of the Inquiry into Prison Disturbances.* London: Prison Reform Trust.

Prison Reform Trust. (2013). *Prison: The Facts. Bromley Briefings Summer 2013.* London: Prison Reform Trust.

Prison Reform Trust. (2021). *Bromley Briefings Winter Factfile.* London: Prison Reform Trust.

Prisoners' Advice Service. (2020). Incentives and Earned Privilege Scheme (IEPS) – Information Sheet [Online]. http://www.prisonersadvice.org.uk/wp-content/uploads/2021/05/IEPS.pdf [accessed 24/03/22].

Prisoner Advisory Service. (2018). Prisoner Advisory Service submission to Health Committee Inquiry on Prison Health [Online]. House of Commons Health Committee. http://data.parliament.uk/writtenevidence/committeee vidence.svc/evidencedocument/health-and-social-care-committee/prison-hea lth/written/85992.html [accessed 24/03/22].

Prisoner Learning Alliance. (2020). Prisoner Learning Alliance (PLA) submission to Education Committee Inquiry on Adult Skills and Lifelong Learning [Online]. House of Commons Education Committee. https://committees.par liament.uk/writtenevidence/9597/html [accessed 07/02/22].

Prisons and Probation Ombudsman. (2014). Risk factors in self-inflicted deaths: learning from PPO investigations [Online]. http://www.ppo.gov.uk/app/uploads/2014/07/Risk_thematic_final_web.pdf.

Prisons and Probation Ombudsman. (2018). Complaints about discrimination [Online]. *Learning Lessons Bulletin*, Issue 9(January).

Race and Equalities Action Group. (2008). *Race Review 2008: Implementing Race Equality in Prisons – Five Years on.* London: MoJ.

Radzinowicz, L. and Hood, R. (1986). *A History of English Criminal Law. Vol. 5. The Emergence of Penal Policy.* London: Stevens & Son.

Ramluggun, P. (2013). A critical exploration of the management of self-harm in a male custodial setting: qualitative findings of a comparative analysis of prison staff views on self-harm. *Journal of Forensic Nursing*, 9(1), 23–34.

Ramsbotham, D. and Gesch, B. (2009). Crime and nourishment. *Prison Service Journal*, 182, 16–17.

Roberts, J. (2007). *Punishing Persistent Offenders: Exploring Community and Offender Perspectives.* Oxford: Clarendon Studies in Criminology.

Roberts, R. and McMahon, W. (2008). Ethnicity, harm and crime: a discussion paper. London: Centre for Crime and Justice Studies.

Rothwell, J. (2015). Drug offenders in American prisons: the critical distinction between stock and flow [Online]. Brookings Institution blog. http://www.brookings.edu/blogs/social-mobility-memos/posts/2015/11/25-drug-offend ers-stock-flow-prisons-rothwell [accessed 03/03/22].

Ruck, S.K. (ed.) (1951). *Paterson on Prisons.* London: Frederick Muller.

Rushchenko, J. (2019). Terrorist recruitment and prison radicalization: assessing the UK experiment of 'separation centres'. *European Journal of Criminology*, 16(3), 295–314.

Rutherford, A. (2002). *Growing Out of Crime: The New Era.* 2nd edn. London: Waterside Press.

Rynne, J. and Harding, R. (2016). Private prisons. In Jewkes, Y., Bennett, J. and Crewe, B. (eds) *Handbook on Prisons.* 2nd edn. London: Routledge, pp 149–168.

Sampson, R. and Laub, J. (2005). A life-course view of the development of crime. *The ANNALS of the American Academy of Political and Social Science*, 60(2), 12–45.

Savage, M. (2021). 'Deep crisis' in British prisons as use of force against inmates doubles [Online]. *The Observer.* https://www.theguardian.com/society/2021/jan/03/deep-crisis-british-prisons-use-force-inmates-overcrowding [accessed 25/08/2022].

Schinkel, M. (2015). *Being Imprisoned: Punishment, Adaptation and Desistance.* Houndmills: Palgrave.

Schwartz, M. and Nurge, D. (2004). Capitalist punishment: ethics and private prisons. *Critical Criminology*, 12, 133–156.

Scott, D. and Flynn, N. (2014). *Prisons and Punishment: The Essentials.* 2nd edn. London: Sage.

Senior, J., Forsyth, K., Walsh, E., O'Hara, K., Stevenson, C., Hayes, A., Short, V., Webb, R., Challis, D., Fazel, S., Burns, A. and Shaw, J. (2013). *Health and Social Care Services for Older Male Adults in Prison: The Identification of Current Service Provision and Piloting of an Assessment and Care Planning Model.* Health Services and Delivery Research 2013. Southampton: NIHR Journals Library.

Sentencing Council. (2022). Determinate prison sentences [Online]. https://www.sentencingcouncil.org.uk/sentencing-and-the-council/types-of-sentence/determinate-prison-sentences/ [accessed 09/01/2022].

SEU (Social Exclusion Unit). (2002). *Reducing Offending by Ex-Prisoners.* London: Social Exclusion Unit.

Shalev, S. (2009). *Supermax: Controlling Risk through Solitary Confinement,* Cullompton: Willan.

Shichor, J. (1998). Private prisons in perspective: some conceptual issues. *The Howard Journal*, 37(1), 82–100.

Sim, J. (2009). *Punishment and Prisons: Power and the Carceral State.* London: Sage.

Skills Funding Agency. (2018). *Further Education and Skills: November 2018.* London: Skills Funding Agency.

Skolnick, J. (1966). *Justice without Trial: Law Enforcement in Democratic Society.* New York: Macmillan.

Smith, I. and Hopkins, K. (2014). *The Impact of Experience in Prison on the Employment Status of Longer-Sentenced Prisoners after Release: Results from The Surveying Prisoner Crime Reduction (SPCR) Longitudinal Cohort Study of Prisoners.* London: MOJ.

Spierenburg, P. (1998). The body and the state: early modern Europe. In Morris, N. and Rothman, D. (eds) *The Oxford History of the Prison: The Practice of Punishment in Western Society.* Oxford: Oxford University Press, pp 44–71.

Spierenburg, P. (2005). Origins of the prison. In Emsley, C. (ed.) *The Persistent Prison: Problems, Images and Alternatives.* London: Francis Boutle.

Sturge, G. (2021). *UK Prison Population Statistics.* London: House of Commons Library Briefing Paper.

Sykes, G. (1958). *The Society of Captives: A Study of a Maximum Security Prison.* Princeton, NJ: Princeton University Press.

Tanner, W. (2013). *The Case for Private Prisons.* London: Reform.

Taylor, D. (2020). Bristol prison race failings led to attack on inmate, says report [Online]. *The Guardian*. https://www.theguardian.com/society/2020/aug/05/bristol-prison-race-failings-led-to-attack-on-inmate-says-report [accessed 25/08/22].

Taylor, S., Burke, L., Millings, M. and Ragonese, E. (2017). Transforming rehabilitation during a penal crisis: a case study of through the gate services in a resettlement prison in England and Wales. *European Journal of Probation*, 9(2), 115–131.

The Guardian. (2019). Britons without a bank account 'pay a £485 poverty premium' [Online]. *The Guardian*. https://www.theguardian.com/money/2019/apr/22/britons-without-bank-account-pay-poverty-premium [accessed 13/03/22].

The Guardian. (2020). Why a bank account can be key to beginning a new life after prison [Online]. *The Guardian*. https://www.theguardian.com/money/2020/aug/23/why-a-bank-account-can-be-key-to-beginning-a-new-life-after-prison [accessed 13/03/22].

The Prison Rules. (1999). UK Statutory Instruments 1999 No. 728. https://www.legislation.gov.uk/uksi/1999/728/contents/made [accessed 08/02/22].

Thompson, B. (2021). The long view – race equality: part of the fabric or just embroidery? *Bromley Briefings Winter Factfile, February*. London: Prison Reform Trust, pp 6–8.

Tidmarsh, M. (2020). The probation service in England and Wales: a decade of radical change or more of the same? *European Journal of Probation*, 12(2), 129–146.

Tomaszewska, M., Baker, N., Isaksen, M. and Scowcroft, E. (2019). Unlocking the evidence: understanding suicide in prisons [Online]. Samaritans. https://media.samaritans.org/documents/Samaritans_PrisonsDataReport_2019_Final.pdf.

Uhrig, N. (2016). *Black, Asian and Minority Ethnic Disproportionality in the Criminal Justice System in England and Wales*. London: MoJ.

United Kingdom Government. (2022a). New drive to tackle terrorism in prisons [Online]. https://www.gov.uk/government/news/new-drive-to-tackle-terrorism-in-prisons [accessed 25/08/22].

United Kingdom Government. (2022b). Getting parole [Online]. https://www.gov.uk/getting-parole [accessed 25/02/22].

United Nations Human Rights. (2021). United Kingdom: UN expert raises alarm over abuse of close supervision centres [Online]. Press release. https://www.ohchr.org/EN/NewsEvents/Pages/DisplayNews.aspx?NewsID=27076&LangID=E [accessed 05/12/2021].

United States Department of State. (2020). *Country Reports on Human Rights Practices for 2015: India*. Washington DC: US Department of State.

Unlocked Grads. (2022). Unlocked Graduate Scheme [Online]. https://unlockedgrads.org.uk/ [accessed 22/02/22].

UNODC (United Nations Office on Drugs and Crime). (2015). *United Nations Standard Minimum Rules for the Treatment of Prisoners (the Nelson Mandela Rules)*. Resolution adopted by the General Assembly on 17 December. https://www.unodc.org/documents/justice-and-prison-reform/GA-RESOLUTION/E_ebook.pdf.

UNODC. (2022). *The Nelson Mandela Rules: The United Nations Standard Minimum Rules for the Treatment of Prisoners* [Online]. UNODC. https://www.unodc.org/documents/justice-and-prison-reform/16-05081_E_rollup_Ebook.pdf [accessed 03/04/22].

UNODC (nd). The Nelson Mandela Rules [Online]. https://www.unodc.org/documents/nigeria/Nelson_Mandela_Rules.pdf [accessed 13/01/23].

Van Ginneken, E., Sutherland, A. and Molleman, T. (2017). An ecological analysis of prison overcrowding and suicide rates in England and Wales, 2000–2014. *International Journal of Law and Psychiatry*, 50, 76–82.

Von Hirsch, A. (1976). *Doing Justice*. New York: Hill and Wang.

Von Hirsch, A. (1998). Rehabilitation. In von Hirsch, A. and Ashworth, A. (eds) *Principled Sentencing Readings on Theory and Policy*. Oxford: Oxford University Press, pp 1–6.

Von Hirsch, A., Bottoms, A., Burney E. and Wikstrom, P.O. (1999). *Criminal Deterrence and Sentence Severity: An Analysis of Recent Research*. Oxford: Hart.

Wainwright, L., Harriott, P. and Saajedi, S. (2019). *What Do You Need to Make the Best Use of Your Time in Prison?* London: Prison Reform Trust.

Walker, N. (1991). *Why Punish?* Oxford: Oxford University Press.

Warr, J. (2016). The prisoner: inside and out. In Jewkes, Y., Bennett, J. and Crewe, B. (eds) *Handbook on Prisons*. Cullompton: Willan Publishing.

Weaver, B. and McNeill, F. (2010). Travelling hopefully: desistance research and probation practice. In Brayford, J., Crowe, F. and Deering, J. (eds) *What Else Works? Creative Work with Offenders*. Cullompton: Willan.

Webb, S. and Webb, B. (1922). *English Prisons under Local Government*. London: Longman, Green.

Weiss, R. and South, N. (eds) (1998). *Comparing Prison Systems: Toward a Comparative and International Penology*. Amsterdam: Overseas Publishers Association.

Welch, M. (2011). *Corrections: A Critical Approach*. 3rd edn. London: Routledge.

Wilson, D. (2000). Whatever happened to 'the governor'. *Criminal Justice Matters*, 40, 11–12.

Wilson, D. (2014). *Pain and Retribution*. London: Reaktion Books.

Women in Prison. (2015). *State of the Estate: Women in Prison's Report on the Women's Custodial Estate*. 2nd edn. London: Women in Prison.

Women in Prison. (2017). The Corston Report 10 years on: How far have we come on the road to reform for women affected by the criminal justice system? [Online]. Barrow Cadbury Trust. https://www.mappingthemaze.org.uk/wp-content/uploads/2017/08/corston-report-10-years-on.pdf [accessed 17/02/22].

Wood, J. (2006). Gang activity in English prisons: the prisoners' perspective. *Psychology, Crime & Law*, 12(6), 605–617.

World Population Review. (2022). Prison population by state 2022 [Online]. https://worldpopulationreview.com/state-rankings/prison-population-by-state. [accessed 25/03/22].

World Prison Brief. (2022a). Highest to lowest – prison population total [Online]. https://www.prisonstudies.org/highest-to-lowest/prison-populat ion-total?field_region_taxonomy_tid=All [accessed 25/03/22].

World Prison Brief. (2022b). Highest to lowest – prison population rate [Online]. https://www.prisonstudies.org/highest-to-lowest/prison_populati on_rate?field_region_taxonomy_tid=All [accessed 25/03/22].

World Prison Brief. (2022c). Australia [Online]. https://www.prisonstudies.org/country/australia [accessed 25/03/22].

World Prison Brief. (2022d). Brazil [Online]. https://www.prisonstudies.org/country/brazil [accessed 25/03/22].

World Prison Brief. (2022e). India [Online]. https://www.prisonstudies.org/country/india [accessed 25/03/22].

World Prison Brief. (2022f). Japan [Online]. https://www.prisonstudies.org/country/japan [accessed 25/03/22].

World Prison Brief. (2022g). Norway [Online]. https://www.prisonstudies.org/country/norway [accessed 25/03/22].

World Prison Brief. (2022h). United States of America [Online]. https://www.prisonstudies.org/country/united-states-america [accessed 25/03/22].

Youle, E. (2020). This is what it's like to be a prison officer during the coronavirus pandemic [Online]. *Huffington Post*. https://www.huffingtonpost.co.uk/entry/prison-guard-coronavirus_uk_5eac347dc5b6995f1400162b [accessed 24/02/22].

Zaalberg, A., Nijman, H., Bulten, E., Stroosma, L. and Van der Staak, C. (2010). Effects of nutritional supplements on aggression, rule-breaking, & psychopathology among young adult prisoners. *Aggressive Behaviour*, 36(2), 117–126.

Zimring, F. E. (2010). The scale of imprisonment in the United States: twentieth century patterns and twenty-first century prospects. *Journal of Criminal Law and Criminology*, 100(3), 1225–1246.

Index

References to figures and photographs appear in *italic* type; those in **bold** type refer to tables.

Index